LIVING WITH BRAIN INJURY

QUALITATIVE STUDIES IN PSYCHOLOGY

This series showcases the power and possibility of qualitative work in psychology. Books feature detailed and vivid accounts of qualitative psychology research using a variety of methods, including participant observation and field work, discursive and textual analyses, and critical cultural history. They probe vital issues of theory, implementation, interpretation, representation, and ethics that qualitative workers confront. The series mission is to enlarge and refine the repertoire of qualitative approaches to psychology.

General Editors
Michelle Fine and Jeanne Marecek

Everyday Courage: The Lives and Stories of Urban Teenagers
Niobe Way

Negotiating Consent in Psychotherapy
Patrick O'Neill

Flirting with Danger: Young Women's Reflections on Sexuality and Domination
Lynn M. Phillips

Voted Out: The Psychological Consequences of Anti-Gay Politics
Glenda M. Russell

Inner City Kids: Adolescents Confront Life and Violence in an Urban Community
Alice McIntyre

From Subjects to Subjectivities: A Handbook of Interpretive and Participatory Methods
Edited by Deborah L. Tolman and Mary Brydon-Miller

Growing Up Girl: Psychosocial Explorations of Gender and Class
Valerie Walkerdine, Helen Lucey and June Melody

Voicing Chicana Feminisms: Young Women Speak Out on Sexuality and Identity
Aida Hurtado

Situating Sadness: Women and Depression in Social Context
Edited by Janet M. Stoppard and Linda M. McMullen

Living Outside Mental Illness: Qualitative Studies of Recovery in Schizophrenia
Larry Davidson

Autism and the Myth of the Person Alone
Douglas Biklen, with Sue Rubin, Tito Rajarshi Mukhopadhyay, Lucy Blackman, Larry Bissonnette, Alberto Frugone, Richard Attfield, and Jamie Burke

American Karma: Race, Culture, and Identity in the Indian Diaspora
Sunil Bhatia

Muslim American Youth: Understanding Hyphenated Identities through Multiple Methods
Selcuk R. Sirin and Michelle Fine

Pride in the Projects: Teens Building Identities in Urban Contexts
Nancy L. Deutsch

Corridor Cultures: Mapping Student Resistance at an Urban High School
Maryann Dickar

Gay Men Becoming Dads: Transitions to Adoptive Fatherhood
Abbie E. Goldberg

Living with Brain Injury: Narrative, Community, and Women's Renegotiation of Identity
J. Eric Stewart

Living with Brain Injury

Narrative, Community, and Women's Renegotiation of Identity

J. Eric Stewart

NEW YORK UNIVERSITY PRESS

New York and London

NEW YORK UNIVERSITY PRESS
New York and London
www.nyupress.org

© 2014 by New York University

References to Internet websites (URLs) were accurate at the time of writing.
Neither the author nor New York University Press is responsible for URLs that
may have expired or changed since the manuscript was prepared.

Library of Congress Cataloging-in-Publication Data
Stewart, J. Eric, author.
Living with brain injury : narrative, community, and women's renegotiation of identity /
J. Eric Stewart.
pages cm Includes bibliographical references and index.
ISBN 978-0-8147-6471-8 (hardback) — ISBN 978-0-8147-6048-2 (paper)
1. Brain damage—Patients—Rehabilitation—Case studies. 2. Women—Health and
hygiene—Psychological aspects. 3. Women—Physiology—Social aspects. I. Title.
RC387.5.S745   2013
617.4'810443—dc23   2013019809

New York University Press books are printed on acid-free paper, and their binding materials
are chosen for strength and durability. We strive to use environmentally responsible
suppliers and materials to the greatest extent possible in publishing our books.
Manufactured in the United States of America
10 9 8 7 6 5 4 3 2 1
Also available as an ebook

CONTENTS

ACKNOWLEDGMENTS

The Greeks warned against counting anyone lucky before he or she was safely dead. Well, Homeric gods, I am very lucky in the friends, collaborators, exemplars, and advisors who have contributed so much to this project (and my life). First before firsts, I owe ultrahumble thanks to the ten women behind the pseudonyms in these pages. The *sine qua nonymous*, their willingness to take a risk on me, their committed openness, and their tough and tender instruction, made the whole thing possible. In a different but similarly faith-based way, the doctors "Larsen" and "Austerlitz" gave me their heavily encumbered time and their preemptive respect. All were willing to go on the record in an unguarded way, even before they (or I) had an idea of what that record would be.

Julian Rappaport and Wendy Heller believed in the project at the very beginning and made it possible as an academic enterprise. That is only one of the reasons I owe Julian more than he should ever expect to get back, but I hope that he recognizes evidence of his intellectual and ethical legacy in this work. Paula Treichler, Peggy Miller, and Mark Aber broadened and deepened my attention and sense of responsibility in important ways. Special thanks go to the great Jim Kelly for reading very drafty drafts of this manuscript, and for bracing conversations about it and so many other important things, particularly the lost art of listening. Rhona Weinstein—she who must be obeyed—my academic father and a stalwart, stern, and funny friend, is my "before-the-beginning."

Thanks plus love to David, my best friend and father of Oskar, who was always there and so is all over this book: he saw the ugly side of—well, enough said.

Thanks to Jennifer Hammer and the two anonymous reviewers for helping me think an audience and move this from ideas to a book somebody could read. Finally, I've never met them, but Tobin Siebers and Rosemarie Garland-Thomson prepared the way.

Research for this book was supported by a grant from the Fetzer Foundation and by a graduate fellowship from the University of Illinois at Urbana-Champaign.

Introduction

NANCY: And this is so funny, constantly doctors were asking me,
"Tell me what this means: People who live in glass houses shouldn't
throw stones." Constantly! They were giving me these little phrases
and asking me what they mean: "Tell me what this means. Tell me
what this means." You know? Those are hard. Those are hard to deal
with.

When Nancy was in her late twenties she began having blinding headaches, tunnel vision, and dizziness, which led to a diagnosis of a congenital arterial malformation on her brain stem. Surgery was scheduled
and she wrapped projects at her job as a financial consultant, assuming
she would be back at work in three weeks. The first surgery was unsuc-
cessful, and complications during a second surgery caused serious
damage to the right side of her brain, resulting in partial paralysis of the
left side of her body and memory and cognitive problems: "I woke up
and there were all these deficits and I was really blown away by it. I was
pretty severely depressed about it." Although she was constantly evalu-
ated in various ways, Nancy's own questions and her distress got little
attention in the hospital; it took a suicide threat to obtain acknowledgment and help for her depression. Her cognitive impairments remitted

significantly during rehab and she returned to work—six months later—
but only after having to threaten a lawsuit under the Americans with
Disabilities Act (ADA). Despite excellent job performance, her physical
impairments were regarded as an "embarrassment" to the "perfect" and
"beautiful" corporate image.

Her post-injury experiences completely changed her relationship
to the corporate culture, which she now sees as "sick," and shifted her
aspirations and values. Despite a lot of anger and uncertainty about her
new future, Nancy's already strong religious faith was deepened. In fact,
she understands the whole incident as a test of her faith. She found her
experiences with other people with disabilities, during and after rehabilitation, to be the most "honest, intimate, and amazing" relationships
she has ever known; a year after leaving rehab, she remains actively
involved with those people and contexts, viewing those engagements
and experiences as an extension of her Christian faith, and as a counter
to the values of the corporate culture in which she still has to work (primarily for the insurance benefits).

Nancy is still working out "what this all means," the larger significance and the day-to-day consequences of her injury. Her account,
and those of nine other women living with severe brain injury, receives
extended and first-person explication in the chapters to follow. This
very brief gloss is meant to provide an opening indication of the ways
an acquired brain injury is not just a personal crisis for an individual
but also entails a major change in social position. Learning how to live
with brain injury is a struggle that revolves around the question of *who
am I?* This is more than a psychological question, because it involves
negotiating the powerful cultural store of narratives and practices relating to disability and to personhood. Identity as a social phenomenon
becomes salient in new ways as one is perceived and positioned as *different.* Whatever else it may involve in terms of adjusting to new impairments, working out how to live with brain injury is a struggle with the
many representations and abstractions that mystify and divide one
in relation to self and others. It involves significant work of personal
reconstruction that will be shaped in various ways by competing systems of meaning, representation, and legitimacy (Garland-Thomson,
2005, 2011; Goodley, 2011; Hogan, 1999; Thomas, 1999). It entails questions about what it is *good* to be, and what are proper relationships to

self and others; living with brain injury is therefore an ethical and inter-subjective negotiation. Furthermore, living with brain injury involves identifying or creating a sense of what it is *pleasing* and enjoyable to be; it therefore entails aesthetic negotiations of being in the world.

This book offers an analysis of extensive interviews conducted with ten women at varying stages of recovery from and living with brain injury. The primary focus is on how the women reauthor identity, meaning, and relationships post-injury. It looks at their strategies for negotiating the complex array of narratives, practices and contexts that support and/or impede that process. The use of terms like "reauthor-ing" and "negotiation" intentionally emphasizes agency, creativity, and complexity in the women's experience of negotiating living with brain injury in an "ableist world." They are also meant to confer value on the accounts, and the ways they might enable a "reimagining" of living with brain injury, and of disability more broadly (Garland-Thomson, 2005). In that regard, it is worth pointing out that the term "negotiation" is used here in the sense of adaptation married to opposition in response to dominant forces (Gramsci, 1971), not in Goffman's (1963) sense of managing stigma and negotiating a spoiled identity within terms and conditions that stigmatize and spoil (Fine & Asch, 1988a; Hogan, 1999).

Dominant narratives about disability, particularly brain injury, negate complexity, agency, and creativity; people with disabilities are generally represented as broken, abject, lacking, unfit, and incapable, or more sentimentally as suffering and brave. Such narratives subjugate the lives and bodies of people we think of as disabled (Garland-Thomson, 2011). They also limit the imaginations of people who consider them-selves nondisabled (Siebers, 2008). The women and their accounts are therefore positioned in this book in terms of human variation, rather than essential inferiority or lack; their voice and their agentive strug-gles are foregrounded in the interests of "formulating a logic that allows people to claim the identity of disabled without having to conceive of it as a diminishment of self" (Garland-Thomson, 2005, 1567).

Meaning, in relation to brain injury and disability, can be under-stood in two ways: in terms of *consequences* and in terms of *significance* (Bury, 1991). As consequences, meaning refers to the practical impact of a disability on roles and relationships in day-to-day life, such as adjust-ing to functional limitations or fatigue and the changes in roles that these may demand. As significance, meaning references the social or cultural connotations and symbolizations that surround and define disability and being disabled. Literary accounts by people with disabilities consistently testify to the fact that adjusting to an acquired impairment ultimately pales in comparison to adjusting to the stigmatization, disqualification and division that comes from being classified as disabled (Garland-Thomson, 2005). Both ways of understanding meaning make embodied experience central: a shifting spatial, temporal, and culturally mediated relationship to the world and, in that, agentive and epistemologically valuable engagements with that world by people with disabilities (Garland-Thomson, 2011; Siebers, 2008).

Consequences and significance are, of course, interrelated: cultural significations and symbolizations of impairments have practical consequences for people with disabilities in terms of frameworks of meaning, representation, and self-understanding; different impairments lead to different contexts and to different vulnerabilities and availabilities to disabling and disqualifying significations (for example, Hughes, 2009). The consequences/significance distinction, though, helps to highlight the shifting terms and contexts in which meaning and identity must be negotiated following brain injury. This distinction also relates to the one drawn by disability rights and disability studies between *impairment*, referring to functional limitations and bodily conditions taken to be impaired, and *disability*, referring to the heterogeneous social processes that mark and marginalize some bodies and minds as deviant and deficient (Garland-Thomson, 2011, Mintz, 2007; Oliver, 1996; Snyder & Mitchell, 2006). Disability, therefore, indexes a broad array of significations that the women we will meet in this book must contend with and negotiate—through compromise, renunciation, or reimagining—in a reauthoring of identity and relationships post-injury, and in striving to reauthor the oppressive social scripts in place for those identified as disabled (Garland-Thomson, 2005).

In the rehabilitation and psychology literatures, concerns with identity and self have recently come to be recognized as endemic to living with brain injury (for example, Gracey & Ownsworth, 2012; Heller et al., 2006; Klonoff, 2010; Levack, Kayes & Fadyl, 2010; Lorenz, 2010; Nochi, 2000). Identity-related issues that have been identified as important in brain injury recovery include: (1) disconnect with the pre-injury identity and learning or reconstructing a new, post-injury self; (2) social disconnect and building new relationships and a place in the world; (3) the need for contexts and resources to engage in meaningful activities and roles; and, (4) "loss of self" in the eyes of others, involving negative perceptions and social categorizations of brain-injured persons by themselves, by others, and by culture in general (Ditchman, 2011; Douglas, 2012; Gracey & Ownsworth, 2012; Jones et al., 2012; Klonoff, 2010; Levack, Kayes & Fadyl, 2010; Lorenz, 2010; Nochi, 1998). With the recent development of frameworks like "social neuropsychology" (Haslam et al., 2008; Jones et al., 2011) and "holistic neuropsychology" (Klonoff, 2010), rehabilitation psychologists have taken a "social turn" in a traditionally individual and biocognitive field, giving recognition to social processes that are the material from which personal identities are constituted (Gracey & Ownsworth, 2012).

Attention to identity and identity processes, and how these are bound up with social factors and contexts, represents a catching up to the rhetoric of a biopsychosocial model of disability and the goal of understanding the interactions between individual and environment that determine life experiences, functioning, and outcomes for people with disabilities (Ditchman, 2011; Dunn & Elliott, 2008; Heinemann, 2005; World Health Organization, 2001). This is certainly a welcome advance over the litany of deficits and the objectifying individualization that has traditionally characterized the medical/rehabilitation literature on brain injury (Klonoff, 2010; Lorenz, 2010; Strandberg, 2009). These advances also represent an overdue, if very preliminary, catching up to the decades of progress in disability rights and disability studies, which began with a "social model" of disability (for example, Oliver, 1990).

Aspects of identity reconstruction following brain injury can be meaningfully addressed within the social identity theory approach employed by rehabilitation psychologists, which focuses on stages of categorization, identification, and comparison (Swain & Cameron, 1999). Social identity, in this model, is defined by social roles and group memberships that provide an important means through which a sense of self is formed and maintained (for example, Jetten, Haslam & Haslam, 2012). Attention may be given to experiences of personal and social discrepancy, or the tendency to view oneself negatively in comparison to both the pre-injury self and to other people (Gracey & Ownsworth, 2012). Attention may also be directed to the loss of identity (the pre-injury self) and disdain for the new, post-injury self (Klonoff, 2010; Nochi, 1998). Moreover, drawing on social psychological research on stigma and identity processes more generally, attention has begun to be directed to the loss of self in the eyes of others due to the negative perceptions and social categorizations of brain-injured persons by others in society (Jones et al., 2012; Klonoff, 2010; Nochi, 1998; St. Claire & Clucas, 2012). For instance, Gracey and Ownsworth (2012) propose that for "many who struggle with the adjustment process, it is the actual or feared negative experience of self in social contexts, and the resulting attempts to manage 'threats to self' that result in a long-term maladjustment process. This is marked by increased self-discrepancy and failure to develop an updated and adaptive post-injury identity" (291).

If social identity theory holds some relevance, the last quote also indicates how the approach is nevertheless limited by its psychological perspective. There is little opportunity there for people with brain injury to work through contested identities and multiple encounters with the subjectifying effects of marginalization, let alone their experiences of multiple selves (for example, Heller et al., 2006; Hogan, 1999). Nor does social psychological identity theory offer an accounting of the toll taken by the emotional labor involved in the assault on the self in response to demands to fit the expectations of others (Hochschild, 1983). People with disabilities, in one way or another, learn to respond to expectations of nondisabled culture and the policing of self-presentation; they are expected to fit the categorizations and fantasies of others, along with social prescriptions and proscriptions of affect and emotion (Goodley, 2011; Marks, 1999; Olkin, 2009; Shildrick, 2007).

From the viewpoint of disabled people, then, their personal and social identities have been preformed within a framework from which they have been excluded, which makes the goal of adjustment somewhat treacherous. In defining parameters that state emphatically what brain injured people are *not* (normal, competent, qualified), dominant cultural narratives and practices determine what their self-reference is measured against (Swain & Cameron, 1999). Because disability is regarded as both a personal attribute and an undesirable quality—one to be managed—there is sparse incentive to view, let alone take up, brain injury as a positive part of one's social identity, except perhaps to appear well adjusted in the eyes of psychologists and rehabilitation professionals. There are, however, innumerable opportunities to become caught up in various forms of self-oppression (Swain & Cameron, 1999). A priori, the process of reauthoring identity and meaning following brain injury is overpopulated with the varied and conflicting intentions of others. Indeed, the terrain is especially constrained and overpopulated for people with brain injury because the institutional constraints are so great and overdetermined. The negotiation of identity, needs, and relationships—and the construal of the meaning of brain injury itself—involves medical and rehabilitation professionals, legislators and policy makers, the media, clergy, employers, academic theorists, support organizations, advocates, friends and family, and others classified as disabled. In addition, people recovering from an acquired brain injury also have to contend with themselves—their prior, "premorbid" selves—and the narratives of self and the world (and of disability) they had held pre-injury. They must take up the ethical and aesthetic negotiations of self-in-the-world while being unable to rely on a lifetime of prior cognitive practices and resources. In addition, they have the daunting task of distinguishing which of the problems they confront—problems of meaning, of access, of separation—are symptoms of impairment and which are the symptoms of culture.

There is little scope within rehabilitation psychology to account for a redefinition of disability or to challenge existing relations, roles, identifications, and categorizations—and even less scope for challenging the dominant ideologies that hold these in place (for example, Corker & French, 1999; Fine & Asch, 1988a; Goodley, 2011; Goodley & Lawthom, 2006). Thus, as Swain and Cameron (1999) point out, the social comparison of importance for disabled people is not a comparison of the attributes of one group (disabled) against another (nondisabled), but rather an analysis of the social structures that favor some people over others. The reauthoring of identity, meaning, and relationships post-injury, then, involves confronting the variety of practices and narratives of exclusion and disqualification that adhere to acquired brain injury. These are the narratives and practices that force invidious comparisons, define and naturalize social categorizations, and spoil identities and identifications. These narratives have legitimacy because they have been authorized by those whose able-bodiedness and able-mindedness legitimize their cultural capital, authority and power (Garland-Thomson, 1997; Tremain, 2005). The very language of adjustment and integration configures disabled people *as* the problem, because it structures an understanding that the disabled person should become more like nondisabled people, rather than offering possibilities for accepting, even affirming, the disabled person for who she is (Garland-Thomson, 2011; Siebers, 2008; Snyder & Mitchell, 2006; Swain & Cameron, 1999).

This is not to say that psychology is unimportant—or inherently dangerous—in making sense of living with brain injury, particularly if it allows us to conceptualize a situated, embodied, feeling, and agentive person engaged with a world of practices and ideologies that variously enable or disable their efforts to construct meaning and identity (for example, Goodley & Lawthom, 2005, 2006; Kelly, 2006; Nochi, 2000; Olkin, 2009; Rappaport, 2000; Thomas, 1999; White & Epston, 1990). While disability studies has helped articulate a counternarrative to the medical model of disability by pointing out the many ways that culture disables certain people, until recently it allowed little ideological room for considerations of personal identity or embodiment; the social model's aversion to individualizing disability and to anything that suggested a psychological determinism rendered individual psychology difficult to address (Shakespeare, 1996). In recent years, however, that field has recognized the need to complement sociocultural approaches with approaches that can make sense of the psychoemotional aspects of life that people with disability experience (Goodley, 2011; Olkin, 2009; Siebers, 2008; Thomas, 1999). The goal is to make sense of these aspects of life in terms of disability rather than in terms of impairment, and to account for the personally or intersubjectively felt effects of the social forces and processes which operate in shaping the subjectivities of people with disabilities (Thomas, 1999; see also Goodley & Lawthom, 2006; Mintz, 2007; Olkin, 2009). That shift has been accompanied by concern about preserving the possibility for understanding and recognizing personal agency (however entangled it may be), variation, embodiment, and situatedness (Corker, 1999; Garland-Thomson, 2011; Scully, 2008; Siebers, 2008).

Confronting the ways that they have been objectified, divided against themselves and from others, and recruited into particular subjectivities engages women with brain injury in struggles that involve and question their status as individuals. These are struggles of identity, and they involve a kind of positive identity politics that if nascent for women with physical disabilities has so far been nonexistent for those with cognitive impairments (Garland-Thomson, 2011; Sherry, 2006; Siebers, 2008). These struggles of identity are complex and paradoxical: on one side they assert the right to be different and to affirm everything that makes the women truly individual. Yet, on the other side, they involve a refusal of everything that separates or divides them, every practice, narrative or positioning that breaks their links with others and splits up community life—everything, that is, that forces them back on themselves and ties them to a constrained and constraining identity (Foucault, 1983). Thus, struggles for a positive disability identity involve an affirmative recognition and valuation of difference *and* a resistance to division from oneself and from others, and to constraining, flattening and isolating forms of subjectification.

Furthermore, and perhaps particularly for brain injury, reauthoring identity also entails struggles in opposition to the effects of power linked with knowledge, competence, and qualification: struggles against the privileges and authority of scientific, economic, political, and social knowledge that operate to define and control people through objectification (Foucault, 1983; Tremain, 2005). This has been true for the struggles against the various authoritative and moral configurations of race, sex/gender, and sexuality; these configurations historically share with disability similar and intersecting forms and practices of exclusion, colonization, medicalization, invalidation, infantilization, and rehabilitation (Campbell, 2009; Connor, 2008; Ghai, 2006; Goodley, 2011; K. Q. Hall, 2011; Leonardo & Broderick, 2011; McRuer, 2006; Michalko, 2002; Sherry, 2004, 2006; Venn, 2000). But the linking of power to competence and qualification may be especially pronounced (though not unique) in the context of brain injury due to the casting of impairments as medical crises in need of cure through technology, the "entry" into an acquired brain injury and sometimes totalizing sequestration in treatment settings, the division from family and self, and the fact that it is one's *brain* in question (Sherry, 2004, 2006; Siebers, 2008; Tremain, 2005).

Finally, the struggle over identity and against attitudinal and physical barriers also involves resistance to the shame imposed on people with brain injuries that divides them from themselves and from others. It involves resistance to the distortions imposed on them by disqualifying narratives and constraining environments. It also entails resistance to the variety of mystifying representations imposed on them, directly and indirectly, by persons and by culture (Foucault, 1983; Snyder & Mitchell, 2006; Tremain, 2005). Recovery from and living with brain injury involves a refusal of the various forms of economic and social violence that ignore who one is individually, as well as a refusal of the scientific and administrative inquisitions that determine and constrain who one is (Foucault, 1983; see also Goodley, 2011; Ghai, 2006; Snyder & Mitchell, 2006; Tremain, 2005, 2006). Rather than a rehabilitative/ therapeutic inquisition into brain injury recovery, this book seeks to recuperate the narratives of these women with acquired brain injury and their strategies for reauthoring a meaningful response to the question of "who am I?"

Identity and Narrative Reimaginings

> CINDY: I'll give you this article that I wrote, for a women's journal. I think you'll like it because you're a community person, because it actually starts off talking about the inability to, I mean the dissociation I experienced from my body, and the dissociation I experienced communally, in the women's community. And I kind of like used the parallel, and then how I reclaimed, you know a sense of community and a sense of personal body and wholeness through my work in disabled women's issues.

Cindy and her fiancé were victims of a violent random attack while they were camping in a state park in Hawaii. Her fiancé was killed; Cindy barely survived, with extensive injuries to her face and the right side of her head. She was partially paralyzed on her left side, with some loss of vision and hearing on the left side. Twenty years after the injury, she has some relatively mild cognitive difficulties and a constant but manageable posttraumatic anxiety. A "gigantic turning point" in Cindy's recovery process was coming to identify with the disability rights community, an identification—in fact, something of a conversion experience—that was initially "very scary, very hard," which she resisted quite a bit as not being her personality. She has gone on to become a nationally recognized advocate for people (particularly women) with disabilities, and has cocreated a very supportive and proactive community in which she feels safe and can work collectively for change. Her membership in a community of disabled women helped her identify and overcome a loneliness and sense of isolation she had been feeling but not quite recognizing since her injury.

Cindy's account illustrates how it might be possible to author an affirmative identity post-injury, an identity that incorporates disability but is not flattened to a medicalized condition or a singular way of knowing oneself and others. A key point is that if dominant narratives and practices surround and animate brain injury and disability in disqualifying and divisive ways, then counternarratives that challenge social norms and configurations can prevent individuals from being isolated, from being "trapped within story-lines of the prevailing narratives" (Thomas, 1999, 55; see also Rappaport, 1998, 2000). In the reauthoring of identities, people with (and without) disabilities can strengthen counternarratives so that oppressive social narratives begin to unravel (Cole et al., 2011; Finger, 2004; Linton, 1998, 2007; Thomas, 1999; Torrell, 2011).

Narrative and an authoring metaphor are useful here for several interrelated reasons. Most obviously, much of the material presented in the chapters that follow takes the form of life histories, which are narrative in nature and structure. Identity is taken here to refer to "an entity that considers itself to remain the same being in spite of changes over time" (Venn, 2000, 98). Identity-as-narrative knits the past of a life (the "having-been") to the "making-present" and to the future (the "coming-towards"), according to culturally stored emplotments of being and doing that enable (or not) the figuration of each "self" (Venn, 2000, 21; see also Ricoeur, 1984, 1991). Identity, then, is not the self-identicalness of a permanent and continuous entity, but a "mode of relating to being that can be characterized as selfhood . . . it is not reducible to the facticity of things-in-themselves" (Venn, 2000, 98–99; see also Ricoeur, 1996). Self is constituted as an identity by the stories a person tells about herself and those that are told about her by others. Every identity is "mingled with that of others in such a way as to engender second order stories which are in themselves intersections between numerous stories. . . . We are literally 'entangled in stories'" (Ricoeur, 1996, 6).

Identity-as-narrative, then, is fundamentally temporal and intersubjective, and therefore also cultural and ethical.

Identities are a means of inserting persons into a social world; they are narrative responses to and creations of social reality (Siebers, 2008). All of us come to be who we are through being located or locating ourselves, consciously and unconsciously, in social narratives that are rarely of our own making (Alcoff, 2006; Somers, 1994). The authoring metaphor in relation to identity emphasizes temporal and social *processes*, ongoing practices, strategies, interactions, assertions and refusals, rather than a once and for all or "true" resolution, and so provides a way of presenting and understanding living with brain injury as a developing, iterative, inter-subjective and "always-already cultural" complex of negotiations (Ricoeur, 1988; Venn, 2000).

Narrative also provides a conceptual framework that crosses disciplinary boundaries, for example between psychology, the humanities, and critical/political theory. Narrative is quite useful for spanning levels of analysis, between the personal, the interpersonal, and the structural/discursive, elucidating their relationships without reducing any one to the other (for example, Holstein & Gubrium, 2005; Mankowski & Rappaport, 1995; Polletta et al., 2011; Rappaport, 1998). Narrative as metaphor and as practice offers the means to handle the private/public, body/culture, and individual/social dichotomies that have been problematic for the conception and study of disability, and of persons and culture more generally (Corker, 1998; Garland-Thomson, 2011; Meekosha, 1998; Shakespeare, 1996; Wendell, 1997; see also Rose, 1992; Venn, 2000). In fact, there is particular usefulness in the possibilities narrative offers for an accounting of the many instances of both/and that define identity and disability: the importance both of agency and of social structure, of both the what and the how of accounting for oneself and the world, both the materiality of body and impairment and the socially mediated nature of our relationships to them, and of both personal and cultural historicity (the "little" narratives of lives and the grand narratives of culture). Narrative offers insights into the powerful role that time and spatial arrangements play in shaping people's lives and embodiment in socially enabling and/or constraining ways (Freund, 2001; Sparkes & Smith, 2003; Venn, 2000). Like experience, body as lived and social is never knowable in unmediated ways, as truth-as-correspondence;

narratives are important because bodily experience is deeply embedded in narrative, and narratives emanate from embodied experience (Garland-Thomson, 2011; Smith & Sparkes 2002, 2005; Sparkes & Smith, 2003, 2005).

When personal and cultural (and scientific) narratives are understood not as transparent representations of reality or interiority but as ideologically mediated and culturally bound (and bound up) interpretive accounts, they can be understood to represent forms of social action (Atkinson & Delamont, 2006; Rappaport, 1998; Smith & Sparkes, 2008). Personal accounts of experience and identity are not private, virtuoso achievements but derive from—and therefore enable—social relationships (Gamson, 2002; Mankowski & Rappaport, 1995; Torrell, 2011). They are—at least potentially—a shared resource that can help guide action and give substance, creativity, and texture to people's lives (Finger, 2004; Gamson 2002; Garland-Thomson, 2011; Smith & Sparkes, 2008). A variety of social narratives, products of particular times and spaces, interact to constitute the ontological narratives of those who live in those times and spaces (Thomas, 1999). Counternarratives can provide alternative emplotments regarding disability and impairment that refuse and displace the tragic abjection story, that resist social oppression and allow different body-self and self-other relationships to emerge (Garland-Thomson, 2005; Smith & Sparkes, 2008; Rappaport, 2000; Wendell, 1996). Finally, narrative inquiry offers promise for engaged scholarship committed to varied and situated possibilities for individual and social transformation, resistance, and living life differently (Smith & Sparkes, 2008).

In relation to social change, disability studies theorist Tobin Siebers (2008) argues for the ways that narrative enables political and practical action by providing a rhetorical form that satisfies the requirements of negotiating a minority or marginalized identity:

> Narratives about disability identity are theoretical because they posit a different experience that clashes with how social existence is usually constructed and recorded. They are practical because they often contain solutions to problems experienced by disabled and nondisabled people alike. They are political because they offer a basis for identity politics, allowing people with different disabilities to tell a story about their

common cause. The story of common cause is also the story of an outsider position that reveals what a given society contains. (104)

Critical awareness about disability requires the ability to abstract general rules based on personal experience while also being able to recognize how one's experience differs from that of others. Narratives of
identity provide the means for such an abstraction—for the critical
negotiations of sameness, difference, and cooperation between people—because they represent "significant theories about the construction of the real," and provide useful information about how one can
make an "appearance in the world" (Siebers, 2008, 105; see also Alcoff,
2006; Moya, 2002).

Fitting Together

Although people with brain injuries may have little power in society—
in fact they may be disqualified in many instances from membership in
society—their accounts and identities hold theoretical power because
they reflect perspectives "capable of illuminating the ideological blue-
prints used to construct social reality. Disability identities, because of
their lack of fit, serve as critical frameworks for identifying and questioning complicated ideologies on which social injustice and oppression depend" (Siebers, 2008, 105). Rosemarie Garland-Thomson (2011)
extends this argument by articulating how "misfitting" represents a
"spatial and perpetually shifting relationship that confers value and
agency on subjects at risk of social devaluation by highlighting adapt-
ability, resourcefulness, and subjugated knowledge as potential effects
of misfitting" (592). Experiences of misfitting, if recognized for their
political implications, make apparent the relational nature and fragility
of fitting: "Any of us can fit here today and misfit there tomorrow" (597).
    The discourse of individuality is a form of oppression that "has man-
ufactured the community of disabled people as a community of 'unre-
lated strangers,' largely without the benefit of a relationship based on
collective co-operation and trust" (Corker, 1998, 223). To the extent that
this changed, the change is due to increased population density, along
with diversifying and increasing forms of communication that have
made it possible for individuals to form recognizably distinct groups

based on different and increasingly diverse relationships. The development of communities, often small enough to allow everyone voice—and a fit—has been important for allowing disabled people to challenge oppression and division (Corker, 1998; see also Cole et al., 2011; Torrell, 2011). Such settings, and the meaning-giving interactions they facilitate, provide people with disabilities places in the world, experiences of fitting (Williams, 1998). Importantly for people with disabilities, the construction of divisions between supportive, nurturing interpersonal relationships or networks on one side, and organized, critical social action opposed to structural and discursive oppression on the other serves to enable social control and various forms of division (Corker, 1998); that is to say that for people with brain injuries, it may be important for "fitting" to be linked to intentional and orchestrated "misfitting." Social contexts in which to develop and be supported in personal and collective identities are critical, in both senses of the term.

Community reintegration and community outcomes have come to be recognized as important in the field of rehabilitation, most recently for brain injury recovery (for example, Douglas, 2012; Heinemann, 2005; Jetten, Haslam & Haslam, 2012; Ylvisaker & Feeney, 2000; Ylvisaker, Feeney & Capo, 2007; Ylvisaker et al., 2008; Ylvisaker, Turkstra & Coelho, 2005). Research has identified strong links between social activity, self-identity, and post-injury adjustment, and some work is underway to focus on these constructs in rehabilitation (Douglas, 2012). But rehabilitation research and practice related to community integration are limited on a number of fronts, including the same limitations that characterized the work on social identity discussed above: a lack of critical attention to aversive physical and social characteristics of community contexts for people with disabilities, and the demands made on them to do the costly emotional labor of adjusting to the disabling expectations of others. That is, the adjustment is all on one side, with no allowance or valuation for "creative maladjustment" (King, 1968) to the oppressive or objectifying experiences and expectations that structure community functioning and restrict the meaning of access (Garland-Thomson, 2011; James, 2011; Sherry, 2006; Swain & Cameron, 1999). While experiences of misfitting can and often do lead to segregation and alienation from community and exclusion from full participation as citizens, they might also produce positive oppositional consciousness, an awareness of social injustice, and the formation of a "community of misfits" that can collaborate not only for a liberatory politics but also for new ways of relating to self and others—including for the able-bodied (Garland-Thomson, 2011, 597). But that is only if the misfits can be allowed to escape the tyranny of adjustment.

Another limitation in the rehabilitation literature is in how "community" and "integration" are understood and measured. "Community" is typically conceptualized broadly and generically, rather than referring to a specific (or meaningful) context (Ditchman, 2011; Kelly, 2006). Integration typically focuses on individuals' access to and frequency within community settings, and to activities like shopping or spending time with friends, with little attention to the influence a person feels she has in communities, her sense of belonging or mattering in community contexts, or an experience of reciprocity in relationships (Ditchman, 2011; Chronister, Johnson & Berven, 2006). These are central aspects of sense of community, or SOC (Fisher, Sonn & Bishop, 2002; McMillan & Chavis, 1986; Sarason, 1974). One of the orienting concepts of community psychology, SOC is an interactionist perspective that aims to link extra-individual phenomena with psychology, with a focus on individuals' experience—rather than simply their physical presence—in specific community contexts. Though SOC promises particular value in relation to disability, very little work has been done in this area (Ditchman, 2011). While offering a significant practical and theoretical advance over the traditional rehabilitation literature on community, the sense of community literature has tended to focus on geographical community (that is, neighborhood), with little attention to other forms of community, such as those based on shared experiences or identities (but see Aber, Maton & Seidman, 2011; Mankowski & Rappaport, 1995; Rappaport, 1995, 2000). Nor has it attended to virtual and "textual" communities, which may be of particular relevance to people with certain kinds of disabilities or people living in rural or otherwise isolated locations (for example, Cole et al., 2011; Finger, 2004; Miller et al., 1993; Torrell, 2011).

The kinds of oppression, marginalization, and invisibility— "attitudinal barriers"—that brain-injured people experience in communities have also received little attention in the SOC literature, which is surprising given its conceptual focus on the experience of community (see Townley & Kloos, 2009, for a notable exception). In fact, it seems fair to say that the SOC literature has so far given little critical attention to how difference in general relates to sense of community. It also offers little by way of assistance in understanding the complexities of people's membership in multiple communities, or the challenges of navigating within and between these identifications.

All of the women in this book referenced community—more accurately communities—as important in various ways and forms: for providing material, social, emotional, spiritual, and/or political support; for performing and audiencing meaningful, competent, and affirmative identities; for providing and receiving information and expertise; and for work. None of the women identified solely as disabled, and they all identified different communities and identifications as important or central: a variety of religious communities; the Black community, both politically and in terms of a specific place and set of relationships; queer women; the women's community; a town or neighborhood; high school or college; professional colleagues; and, family. There was also significant variation and complexity in how they talked about what their disabilities meant for fitting or misfitting those communities. Two of the women, both fairly early in the recovery process, had no relationship at all to what could be called a disability community; the other eight women did, but each held differing, sometimes fluid, degrees and forms of relationship or identification with it and with a disability identity. Those women who identified connection to other disabled people as important discussed those relationships and identifications in varied and complicated ways.

The complex fluidity of community identification gets specific attention in the chapters that follow, but it bears preliminary mention because it is relevant to framing the women's reauthoring of identity, particularly their strategies for negotiating the variety of narratives, practices, and contexts that enable or disable that process. All of the women were members of multiple communities and relationships, and they discuss varying experiences of fitting and misfitting across and within those social locations. That is, misfitting was a common, if variously interpreted experience, both inside and outside "disability community." In some cases, it was what these women brought of their experiences with disability to their other, "able-bodied dominated" relationships and settings that generated critical consciousness both in themselves and in those others. And vice versa: some of the women brought experience with the women's movement, queer politics, Black consciousness, or spirituality to bear in constructing a positive, critical consciousness about disability. All of which is to say that people are generally part of multiple communities and negotiate multiple and complexly interrelated identities, and they do so in situated, affective, and embodied—rather than just theoretical—ways.

The field of rehabilitation has given little attention to the relevance of developing an affirmative disability identity, or to the need to confront—not adjust to—the ubiquity of disabling practices and narratives. Conversely, disability rights has made identification with and participation in disability community central to positive personal and social change, but the emphasis has largely been on disability community and identity. Feminist disability studies have done considerable work on illuminating the intersection of woman and disability, in both critical/theoretical and experiential ways. That is, the field has explicated the ways that sex/gender ideology intersects—overlaps and is reciprocally structured by—ableist ideologies, while also examining the life experiences and strategies of women negotiating that intersect (a list of citations would be long and surely incomplete, but points of entry will be found in Fine & Asch, 1988b; Fries, 1997; Garland-Thomson, 2002, 2005; Ghai, 2006; Gonzalez, 2008; K. Q. Hall, 2011; Klein, 1992; Linton, 2007; Meekosha, 1998; Mintz, 2007; Morris, 1996; Schriempf, 2001; Wendell, 1996, 1997). Recent work has begun to articulate the intersection of queer theory and disability (for example, Brownworth & Raffo, 1999; Clare, 1999; McRuer, 2002, 2003; 2006; Sherry, 2004, 2006; Shildrick, 2007), though with a heavier emphasis on theory and as yet little life writing or accounts of experience. There is a burgeoning of work on the intersection of race and ableist ideologies, particularly in the context of colonialism and postcolonial studies (for example, Connor, 2008; Ghai, 2006; Leonardo & Broderick, 2011; Meekosha, 2012; Michalko, 2002), but as yet there is little critical work on personal or situated experiences of navigating lived identities as, say, Black and disabled (James, 2011; see also Balcazar et al., 2010). All of this work (and others that are not cited here) is important in illuminating the ways that ideologies of race, sex/gender, sexuality, and the political economy intersect in mutually supportive and informing ways, thereby exposing the similarities between different and differently marginalized identities and their relation to oppression. It also helps lay bare the complicated workings of ideologies that split up community life and divide us from ourselves and others while also denying everything that makes us truly individual.

Because this work is largely highly theoretical and complex it is not just difficult to navigate but also raises critical concerns for representing and theorizing the experience of people with disabilities (Corker, 1999; Davis, 2001; Hughes, 2009; Mitchell & Snyder, 1997; Sherry, 2006). If the literature and questions of representation and theorization are difficult to navigate, the lived experience of people whose lives involve negotiating these intersections are particularly complex, sometimes treacherous, in the context of brain injury and disability, as will be clear from all of the complex permutations of identities and social positions that just the ten women in this volume represent. Work on intersecting and multiple identities does, however, underscore the complexity and power-laden nature of identity and community (and their representation), which needs to serve as contextualization of the women's difficulties (and solutions) in navigating them. The experience of multiple selves can provide a critical point of analysis for understanding how the taken-for-grantedness of everyday interactions and the stability of social practices are actually not at all granted or stable (D. E. Hall, 2004; Hogan, 1999). Also, and germane to the interests of this book, multiple identities and intersecting forms of oppression point to the theoretical and practical power to be gained from sharing and representing the experiences of oppression and struggle—of misfitting—lived by minority or marginalized people, both separately as individuals or groups and in relation to others differently marginalized (K. Q. Hall, 2011; Scully, 2008; Siebers, 2008). That is because, as the accounts in this book demonstrate, attention to the similarities between different and differently marginalized identities exposes their relation to oppression while also increasing the chances for common cause (Alcoff, 2006; Collins, 2000; K. Q. Hall, 2011; Johnson & Henderson, 2005; Kelley, 1997; Moya, 2002; Moya & Hames-Garcia, 2000).

A final theoretical point needs to be made because it is closely related to the aims, methodology, and reading of this book. What follows are accounts of reauthoring identity. There is a risk that in presenting these authorial processes that the singular nature of the autobiographical voice might reinforce a pejorative assumption about disability: that the experience of disability is an isolated one and that the issues addressed are personal problems that do not require social and political action (Mitchell, 2002; Stewart, 2011; Torrell, 2011). In the employment of the narrative and authoring metaphors here, and in a focus on identity and experience, there is the risk of reinforcing a singularity of disability, of severing the connection between the personal and the political dimensions of both disability and the authoring of identity. That is, there is a risk of reinscribing the individualizing and isolating practices of medical/rehabilitation discourses and practices in relation to disability. As Lennard Davis argued, "by narrativizing an impairment, one tends to sentimentalize it and link it to the bourgeois sensibility of individualism and the drama of an individual story" (1997, 3–4). However, the goal in the presentation of these accounts is not to elucidate the struggle against impairments or a singular and heroic overcoming of deficits but to foreground the highly social negotiations of ableist and individualistic ideologies. The intention is to employ autobiography and voice—specifically the voices of brain-injured women that have been absent in the literatures of rehabilitation, psychology, and disability studies—toward a conception of individual lives in the service of creating positive, even liberatory, resources for living and identity for disabled people, on both a personal and a socio-political level (Finger, 2004). In other words, the narratives of individuals can affirm the potential of "singular" voices for constructing community—in a variety of forms and combinations—and contributing to personal and social change (Crossley, 2003; Frank, 2004; Linton, 2007; Smith & Sparkes, 2008; Torrell, 2011). And, because brain injury and disability are so seldom presented as an integral part of one's embodiment, character, life, and way of relating to the world, and even less often as part of the spectrum of human variation, the women's accounts might enable a "re-imagining" or "resymbolization" of disability and disabled people (Garland-Thomson, 2005). They may also enable a reimagining for (currently) nondisabled people.

What Follows

This book gives priority to the voice and experiences of women living with brain injury. When women (or men) with brain injury are spoken of, it is almost invariably by and in the terms of others—doctors, researchers, family members—and so often become stories about *others*. The person with the brain injury is typically framed as a problem, something about which something must be done. Therefore, it is a central aim here to present the women as artful, if entangled, agents, strategists, and epistemologists. The accounts present the women's work and art—and difficulties—in creating and refashioning selves and identities in multiple ways and forms and in different contexts. To that end, the interview material is presented to preserve the length and form of the women's narratives.

A second aim, however, is to attend to the dominant cultural narratives and practices that the women struggle against—with varying forms and degrees of critical consciousness—and to how they do it—successfully, unsuccessfully, or figuring that out. There is, then, a dialogical back-and-forth between story telling and story analysis, attention to what the women say and critical attention to constitutive, entangling and dividing effects of cultural discourses and practices (Smith & Sparkes, 2008). This means there is a self-conscious attention to interpretive practices—the women's, both singly and in relation to one another's accounts, and my own, which also extends to subjecting theory to the women's accounts, not just the more usual other way around. But, the commitment is to always being on the women's side in that analysis, as well as a theoretical and methodological desire to clearly distinguish between the women's interpretive resources and aims and my own (Holstein & Gubrium, 2005).

Examining data from different viewpoints is intended to value the complexity and diversity of the women's accounts of disability and impairment, but it does also construct that complexity (Coffey & Atkinson, 1996). The goal is an evocative, empathetic, multivoiced presentation in which the construction of meanings remains open and unfinalized, and the reader will not just know the facts but can also keep in mind the complexities of culture, society, and concrete moments of lived experience (Ezzy, 2002; Frank, 2004; Richardson & St. Pierre, 2005). The third aim—one that should be accomplished in effectively documenting how identity, meaning, and social reality are constructed, sustained, and altered, and not once and for all or all at once—is to link these political and aesthetic accomplishments of meaning to social action, and to the development of resources and perspectives for personal and social change.

Organization of the Book

Chapter 1 ("People and Methodology") introduces the ten women who are the focus of this book along with two medical professionals, a physiatrist and clinical neuropsychologist, who had first hand knowledge of the women's "cases" over a significant period of time. The women are introduced in brief biographical sketches that also provide information about the nature and severity of their injuries, number of years since those injuries, and other biographical information drawn from their accounts. I position myself, as participant and researcher, in terms of my relationship to the women and in terms of methodological and analytical approaches. The chapter describes the procedural methods for interviewing, transcription, analysis and presentation of data. It concludes with some words about words, and some of the challenges of vocabulary and connotation related to researching, writing and talking in the context of disability.

Chapter 2 ("Meeting Post-Injury") takes up the influences and experiences of early recovery and rehabilitation settings, practices, and communications. Drawing on interviews with rehabilitation professionals, the chapter begins with some perspective on rehabilitation practices and contexts, including their changing climate under managed care. The major portion of the chapter draws on the women's discussion of their experience and the effects of early recovery in inpatient and outpatient rehabilitation settings.

Chapter 3 ("Oneself as Another") discusses coming to terms with the disconnect or division between the pre-injury and post-injury selves. It serves as bridge between consideration of rehab in chapter 3 and of the "outside world" experiences of the subsequent chapters, and shifting the site of fighting from one's body and brain to the disabling narratives and arrangements of the ableist world—as well as decisions about when to fight and when to let it go—a theme picked up in chapter four.

Chapter 4 ("Fighting") addresses challenging or resisting cultural barriers in place for people with brain injury: at work, at school, and in the range of contexts in which the women did or wanted to participate. This involved specific fights to gain access, agency, or legitimacy, for example against transit systems, employers, or universities. The women's accounts also attend to more diffuse and pervasive fights, including the fight to identify and name forms and instances of oppression or exclusion, as well as struggling with identifying as disabled and/or with other disabled people.

Chapter 5—"Sense (and Sensibility) of Community"—considers the importance and value of finding a fit, creating or locating place and company within community. Again following the women's accounts, this often meant finding a place and identification in a disability community, including the benefits and discontents of heterogeneity within and intersecting that community. Finding a place within or in relation to a disability community involves differences in types and severity of disability: "invisible" versus visible disabilities; primarily cognitive versus primarily (otherwise) physical impairments; and so on. But finding "place" also involves intersections and tensions with other identifications or positions, and finding a location or fit within the disability community also entails marking distance and differences within it. However, as mentioned earlier, two of the women had no connection to or identification with a disability community or identity, and those who did also pointed to central importance of other identities and communities. Thus, this chapter also considers finding or re-creating a place in other communities and the intersections of several identities.

Chapter 6 ("Wrestling with an Angel") addresses the metaphysics of brain injury and disability. Metaphysical questions and commitments cut across most of the themes, relationships, and dilemmas discussed throughout the book, this chapter brings them—and their varied forms and functions—forward for direct attention. Chapter 6 focuses on the variety of spiritual and religious narratives and affiliations the women discuss, from the resolutely materialist to the most mystical, the positive or complicating roles those have played in their authoring processes, as providing the grounds for refusing forms of division and subjectification, and as a "place aside" for asserting the immanent (thereby returning to and consolidating some themes and arguments of preceding chapters).

The brief concluding chapter ("Coda") revisits and links the main themes of the book and its goals and considers some practical, theoretical, and ethical implications for research, practice, representation, and/or social action.

1

People and Methodology

The first interviews conducted for this study were with Rose and Cindy, both of whom asked many questions about the study, its aims and methods. Both women also offered specific advice about how I should (and shouldn't) proceed. Cindy, who had conducted life history research on people with disabilities for her (post-injury) master's degree, first corrected my notion that people with acquired brain injuries would divide their lives into "before and after" chapters or selves:

> CINDY: There usually—my research, and you can quote me on this
> [ES: Okay]—there are several turning points. There's never one. I
> would advise you to encourage people to talk about some of the
> turning *points*. Um, and there are many. What I was doing, and I
> don't know if this would help you at all, is that when I interviewed
> people I talked about the first year prior to the injury, I did like the
> year pre-injury, then I asked the same questions and moved to a
> year post-injury, and then I jumped way ahead to like the present.
> [ES: Okay] And I did some of the same questions, to try to, to have a
> context to stimulate conversation. And I would get different turning
> points—because you *do* have different turning points. I mean at the
> beginning, there's just such um, I'd say one of the benefits of having a

traumatic brain injury in one's life [*Cindy then ES laugh*] is that—for me—and I think this might be head injury [*Cindy laughs*] I don't know, but there were so many things I still hadn't done, um, pre-injury, and that I'd be doing post-injury. I don't know if everyone is dominated by this need to do all these things post-injury, but I think I find a thrill in doing something new, different. Like I remember the first time I travelled on a business trip *on my own*, was just, um it was fourteen years later, um, after. I had been on a plane, I had done several trips, but I had people meeting me both ways, you know. But I hadn't done the whole shot where I did the taxi to the airport, gone through the airport—the airport script [*laughs*]—that script had not been rescripted at all, for fourteen years. So it really changed how I looked myself, it added meaning and, um, dimension. The quality of oneself and how one looks at oneself, and what one is able to achieve. So, um, yeah, try to find out about the many turning points.

Within a few minutes Cindy had: apparently decided I was worth talking to; checked any misconceptions about who could claim expertise in the relationship and in regard to brain injury recovery; troubled, even displaced, the construction of pre- and post-injury identity in the medical/rehabilitation literature as the defining turning point; and offered methodological advice for asking about many turning points and making room for participants to discuss a whole life. Furthermore, her account clarified an important, easy to miss distinction between the deficit-driven "heroic overcoming" narrative and what Frank (2004) would call a "quest narrative," which, as Cindy's telling illustrates, is driven by a creative becoming. The intervention always steered me clear of the claustrophobic tendencies of most brain injury research and toward a greater attention to and facilitation of capaciousness.

In fact, many of the women offered advice—prescriptive and pro-scriptive—for talking to women with brain injury. This advice usually came after they had already asked me, in one way or another, a lot of questions about me, my interest in them, and who else I had talked to. These interactions are significant on a number of counts, some of which were implied in the previous chapter: the women were concerned about how they would be represented, what the interview experience would be like, and maintaining some control over that experience and over how they would be represented. Many of them were concerned about the experience of the other women I had been or would be interviewing.

The interactions were significant as well because the initial "testing" process and the information the women offered provided methodological and epistemological direction. As an academic, I knew there would be a critical turn when it came time to analyze and interpret the transcript material, a turn that can represent a moment of objectifying betrayal in ostensibly collaborative qualitative research, particularly with marginalized voices. The initial interrogations established frank relationships that allowed both an asking and answering of critical, even confrontational, questions as the interviews progressed. That is, critical analysis could happen in the context of interviews, not just in the after-the-fact transcript analysis and write-up. Being able to be reciprocally critical throughout mattered because it facilitated many shifts in epistemology and theoretical direction over the research process. It mattered too because at the time critical disciplines were ambivalent about the use and value of voice and experience. For instance, within disability studies there were controversies about the naïve deployment of first person accounts and life history work, about singularizing or sentimentalizing disability, and about reinscribing disabling ideologies and subjectifications. The possibility for engaging in a mutual troubling and exposition of perspectives and interpretations resolved some practical and theoretical concerns about voice, representation, and the relationship between experience and critical theory.

Participants and Settings
Locating the Women

Because this was an in-depth, extended interview study, the number of participants was necessarily small. The first people I interviewed (Rose and Cindy) were women, and I decided to keep the focus on women in order to avoid one set of complications in interpretation. Including men would have made comparisons extremely hard to avoid, and with a small group of people comparisons would have been misleading at best. Furthermore, women with brain injuries are particularly underresearched. The language demands involved in an interview study dictated an inclusion criterion of fairly high language abilities, excluding women with serious speech-production problems or aphasias. This meant that most of the women had right-brain injuries (RBIs), although several had more diffuse injuries that included areas of the left hemisphere.

The primary (or most convenient) place to find brain injury survivors has always been medical and rehabilitation settings. In these settings, however, one is likely to find people in the early stages of recovery and rehabilitation leading to a truncated, deficit-focused understanding of recovery, particularly in regard to questions of identity and identification. Working with people in these settings also likely exaggerates the role and importance of medical discourses and practices in the processes of living with brain injury. Therefore, it was important to identify women further along in living with brain injury, and so removed from rehabilitation settings.

Finding and making connections with these women was no small part of the project. It is difficult to gain access to a "network" of brain-injured people for several related reasons. First, they aren't particularly interested in being found. That is, as many of the women here noted, academic interest in them has been largely exploitative and objectifying, with little interest in their experience and lives, so they aren't especially eager to be "subjects." Second, brain injury is often an "invisible" disability, and many of the women like it that way in many contexts of their lives. Identification as brain-injured is often selective and strategic, and not particularly public. This relates directly to a third point, one that may underlie all the others: trust. I would not have made contact with most of the women without being vouched for by somebody they knew. My first and key contact, Cindy, was the first link in a chain of connection to six of the women, and I only met Cindy through her public role as an advocate for women with disabilities. That is, in relation to the factors I just enumerated, Cindy was intentionally visible and public, and she was also adept at negotiating the terms of research relationships. In the different context of a hospital in a small city, the women participated because they trusted a friend of mine who worked in the neuropsychology clinic there and advocated for the project and for me. The spaces these women and other people occupy as brain-injured people are not public spaces in the usual sense, and strangers did not have easy access. Once I was in I was in, but it took some time and some self-accounting to establish that status.

Ten women with brain injuries participated in formal interviews. Three came from a small midwestern city or one of the very small towns nearby. The other seven women came from a large midwestern city and its suburbs. The women ranged in age from seventeen to fifty-three, and at the time of the first interviews they ranged from six months to around twenty-eight years post-injury. Two of the women were African American and the others were white. Three were married, two were engaged, and one self-identified as lesbian or queer. Nine of the women had at least two years of college, and one was still in high school; six had attended or were attending graduate school. (Many of the women began or completed their graduate work after their injuries, a fact involving a number of considerations and will be discussed in subsequent chapters, particularly chapter 5).

All of the women's injuries were classified as severe, but there was considerable variation in the effects of those injuries. For the most part those injuries and their effects had little impact on the interview process. What effects there were or might have been varied by participant, context, and topic and do not allow for any general characterization. The women were all quite fluent and had few problems presenting their accounts. In the instances where the effects of the women's injuries did in some way or another figure in the interview process, or in communication more generally, those dynamics are discussed in the context of their accounts.

What follows are brief thumbnail biographical profiles of the women, drawn from their interviews and autobiographical accounts. These short sketches are meant to provide an orientation or reference point for the reader, not to capture the women's lives. (The appendix provides a table of briefly summarized characteristics of each of the women, which may be handy as a kind of program of players in reading the chapters to come.)

Rose. Rose is a single African American woman in her mid-forties, from a working-class background. She was living in a midwestern university town where she was working toward a master's degree in oral history. Rose received right parietal damage in a closed-head injury as a teenager, but she was not correctly diagnosed until twenty-four years after the fact (about four years before the interview). In the meantime she received numerous misdiagnoses, from learning disabilities to schizophrenia. It was only by a series of "fortuitous connections" that she was eventually correctly diagnosed. She continues to hold some anger toward mental health professionals in general, an anger that she feels kept her going.

Rose describes the years following the injury as frequently "nightmarish," marked by posttraumatic symptoms and "low self-esteem and self-blame." She got a BA with the help of "people who had no understanding at all of [her] problem," who believed in her and took her eventual success as "an article of faith." Her mother died about four years before our meeting, and that event precipitated her worst encounters with the mental health system: her "flipping out." Since obtaining a correct diagnosis, she has been involved in some rehabilitation work with a neuropsychologist, and she has become involved in head injury support and community education. At the time we met, Rose was engaged in her own research on the oral histories of people with traumatic head injury and their families (this will be discussed in chapter 5).

Tracy. Tracy is a single seventeen-year-old white woman living in a very small midwestern town. Approximately six months prior to the first interview, she was involved in a car accident that resulted in a right parietal fracture, right and left occipito-parietal hematomas, and a left frontal concussion. Her condition deteriorated while in the hospital (due to the hematomas) and she was in a coma for a few days; she had posttraumatic amnesia of three days, and pretraumatic amnesia of less than an hour. At the time of the interview she was experiencing some emotional problems (depression and irritability), aggravated by difficulties with social perception, and some cognitive difficulties mostly involving memory and attention. Her main concerns however were about "how people are treating [her] differently" since the accident, and that her doctors "don't want [her] playing basketball because it could kill [her]." Sports are a key part of Tracy's identity and social life.

Tracy has lived in the same small town since she was born, attending school and church with many of the same people for much of her life, and she is quite embedded in her particular cohort of friends. She characterizes herself as an average student. She was highly active in varsity sports prior to the injury (track, softball, and basketball) and just tentatively returning to play at the time of the interview. Tracy has two younger brothers; her father is a farmer and her mother has a white-collar position at large company. Her parents divorced about five years prior to the injury; she spends half the week living with her father and stepmother and half with her mother and stepfather. At the time of the interview, she was still involved in rehabilitation and on half-time schedule in her senior year of high school.

Sarah. Sarah is a forty-nine-year-old white woman who was about a year post-injury (six months out of the hospital) at the time of the first interview. She had moved to a very small midwestern town when she married her third husband about a year and a half prior to the injury. Her husband is a farmer, but he is also a volunteer paramedic who was called to respond to the accident in which his wife was injured, a car collision near her home that happened en route to a wedding rehearsal with four other women. Sarah received extensive injuries to right frontal-parietal and temporal areas, was in a full coma for about three weeks, and had pretraumatic amnesia of one week (much more according to her husband) and posttraumatic amnesia of approximately six weeks. Her pelvis and right rib cage were crushed and her right eye cut through in the collision. At the time of the interviews, she had some persistent sensory perception and motor deficits in her left side, and her vocal cords were partially paralyzed so that she required a tracheotomy tube for breathing. Speaking required her to cover the tube with her finger and pull air up over her vocal cords. She was still experiencing cognitive problems, particularly with distractibility and short-term memory.

Sarah and her two sisters were raised in the Church of the Nazarene in small towns in the West and Midwest. After graduating from a Nazarene college, she worked as a model and as an interior decorator. She adopted an infant son as her first marriage was ending. When she divorced her second husband, a military man like her first husband, she turned to professional motivational speaking and image consulting. Following her "spiritual calling," she moved to the desert Southwest around nine years before marrying her current husband (also on a spiritual calling), where she became a leader and teacher to an extended circle of people. Although she disavows official membership with any one church or religion, she is a licensed minister and had been a substitute minister in one of her town's churches prior to the collision. She and her husband hold strong but somewhat nontraditional Christian spiritual beliefs that also define their relationship to the accident and injuries, as well as many of their social relationships.

Cindy. Cindy is a white woman in her early forties and was nearly fifteen years post-injury at the time of the first interview. She lives in the suburbs of a large midwestern city. Her husband is a bank executive whom she had known prior to the injury, but she only became romantically involved with and married him several years after it; they have a young son. Cindy and her then fiancé were violently attacked in their sleep during a camping trip in Hawaii. The attack left her fiancé dead and Cindy with extensive open-head injuries to most of the right hemisphere. The injury left her partially paralyzed on her left side and with loss of vision in the left visual field and hearing in the left ear. She is able to walk with a leg brace and cane but increasingly uses a motorized scooter, in part because of rheumatoid arthritis. Cognitive difficulties were not readily apparent to me, but she reported problems with short-term memory, distractibility, and attending to more than one source of input at a time. She described a feeling of constant but manageable anxiety, which she identifies as related both to organic effects of the injury and to the violent way in which it occurred.

Cindy was raised in various places around the country. Her parents were middle-class Catholics and children of Eastern European immigrants, but she converted to Judaism when she married. Cindy had achieved success in business but was looking to make a career change immediately prior to her injury. After the injury, she acquired a master's in philosophy and another in communications. She cofounded and directs a resource center for women with disabilities (the Women's Center) at a major midwestern rehabilitation center (the Rehab Center), edits its newsletter, speaks publicly on disability issues, and has received several awards and grants for her work in disability services.

Abby. Abby is a single African American woman in her early thirties, from a small-town working-class background, living at the time in a large midwestern city. During her senior year at college she had a stroke caused by a congenital arteriovenous malformation (essentially a missing capillary bed leading to ruptured veins), which affected occipital and parietal regions of both hemispheres, though left hemisphere, especially occipito-parietal, problems are most apparent. Abby is partially hemiplegic on her right side and has some mild to moderate cognitive difficulties, mainly with reading and occasionally with fluency and word finding.

Abby chose to attend a prestigious private college over the historically Black university that her family had expected she would attend. She holds strong Southern Baptist beliefs, which figure prominently in her account. At the time of the stroke, she was majoring in communications and preparing for law school and a career in politics; in fact, she was delivering a public lecture when she collapsed from the stroke. She lived with her mother in her hometown during recovery and rehabilitation; when she began to realize that "everything was returning to normal except for me," she went back to the college and finished her degree, three years after the stroke. At the time of the first interview she felt that she had been doing "badly" and discussed a few prior suicide attempts and an apartment fire. She was, however, working part-time at a direct social service agency and active in programs for women with disabilities. At the time of the third interview two years later she had begun a graduate program in rehabilitation services, was involved in a "maybe serious" relationship, and talking much more about "moving forward."

Lydia. Lydia is a single white woman in her late forties, about twenty-eight years post-injury. She lives with her elderly, wealthy parents in a suburb of a large midwestern city. She was injured when her car rolled off the road and she was ejected through the sunroof. The accident caused a long fracture and resultant hematoma beginning behind the left ear and wrapping around the base of the skull to the right temporal lobe. Injury to the brain was diffuse but primarily affected parts of the left temporal and parietal and right parietal areas. She was in inpatient rehabilitation for ten months and continued intensive outpatient therapy for about five years. However, she reports it taking twelve years to finally reach her current level of functioning. She has persistent motor difficulties and partial paralysis to the right side, which also affects her speech production. Lydia also has some memory deficits and has to write and keep track of notes about appointments, tasks, and phone calls.

Prior to the injury, Lydia was a registered nurse, a career that was quite important to her. She is now trying to develop her business as a freelance massage therapist and volunteers part-time at Cindy's women's center. Although her parents have made sure that she won't have to worry about money, Lydia is concerned with finding a meaningful career post-injury (her memory and motor problems prevent her from returning to nursing). After having to "keep trying different ones out" she finally found a church that felt comfortable to her, where they don't treat her "like a charity case" and let her sing in the choir "even though [she] doesn't pronounce the lyrics perfectly." She is quite active in her church, including teaching Sunday school and attending singles' groups. Lydia credits the accident for bringing her "back to God" and "responsibility," and she frequently gives people—like me—the testimonial she wrote about God's miracles.

Nancy. Nancy is a white woman in her late twenties. She lives with her fiancé near a major university in the suburb of a large midwestern city. She works as a consultant for a large accounting/auditing company. She returned to work six months after her injury, though not without having to threaten the company with an ADA suit, and not to her original position. One year before the interview, almost to the day, Nancy began having severe headaches, tunnel vision, and dizziness. She was eventually diagnosed as having an arteriovenous malformation on her brain stem. Complications during a second surgery interrupted blood flow to major portions of the right hemisphere, particularly the occipito-parietal and temporal regions. The incident caused partial left hemiplegia and the loss of part of her left visual field, both of which may be permanent. She initially had memory and cognitive processing difficulties, but these have remitted to near pre-injury levels. Nancy also suffers from periodic major depression perhaps aggravated by the injury, but which is responsive to medication.

One month before the second surgery, Nancy made a "spontaneous decision to be baptized" in the Episcopal Church. She feels that this was "no mere coincidence" and believes that, while she is uncertain of its ultimate nature or purpose, what happened to her is "test of faith." Since the injury, she has become active in her own church and in her fiancé's Catholic church. Nancy is also an active volunteer and fundraiser at the same Rehab Center where she was a patient. After her fiancé finishes his PhD in history, Nancy plans to return to school for a master's in education and then to teach high school.

Elise. Elise is a white self-identified lesbian in her mid-twenties. She lives with her mother and brother in a large midwestern city. She is currently attending college as a music education major. Seven years before the first interview, soon after her high school graduation, Elise's car was hit by a drunk driver who fled the scene. The accident caused a closed-head injury to the base of the right side of the skull, causing trauma and swelling in her brain stem and temporary loss of blood flow to areas of both hemispheres. She has persistent memory and cognitive processing difficulties (though these were not immediately apparent to me), including social perception problems, sensory and motor deficits on the right side, and paralysis of her right vocal cord (causing difficulties for her career as a vocalist).

The first years after the injury were particularly difficult for Elise. She feels that her doctors and therapists gave her "unrealistic" "misinformation" about her limitations, her recovery process and potential. She dropped out of college after one semester because she was unable to sing or keep up with course work. After training in sign language and interpreting for a year and a half, she gave that up as career because it had "lost its flair" and returned to college. She is still fairly active in the deaf community, however, and volunteers to sign at many events. Having "lost music and mourning it like it was dead," she felt she had lost her "purpose and identity." She also lost faith in the church, which had also been an important part of her identity, a loss of faith cemented by her reading of the book of Job. She credits her introduction to Buddhism and her involvement in the Buddhist cultural center with pulling her out of her feelings of "angst, confusion, and being stuck."

Susan. Susan is a white woman in her mid-thirties, engaged to be married to man who also had a serious brain injury. She lives in an assisted-housing complex in an affluent, predominantly Jewish suburb of a large midwestern city. Her parents live nearby and are still very involved in her life. Thirteen years prior to the first interview, Susan and a friend riding with her were seriously injured in a car accident, for which she was found to be at fault. Susan suffered an open head injury that caused extensive damage to the right parietal and frontal areas and put her in a coma for nine weeks. Consequently, she has partial paralysis in her left side, motor deficits, and some executive-function and social perception difficulties. She was in rehabilitation for over seven years at various rehabilitation centers in the Midwest.

Susan is currently working as a clerical assistant at her city's Center for Independent Living and is hoping to be certified as an Employee Advocate Professional for people with disabilities. She enjoys counseling people with brain injury, especially working with the parents of young people who have brain injuries. Of all the women participating, Susan's cognitive difficulties are the most obvious. She relies on her parents, particularly her mother, and a visiting social worker to handle many of the details of her life. Despite that, she is ambitious, proud of her work and of how much she reads, and proud of her success with men ("I've always had guys knocking on my door, pounding on the door, and I keep telling them to go away!"). She believes that when she and her fiancé are married, they'll be able to look out for each other and "keep each other straight." Both families are wealthy enough to insure their children's financial security.

Beth. Beth is a married white woman in her late forties, about six years post-injury at the time of the interview. She lives with her husband and college-age daughter in an affluent but diverse suburb of a large midwestern city. Prior to the injury, she was a well-established orthodontist and taught at a university. In fact, she was driving to address a dental association meeting when she was caught in gun cross fire. A bullet penetrated her head at the right temporo-parietal area, traversed the third ventricle, and lodged in the left temporal lobe. She lost control of the car and collided with parked cars, causing additional injuries. The injury caused widespread motor, sensory, memory, attention, and cognitive processing problems, as well as temporal lobe epilepsy (now controlled with phenobarbital). As she describes it, "nothing is automatic anymore," and she has to talk herself through even routine activities such as getting dressed: "Cooking dinner for the family is quite a project. I'm ready to call it a day afterward."

Beth still attends dental and orthodontics conferences and develops and explains orthodontic plans at her former practice, but she does not expect ever to be able to practice again herself. She also volunteers a great deal of time for the Epilepsy Foundation. Beth and her husband both come from "stoic, nondemonstrative, Midwest backgrounds"; their marriage had been "formal" for many years prior to the injury.

However, she believes the individual and couples' therapy, support groups, and volunteer activity she became involved in post-injury, along with the enforced "slowdown" in her life, have increased her "sense of relatedness to people" and community, made her more "insightful," and greatly improved her marriage.

* * *

Because I was working in a psychology department and working with two hospitals, and because brain injury classified the women as members of a sensitive population, the research involved approval processes from Institutional Review Boards (or Human Subjects Committees) at each of the three settings involved. All of the women involved in the study gave informed consent for their involvement, including an option of anonymity. Pseudonyms are employed throughout this text, but this choice was based less on the participants' concern for anonymity than on concern for the anonymity of people and settings that the women refer to in their interviews (who did not give consent to be participants). That is, most of the women were willing to be fully on the record, but as the interviews proceeded some concerns arose about other people discussed in their accounts. Protecting the identities of settings and of people named in interviews became an issue, and the only way to deal with this was change everybody's names, including the names of people the women discuss in their interviews. The precise time frame of the project and interviews has also been left ambiguous to help blur the identities of the actual sites and people discussed in the interviews. The anonymity so provided is probably penetrable to anybody directly involved in these settings, but that will at least remain a function of inferential and unconfirmed deduction.

The process of recruiting the participants was uneven and spread out over time, so some of the women were involved in the study for five or more years, others for only a few months. Some of the women were simply less available for extended participation because of their own time constraints, other commitments, relocations, or their interest in discussing their experience with their injuries. Therefore, although all of the women's accounts form the interpretive and analytic framework, some of the women came to play the role of "key informant"; they provided more material than did others, so their accounts get more representation in this book. Some of the women gave more or more elaborated discussion to certain experiences or contexts than to other themes addressed in this book, so some women's accounts get more representation in some chapters than in others: Cindy in the chapters on disability community, for example, and Sarah or Abby in the chapters on metaphysical narratives and religious community, as other examples.

In the cases where there was less interview material to present, at appropriate locations I have tried to incorporate passages, however brief, from those participants in relation to or in conversation with passages from other participants, to help amplify or elaborate their points or experiences. In other words, I tried to insure that some of the women's perspectives and experiences were not under- or overrepresented based solely on how forthcoming or eloquent they happened to be, where they were in the recovery process, or on how well their perspectives matched the structuring of analyses. Some of the participants did have more to say, for a variety of reasons including age and amount of experience living with disability, or simply interest in saying it; to me that is reflective of the diversity of people with disabilities, and that diversity is reflected in what follows.

Medical Opinion

To help contextualize the women's accounts and elucidate something of the professional institutional terrain of rehabilitation and neuropsychology, two relevant rehabilitation professionals were interviewed in some depth.

Dr. Austerlitz. Dr. Austerlitz is a clinical neuropsychologist at a regional hospital and trauma center serving a broad, largely rural area of the midwestern state (Doctors Hospital). The hospital is located in a small university city and, though not university affiliated, has established some training and research relationships with various departments and schools at the university. Dr. Austerlitz became a key informant for several reasons. First, he often works with patients from admission on through years of neuropsychological evaluations, rehabilitation, and psychotherapy. Second, he had worked with and helped identify two of the participants (Sarah and Tracy), which made it possible to contrast his account directly with theirs. Third, Dr. Auster-litz has interest in—and is inclined to philosophize about—living with severe disability, mortality, meaning, and identity. He was somewhere in his fifties at the time of the interviews and had been working in neu-ropsychology long enough to have seen it through some major changes and developments, as well as to have worked with a large number of patients. Having come from the East Coast and being Jewish, Dr. Aus-terlitz feels that living in a small midwestern and largely Christian town has given him insight into the experience of being "other" (he reports not being allowed to join the country club when he first moved to town, for example). This insight, he feels, allows him to better identify with his patients' experience.

Dr. Larsen. Dr. Larsen is a physiatrist, or doctor of rehabilitation medicine, at a large, highly respected rehabilitation hospital affiliated with a university medical center in a large midwestern city (Rehab Cen-ter). As a physiatrist, she generally has a closer and longer-lasting rela-tionship to patients than might other rehabilitation professionals. She has been seeing some of her patients for many years after their release from inpatient treatment, making referrals to other medical or mental health services as well as to community-based services and organiza-tions. Dr. Larsen is also cofounder and codirector of Cindy's Women's Center and has a particular commitment to women's health and access to services. Partly in relation to this commitment, she is active in the Rehab Center's policy development and ethics committees. She is con-cerned and very well informed about the social and structural issues people with disabilities face, as well as the resources available (or not) to assist them. At the time of the first interview, Dr. Larsen was probably somewhere in her mid-thirties.

Aside from the very different settings, with differing public and research functions and in different geographical and institutional loca-tions, the doctors' roles in those settings and relation to their patients also differed. Perhaps because he is a psychologist, Dr. Austerlitz attends to psychological and existential concerns quite a bit in his discussions of and with his patients, and he does psychotherapeutic work with his patients and their families. By contrast, Dr. Larsen gives considerable attention to policy concerns and broad structural changes and factors, particularly as these relate to health care and access to services, which may be reflective of her position at a research- and policy-directed center, as well as of the fact that she is doctor of rehabilitation medicine. The two doctors also knew different women participating in the study. These factors mean that there are differences in their roles as informants and the themes and concerns they discussed. Therefore their accounts figure in different ways and in different chapters in this book, for instance, Dr. Larsen in chapter 3 (on managed care) and Dr. Austerlitz in chapter 6 (on metaphysics and brain injury as an existential phenomenon).

Settings

Locating and working with the women involved several settings other than the interview locations. Two of these have been alluded to already. The first is Doctors Hospital, which serves as the major trauma center for large, mostly rural area around a midsize university town and provides what rehabilitation services are available in the area. I met with Dr. Austerlitz for formal and informal conversations at the neuropsychology clinic he runs at the hospital. I was also given access to the clinic files for Sarah and Tracy, as well as to some of the staff involved in their cases. The other settings were the Rehab Center where Dr. Larsen works and where Cindy's Women's Center is located (though it operates fairly autonomously on its own grant funding). All of Cindy's interviews were conducted at the Rehab Center, in her office at the Women's Center or in the cafeteria, as were a number of other informal conversations. Dr. Larsen was interviewed in the Rehab Center's cafeteria, and Lydia was interviewed in the Women's Center library. I also spent a fair amount of time simply hanging around the Rehab Center and the Women's Center, which, because they are usually busy with volunteers, staff, and clients, meant that I had the opportunity to listen in on or participate in many informal conversations and interactions. Cindy invited me to sit in on a meeting of the Rehab Center's ethics committee, which included the outgoing and the incoming directors (most of the discussion dealt with managed care and insurance company–imposed capitation and stay limits, and the Center's handling of them).

My relationship with Cindy (spanning more than six years) led to involvement in two conferences, both sponsored or cosponsored by the

Rehab Center and both highly relevant to this work and to women with disabilities: one on managed care and its implications for women with disabilities, the other addressing the implications of assisted suicide for people with chronic illness or disabilities (or the "duty to die" as many of the activists there defined it). At both conferences I worked as a volunteer, which meant doing anything needed, from trying to make restrooms accessible to finding mayonnaise, from running the microphone to helping people get around. At both conferences I was introduced to and got to hear from a number of people involved in disability concerns or communities, including doctors, lawyers, radical and not so radical activists, and many women simply navigating their way through the issues related to living with disabilities. I include mention of these settings, as well as those of the interview locations below, for several reasons. First, the settings, and the time spent and interactions occurring in them, informed the interpretations of interview material and provided context for the analysis. In some cases, these interactions alerted me to particular questions or directions of inquiry that would otherwise not have occurred to or crystallized for me. Second, and related to the first point, contacts and discussions with others in some of these contexts (for example, hospitals) provided a check on some assumptions and stereotypes (for example, of the medical profession). Third, the settings in which the interviews took place communicate something about the women themselves, their circumstances, and the kinds of relationships I formed with each of them.

All participants chose the interview locations, and with the exceptions just noted and Rose, all interviews were conducted in the women's homes. These ranged from small, urban apartments to large suburban or rural houses. Sarah and Tracy both live in very small farming towns. The rural location is noteworthy because of the limits it imposes on access to the disability-related services, information, and affiliations available in larger urban areas. (However, urban location is no guarantee of access to or even awareness of such resources, as many women in the study pointed out. Similarly, small towns and rural communities may provide different kinds of support and resources, as is evident in Sarah's account.) At each of Sarah's interviews she chose to have another person present, her husband for two of the interviews and a friend visiting from out of town for another. This was because her tracheotomy tube made it possible that she would experience breathing difficulties requiring informed assistance. But in each of the interviews the other party participated in Sarah's accounts, adding his or her own perspectives and some occasional memory prompting.

I interviewed Abby at Cindy's house on one occasion, when she was taking care of Cindy's son for the afternoon. The other interviews with Abby were conducted at her home; the first was at her small studio apartment near the private university she had attended as an undergraduate. The third time was at her new apartment, near another university she was currently attending, which she shared with her boyfriend. Susan was interviewed in the commons room of the assisted-living building she lives in. Beth and Elise were interviewed in their homes. I met with Rose at a campus-area vegetarian cooperative restaurant in the university town where we were both residing.

Positioning Myself

I have not experienced a brain injury, at least not beyond the types of injuries that are actually quite common in the general population (namely concussions), and by most standards I don't qualify as disabled. I am also, for the record, not a woman. I have to defer on the question of men without brain injuries doing research on women with brain injuries. These do represent critical and asymmetrical social axes of difference and power, and they therefore must be acknowledged, if not foregrounded, in research and interpretation. Something different does emerge from my interviewing these women than would be the case if a woman, a person with a brain injury, or a brain-injured woman were to conduct the research. I am equally certain that there is value in a variety of arrangements and in their intertextual dialogue.

While they may not be foregrounded in this study in quite the same ways, other axes of social identity and experience were also involved in some or many of the interactions. I am white and two of the participants are Black. I identify as queer, and only one of the participants would identify in that way (and I'm not certain that "queer," versus "lesbian" or "dyke," would be her consistent choice). I am the approximate age of only a few of the women. I am pretty resolutely nonreligious, but many of the women hold fairly firm religious or spiritual faith. And so on. Obviously living with brain injury and disability are a central focus here, and gender becomes salient in its own complex way because of the participants. These topics will be discussed throughout the following chapters; so too will the ways they inflect my interactions with the women participating, their experiences and interpretations, and my interpretations of those accounts. But most of the conversations crossed several lines of difference—and ostensible sameness—simultaneously and unavoidably. Conversations across these lines of difference are desirable in that they push or pull for more articulation and explication of experiences and interpretive frameworks than would be the case if both parties shared an "implicit" understanding (Kögler, 1999). My presentation of lengthy and only lightly edited transcript passages, which often include my own questions or responses, should enable the reader to evaluate how the differences in subject positions affected the process and product. Furthermore, much of interpretive process has been put "on the page" and made as transparent as possible, including stating when I simply didn't know how to understand something.

Disciplining Myself

Gareth Williams (1998) warns researchers against the urge, when writing about disability or chronic illness, to resort to abstractions or universals, to use the experience of participants "as a vehicle for exploring basic questions about the nature of the self in the world" (241). Such solipsism—as he characterizes that urge—tends to erase or obscure not just the embodied experience of people with disability but also the structures and contexts that make that experience what it is. There is here an interest in broader, more general processes that I believe apply to other marked statuses, particularly in regard to language practices and renegotiations of identity. The accounts are used to elucidate those processes, but I believe this is done without reducing those accounts to mere allegory or taking the participants as devices. Furthermore, although I am sure I couldn't catalog them all, I know I have assumptions about what are and are not liberatory or positive narratives and contexts. I like to believe, however, that these were subject to change or at least bracketing in relation to the women's experience, beliefs, and accounts. This is a study of women living with brain injury and not in a conscious way a metaphor for other, "universal" meanings or experiences. Yet I would like to point out that while we will not all experience a brain injury, our status as nondisabled and cognitively unimpaired is provisional and temporary. Following Siebers (2008), the experiences, theories, and practices of the women here are assumed to elucidate something about our culture, and they do have relevance for problems experienced by both disabled and nondisabled people.

My training and disciplinary perspectives have influenced the methodological and interpretive choices made throughout this book. First, I generally identify as a clinical-community psychologist, a hyphenate that involves inherent disciplinary tensions and critical concerns. As a psychologist, I have an interest in the strategies and tactics that individuals employ in conceptualizing and extricating themselves from cultural binds. Like most community psychologists, I am interested in the transactions between people and their local and cultural contexts, and in processes of setting or social change rather than individual therapy or normalization. The field emphasizes diversity and variation rather than universals and single standards, and views people and communities in terms of strengths rather than deficits or deviations. Community psychology is also committed to working outside of traditional professional settings and disciplinary boundaries, and to fostering a variety of community-based and community-driven support and change efforts, to collaborative and participatory research and intervention methods, and to promoting optimal personal and community development rather than treating pathology. There is, then, an interest in actual people and in actual social contexts, rather than persons as ideas or as an aggregate, standardized "everyman" or the "averaged" person. (For fuller, more detailed discussions of community psychology see Aber, Maton & Seidman, 2011; Goodley & Lawthom, 2005, 2006; Kelly, 2006; Nelson & Prilleltensky, 2004; Rappaport & Seidman, 2000).

My approach to the interviews, I suspect, bears the imprint of clinical training and experience, not least in the attention to use of language and handling of contradictions. And, I hold an interest in how persons solve problems and in individual interpretive strategies. Those proclivities, however, actually led to the foregrounding of the critical perspectives developed by disability studies, already explicated in the introduction and returned to in subsequent chapters. Everything on that list sits side by side with commitments taken up as a queer in the world, and in teaching cultural studies and queer theory. Although narrative offers a more or less common ground among those disciplines, there is an interdisciplinary back-and-forth across these boundaries in what follows, and in attention to the tensions in the women's accounts and my analysis of them. There are tensions that I don't pretend to have resolved, for example between humanistic, even realist, commitments and those to poststructuralist critiques, consideration of which is beyond the scope here, but see Plummer (2005) for a discussion in the context of queer theory. The general approach is, in the end, an emergent methodological and interpretive bricolage (de Certeau, 1984; Kincheloe, 2001; Weinstein & Weinstein, 1991) pieced together to fit the specifics of the complex, shifting "situation" of identity reconstruction and meaning making following brain injury.

Methods

The general procedural approach draws from critical interpretive and cultural methods in that "narrative" applies here not only to the autobiographical experiential and interpretive accounts of the women but also to theories and rationales that structure the cultural (for example, social scientific, critical-theoretical, and medical-rehabilitation) practices that constitute and "speak through" those accounts and that the women negotiate in various ways (Chase, 2005; Coffey & Atkinson, 1996; Goodley et al., 2004; Riessman, 1993, 2002; Smith & Sparkes, 2008; Todd, 2006; Torrell, 2011). Narratives here are taken to be forms of social action: they constitute, maintain, and/or challenge modes of knowing, doing and being. The women telling them are taken to be social agents, though not completely in or on their own terms (Marx, 1956), developing understandings of meaning and social action in ways and frameworks that are in process and unfinalized (Ezzy, 2002; Frank, 2004; Holstein & Gubrium, 2005). Therefore, the language used by the women conveys meaning and how the story is told is as important as what is said (Esterberg, 2002; Riessman, 2003). Finally, because narrative is social action—and social interaction—I give conscious attention to the ways I construct the women's narratives into another of my own, from the context of the interviews, to the selection, analysis, and arrangement of passages, to the authoring of this book (see, for example, Chase, 2005).

Interviews and Transcription

Despite Cindy's advice, the interviews were largely unstructured, with no formal protocol or predetermined questions. It was priority to give control, the upper hand, or expertise in the interview process to the women (for example, Chase, 1995, 2005; Mishler, 1986; Paget, 1983). For all of the reasons outlined in the introduction, particularly because people with brain injury are typically objectified, it was important to make the interviews an empowering experience. Following Chase (2005; see also Gubrium & Holstein, 2002), I wanted to position the women *as* narrators rather than respondents or informants, and I wanted to position myself as a listener who could also ask questions about those narratives and meaning-making and meaning-challenging strategies, to draw out specifics rather than a general phenomenon or trajectory of brain injury. The aim, then, was elaborated, situated, and relatively full interpretive accounts, in whatever way the women would structure and develop—or narrate—them. Frankly, and as a matter of practical fact, there seemed to be no need to develop specific questions to elicit such accounts—brain injury was obviously the issue at hand—or any way to anticipate what would be the salient framing and features of those accounts for each woman. Because the study entailed a critical/analytic approach it was important to obtain as situated, contextual an understanding as I could in the interviews, and to arrive at as collaborative a relationship as possible with the participants (Kögler, 1999).

As the interviews progressed and relationships became better established, it began to feel appropriate, or easier to know when it would be effective, to ask direct or confrontational questions and to investigate seeming contradictions in the accounts. I would sometimes offer my own perspective or the experience of other participants as parallel and/ or better contextualization of particular experiences or interpretations. The process allowed for exploration/elaboration of specific themes or topics, for some in-the-moment critical analysis, for checking my interpretations, and for comparing interpretations across participants.

The formal interviews lasted between one and a half and four hours and were audio recorded. Interview tapes were transcribed within two weeks (most often one week) of the interview; I performed all interviews and transcriptions. As soon as they were completed, copies of transcripts were given to participants to allow them to clarify or add any points if they wished. In the cases where multiple interviews were done, this also allowed an opportunity for participants to think about what they might want to add, qualify, or elaborate in subsequent interviews. Abby and Cindy were interviewed three times over a period of nearly five years, in addition to numerous informal conversations at conferences, by phone, and/or e-mail. Sarah was interviewed three times over a period of about two years. All of the other participants were interviewed once.

Transcription was verbatim, though turning spoken language into written text involved a fair amount of interpretation just, for instance, in making decisions about punctuation or the handling of overlapping utterances. The transcripts were not cleaned of elements such as false starts and the nonlexical or performative utterances (such as "um" and "uh") of normal conversation (and these are preserved in the presentation of excerpts). This is noteworthy for two reasons. These are part of normal speech and part of the "how" of the women's telling; in many of the excerpts presented they help convey the emotional valence of what is being said and/or the difficulty of the recounting. These false starts and nonlexical utterances more often than not have nothing to do with the women's injuries, but sometimes they do (though it may be surprising to see how much they characterize normal spoken speech, as they do my own questions and responses).

Analysis and Presentation

Analytic strategies were roughly grounded in a sociological interactionist approach, attending to the identity or self-construction work that people engage in within institutional, discursive, and local cultural contexts, and which takes narratives of identity to be lived experience and social action (for example, Gubrium & Holstein, 2001; Holstein & Gubrium, 2000, 2004; G. Miller, 1997). In this context the focus is on a more or less specific *aspect* of the women's lives—brain injury and disability—along with particular institutional/organizational settings (for example, Riessman, 2003; Smith & Sparkes, 2002, 2008; Sparkes & Smith, 2003, 2005). The general aim is to explore and show the ways people create a range of narrative strategies in relation to institutional and discursive environments and positions, the ways that individuals' stories are constrained by but not determined by coercive settings and dominant narratives (or hegemonic discourses). A twinned goal is to examine the women's narratives for the ways they can illuminate the contradictory, shifting, and unstable nature of those discourses, and so begin to expose and unravel them. I have, however, employed narrative psychology approaches in attending to the formative effects of narratives, and an assumption that some stories enable and some disable self in relation to life problems (see, for example, Rosenwald & Ochberg, 1992; White & Epston, 1990).

Analyzing the transcript material, therefore, entailed a back and forth between the "whats" and the "hows" of the women's accounts, or between what Smith and Sparkes (2008) term "story analyst" and "storyteller" conventions. On the one (storyteller) hand, the women's accounts are taken as analysis (Ellis, 2004). Their accounts are presented and considered for what they illuminate about active, agentic construction of meaning and identity and the power of narrative to refashion identities in different contexts and presentations. Their accounts do significant work of analysis and theorizing because they are engaging analytic strategies to interpret their world and experiences. On this side, there is a foregrounding of evocation, engagement, and intimate involvement over abstraction, with the aim of creative representation.

On the other (story analyst) hand, there is an attention to the analysis of the narratives as data that do not fully speak for themselves. This entails stepping back from the accounts to think about, explain, or compare certain features or contents, and theorizing them from one or more disciplinary perspectives (Smith & Sparkes, 2008). There are, then, moments or angles at which the women's stories are taken up as an artifact for formal analysis, for extrapolation into theoretical or general propositions, and a concurrent switch into a critical analytic mode. For the most part, the critical, generalizing mode is focused on the institutional and discursive regularities presumed to structure and inform—enable or disable—the women's construction of meaning and identity.

Holstein and Gubrium (2005) emphasize that because interpretive practice is two-sided, there is a tension that cannot be completely resolved. Reducing the analysis of the narratives to the "what," or the

telling, ignores the constitutive, entangling effects of institutional differences and cultural configurations, and so elides the effects of power
and ideology on living with brain injury. Conversely, focusing on just
the "how," or analysis, taking the women's narrative practices as the
mere residue or effect of institutional discourse "risks a totalized marginalization of local artfulness" (495) and reduces participants to cultural dopes. The analytic interplay between the two sides of interpretive practice "mirrors the lived interplay between social interaction, its
immediate surroundings, and its ongoing concerns" (496).

However, I take it as a given that my perspective or position—my
"knowing"—is as entangled in and constituted by cultural narratives
and institutional configurations as the women's are presumed to be.
In establishing relationships, in the interviews, and in analysis of the
material, therefore, I made an intentional effort to engage in a kind of
critical hermeneutics, a mutual illumination of what might be operating behind my back as well as theirs (Kögler, 1999). This related to
the choice to favor what Chase (2005) calls the "supportive voice" as
researcher, to foreground the women's narratives and their epistemological strategies, and to maintain a respectful distance between the
women's voice and my own.

Despite or alongside any a priori methodological choices and strategies, much deciding, choosing, and resolution took place along the way,
especially in the writing. This was salient, for instance, in figuring out
how to be sensitive to and respectful of the diverse stories being told
and the contradictions and tensions between them. The end product is
what Smith and Sparkes (2008) refer to as a "creative representational
project" that rests on the presentation and juxtaposition of extended
passages from the interview transcripts.

While the division and arrangement of the chapters might be taken as
thematic, they are better understood as sites. Analysis was not thematic,
properly speaking, but built outward from the voice and the structure
within the accounts (nobody told her stories thematically) and looking
for threads of connection and contrast between the accounts. The process did support a more or less structured arrangement and analysis of the
accounts by locations or moments, but it will be clear that there is significant cross-cutting, cross-reference, and complexity. Rehabilitation experiences, fighting social barriers, finding a fit in community, and spirituality/

metaphysics should not be taken as "research constructs" in the usual sense, but as data-suggested and not entirely arbitrary textual arrangements for presenting complex linkages within and across the women's accounts. They are, in important ways, as unsettled, nonunitary and open to revision as the women's identities (see Chase, 2005; Stein, 1997).

Words

I don't know if it is possible to make language neutral or fully nonevaluative, particularly as it is taken up by readers. If it is possible, I don't know how to do it. The contested history of the usage of words like "disabled," "impairment," "identity," "agency," or even "interpretation" illustrates how the valuation and effect of words change over time and across contexts. In the context of disability, Oliver (1996) argues that struggles over language are never merely semantic. I have avoided the use of "deficits" in favor of "impairment" or, more often. "difficulties." I mostly use the term "disability" rather than "brain injury," in part because many of the women saw mobility impairments as more salient than cognitive impairments but also to keep the linkage to disability rights/studies upfront. For various reasons usage is not consistent, and the women use a variety of terms in their accounts (such as "handicapped," "retarded"). Sometimes certain words are bracketed, situated, or made ironic with quotation marks and/or some interrogation. But repeated use of quotation marks would have been tiresome or distracting, and sometimes would have had the effect of making the women's choice and use of terms appear to be the object of ironic or critical comment.

One term that I had some trouble with but that seemed unavoidable for a number of reasons, is "activist" or "activism." My discomfort arises from the implication that women here who aren't involved in particular organizations or activities aren't critical or resisting, that they lack commitments or somehow labor under a false consciousness. Most of the women here fight quite a bit and resist quite a bit, though only three or four would be called "activists" in the general sense of the term. The terms "disability" and "disabled" also raise a number of possible questions and problems, versus more precise but cumbersome constructions like "people classified as disabled." I follow the women's usage most of the time, though I generally use disabilities or difficulties, versus impairments; in part because these are the terms most of the women here used most of the time, and in part because the impairment/disability distinction presents its own difficulties (see, for example, Sherry, 2006).

As another example, I had been advised (by Cindy) that I should always call to confirm interview appointments a day or two before the date, just to prevent memory from becoming an issue. I made the mistake with a few participants of saying that I was calling to *remind* them of our appointments. Elise corrected my lapse:

> ELISE: You know what, it's interesting, when you called last night, I don't know if you noticed this but I notice these things. You said "I'm calling to remind you of our meeting tomorrow." And, um, I thought, how funny he should say that because it's common courtesy that you call and *confirm* appointments like this. It's not an accommodation of my disability that you're calling.
> ES: Oh. I think I didn't think about it, I probably use them interchangeably, but—
> ELISE: You may, but *remind* was, you know, it was interesting. I thought, hmm, I don't know about this, I'll have to mention it to him.
> ES: I'll have to watch that, then. I can see—
> ELISE: It's interesting to discuss words, since I'm in the business of words as an interpreter. Um, but to remind someone of something really takes the position of, not to be too serious, kind of takes the position of power. You know, to *remind* somebody? And I'm not trying to come down on you, that's why I don't want to state it too seriously, too harshly. But to say I'm calling to remind you, it sounds parental: you must remember this rather than I need you to do this for me. Does that make sense? [ES: Sure, *now*] It's kind of authoritative I guess, is what it sounds like. I don't know. Just a philosophical discussion about words.

I always said *confirm* after that. Words were important, sometimes contentious, for many of the women (and the doctors). *Recovery* turned out to warrant interrogation, for what it implied about "restoration" and for its oppressive looming as the only acceptable outcome. *Lucky* is another word that got me in trouble on a couple of occasions. Other instances come up in the chapters that follow.

2

Meeting Post-Injury

There is no universal rehabilitation experience. The site and severity of brain injuries vary greatly, as do the effects those injuries will have in the short and long runs, and these are difficult to predict (Doidge, 2007; Lezak, Howeisen & Loring, 2004). Diversity defines pre-injury, for instance in terms of experience and achievement, geographic and social location, sex/gender, age, cultural background, financial and other resources, and so on—the list is long and its itemization is fraught with all of the traps of categorization and division. It also certainly matters how and in what context the injuries were incurred (such as combat, domestic violence, DUI, stroke). Related if not reducible to those factors, there is considerable variation in context, type, quality, and duration of rehabilitation services, and variance in information and expectations conveyed, even within a single rehab setting. There is no unitary discourse about brain injury and brain injury recovery; the field is in a process of reinvention, in part because technological advances have dramatically increased survival rates of brain injury (Smart, 2001; Sneed & Davis, 2002) and life expectancy post-injury is now similar to that of the general population (Warren et al., 1996). The wars in Afghanistan and Iraq, with their high rates of head injuries (Singer, 2008), often comorbid with posttraumatic stress disorder, will continue to affect the field of brain injury rehabilitation for many years to come.

Variation figures prominently within and across the women's accounts. It is worth foregrounding heterogeneity here not only to describe the facts of this study but also as a counter to the convergent, standardizing, and normalizing pressures in rehabilitation research and practices. Brain injury is not just a personal crisis and medical condition; it also involves a sudden and dramatic change in social position, and so brings with it experiences of new social categorization and social interactions; it is a social condition. The crisis, the new social position, and experiences of social categorization will be encountered newly and simultaneously in rehab.

HMOphobic

Managed care—or "mangled care" as it was referred to by a number of people I talked with—is effecting a shrinking of time and services, particularly social and community-focused services, that can be offered or supported in most rehabilitation settings, even the best of them. "HMOphobic" comes from the bumper stickers I noticed on the cars, wheelchairs, and motorized scooters at the Rehab Center and at a couple of disability conferences (I had not seen them anywhere previously). For rehabilitation settings and practices in general, whatever advances in knowledge and technology—or even in political consciousness—have been made in recent years have been counterbalanced by shrinking budgets, increased costs, and the stay limits and capitations imposed by managed care. That is assuming one has insurance or access to rehabilitation services at all.

Managed care and capitations affect whether or not people can get medical attention, in-home care or assistance, sufficient physical therapy, or even obtain a wheelchair. Dr. Larsen, a doctor of rehabilitation medicine (Physiatry) at the Rehab Center, here discusses what she sees as the most pressing issue for people with disabilities in the current cultural terrain:

> DR. LARSEN: I mean the managed care issues, I just find overwhelming. I'm so angry. *So* angry with the health care system. I'm fighting a

battle today where I've had a patient who's been in bed, at home, for over three months, almost four months now, doesn't have a wheelchair, hasn't been able to get out. Her husband called and we brought her in by ambulance. I wanted to admit her, and she doesn't even have an HMO, she has a PPO that will approve her for three days. And that's a gift they tell me. And they won't let me talk to the medical director. I'm furious. I am absolutely furious. And the appeals mechanisms and the recourse that people have, I mean the family's terrified of getting dumped with the bill, *of course*. So, I feel like right now a lot of the fight has to be on a public policy level, because we have sweeping changes in this country that are having a very profound and negative effect on the lives of people with disabilities.

It is important to know that Dr. Larsen is not at all given to hyperbole. Her story illustrates how, already in early rehabilitation, people get the clear message that getting medical and rehabilitation services involves a fight, yet these are also a "gift" that they are given. Even for people with health insurance, like Dr. Larsen's patient, hours of patient, family, and doctor time are spent negotiating and navigating policy and bureaucracy. Time and fighting devoted to acquire the "gift" of services. These are battles that have to be fought during the acute stages of recovery.

There has been considerable critique of the medical model and the biomedical narrative that cast disability as a physiological problem requiring normalizing technology and expertise. Dr. Larsen articulates here how meaning and identity are cast not only in terms of bodily and cognitive deficits but also, maybe preeminently, in terms of economic deficits. Disability is structured by and embedded in an economic narrative of cost and (nonproductive) expenditure. All of the fights—against one's brain and body, against invidious comparisons, against objectification and marginalization, against built and cultural barriers—may be preempted by the fight for care and against being cast and casting oneself as a burden, an expense, and a lot of trouble. And, this sense of being a burden is not helped when your problems with HMOs or with your lack of insurance are framed and treated as singular, individual problems rather than problems of the political economy and of entire classes of people.

Dr. Larsen went on to highlight what she sees as the most frightening problem facing people coming into rehab in recent years:

DR. LARSEN: One of the things that is really troubling to me right now is how quickly people are becoming outpatients. You were talking about the outpatient setting as where more of the interesting work takes place. Well, it used to be that you were in a very supportive environment as you went through certain stages of adjustment. That no longer exists. And, you talk to people like Cindy, or Pepper and Cara, who've been, who've made careers, they were in the hospital six months to a year. And what happens is that there is a psychological process, adjustment process that they were supported with in the hospital. And we had a lot of time to start looking at community adjustment, you know. [ES: Yeah] Getting out into the public transportation system and figuring out how you're going to work the personal care system, and if you wanted to go to a museum, how would you do it. And you want to get on an airplane, and actually helping people walk through these processes. We're not being allowed to do these things, like we used to be able to. And people who would stay in the hospital nine months, you know twenty years ago, are now in and out in eight weeks.

ES: Wow, that's dramatic.

DR. LARSEN: So I really fear because I don't feel like we have the safety nets in place, the outpatient support services—which has always been the argument: "Well, we'll just provide more in terms of outpatient support." Well, it doesn't happen. So, I think we're putting more of the onus on patients and families, to do more work on their own. And, um, I'm fearful of what's happening to people right now who are struggling to do that kind of adjusting. When you're fighting for your health care benefits, I mean *fighting*, and you may be told by your insurance company that you can only stay in the hospital two months because you've only got thirty outpatient treatments, I mean what *despair* people feel. So I feel like a lot of the psychological, spiritual and social aspects of being disabled are getting neglected because we're talking about *pure survival*. I mean I think beginning to be able to accept the fact that you're disabled, beginning to be able to talk to other disabled people, is something that a lot of people need time to get to. And that piece is not addressed at this point.

ES: So, if that's the case, and to the extent that there are community resources out there—*when* there are—that would help address those aspects of recovery, uh, how do you, for instance, as a physiatrist—or the Rehab Center as an institution—help people make those sorts of community connections? Or are they on their own?

DR. LARSEN: I'm afraid a lot of times I think that they're on their own more than they should be. Because the stresses on staff, now in terms of cutbacks, in terms of staff ratios, fewer people are doing more things. It's more crisis management sometimes. I mean, our psychologists try to make sure that people have as many social and community support systems in place as possible. And the outpatient setting, I refer a lot of people to the outpatient social worker, uh, or to Center for Independent Living. I mean I try to make sure people get connected with Independent Living, that they get peer support— which is so necessary. And, um, through the Women's Center, I think that's a really valuable resource, for my younger female patients especially, um, the educational seminars and the newsletters. But I think, again, it's one of those things that's probably not getting the care and attention, universally, that it should.

ES: Yeah. I don't mean to put you on the spot, but this is sort of a premiere facility and so I'm curious to know what you all do, how you think about these things? I guess I'm trying to get sense of what's the optimal situation, the current best case scenario.

DR. LARSEN: I think we do a lot more than a lot of hospitals. I just think it's far short of what we should be doing. Um, I really worry about people who are in rural areas of the country, or in facilities that isolate their disabled patients. I think there are a lot of isolated people out there, people ending up in nursing homes that shouldn't be. Um, my patient at home, [ES: Yes] whose family doesn't know what resources are available or even how to advocate on her behalf. Um, I think that there are a lot of people that are falling through the cracks. As an institution, I think one of the things that the Rehab Center does that's extremely important is the advocacy work, it's always been considered a leader in advocacy issues around the disabled. And, uh, again to me that's one of the most important things we can do. Um, trying to get the message out there about changes in health care and insurance, about how changes in Medicare—I mean the changes in

Medicare have been *frightening*. The implications for our patients are
profound. We do a lot of work trying to talk to legislators and getting
messages out there about the effects on a practical level. Um, I think
very few hospitals or rehab facilities have the capacity to do that.
Part of it's our reputation, part of it's that we've always had very well
connected leadership, who have built a lot of important relationships.
But, even so, it's not like we're even holding a line.

Dr. Larsen makes clear that for questions of mobility, obtaining personal care assistance, identifying and obtaining available services and
entitlements, the simple logistics of disability—let alone identity, meaning, and establishing relationships and social networks—community-
based resources are an increasingly critical piece of the process. Yet, as
she points out, while rhetoric about outpatient services and community resources has proliferated, in most places the actual services and
resources have not. Furthermore, those community-based organizations and settings that at one time were somewhat free to develop mis-
sions of political and social action or other kinds of cultural work, find
that they must devote time and resources to patient advocacy and case
management services.

When Dr. Larsen describes the experience of many of her patients as
one of "despair," that should be taken as a considered estimation. The
scenario she describes as frightening is for one of the best facilities in
the country, in a large city where there are community-based resources
like a Center for Independent Living and a dedicated women's resource
center. If the Rehab Center, with its significant financial and political
resources, along with its professional and ethical reputation, is sometimes operating on a footing of crisis management, it is quite frightening to consider the situation in other areas of the country, in less public
spirited and wealthy facilities—the nursing homes and "facilities that
isolate their disabled patients." Most people with severe brain injuries,
as she points out, do not have these same or even approximate resources
available, because of geography or of mobility, and because of policy
and the political economy.

As or even before one begins to confront objectifying medical narratives, or the heroic overcoming, sentimental, or abjection narratives
that may configure interactions with self and others post-injury, one

confronts being cast in the dollars-and-cents terms of economic burden or liability. I dwell on this for a few reasons. It is a narrative that carries through rehabilitation and beyond: in the time and situated attention caregivers can give to patients ("fewer people doing more things"); in the emphasis on independence and productivity that defines good outcomes for people with disabilities; and, in every encounter with a gatekeeper of services, for whom the women must "perform" and prove their disability and worthiness (Marks, 1999; Shildrick, 2007). It matters because the logic of pragmatism and instrumental rationality drives a quantitative orientation that converts cultural, interpersonal and psychological considerations into monetary values. That logic doesn't drive just managed care, it also increasingly drives program development, standardization, and evaluation metrics and goals in social services and the social sciences (Fineman, 2005; Nafstad et al., 2009; Nelson & Prilleltensky, 2004; Scully, 2008; Seidman & Rappaport, 1986).

The material world of economics and the sociocultural world as mediated by discourse are intricately enmeshed (see Laclau, 1990); the political economy structures ideologies of race, gender, sexuality, and disability, and vice versa, in deeply historical and often naturalized ways. Identity, meaning, community, fitness, and citizenship—as well as caring and interdependence—are caught up in colonialism and capital. Too often theories and practices focus on one or the other—identity politics or economic politics; discourse or materiality—or reduce one to the other (Corker & French, 1999; Duggan, 2003), including (North American) disability studies. Political economy has to be kept in mind as structuring the women's experiences in more and less obvious ways—here in relation to access to services and how the women are positioned in medical/rehabilitation practices and outcome emphases, but later in terms of valuations of caring, labor, community and interdependence, as well the meanings of citizenship, personhood, and rights, not to mention constructions of race and gender.

If there is an upside to Dr. Larsen's account it is that doctors and other rehab professionals are coming around to some political consciousness, beginning to see disability (and health care generally) as a social and political issue, and developing relationships or even coalition with disability rights organizations and activists. It is encouraging to find doctors who are "absolutely furious" about their patients' difficulties accessing services and support. Dr. Larsen may be fairly exceptional in the extent of her actual participation in policy work and developing alliances with community-based and activist organizations; at Doctors Hospital there was less concern over these issues, but there was concern. Doctors and other rehab professionals may be acting out of a sense that their professional and guild territories are being encroached upon, their status and power being diminished by bottom-line considerations and managed-care bureaucracy, but, as Cindy says: "Hey, whatever gets them on board."

My Rehab

Most of the women aren't in a position to reflect in a generalized or institutional way on the rehabilitation experience as they have no basis of comparison. Most people only go through rehab once and usually only at one place. Particularly during the early period of recovery when patients are experiencing new impairments and acutely feeling the loss of prior abilities, it is hard to know or articulate what an optimal rehabilitation experience might be. Even within this small group of women and a few rehabilitation facilities, there is considerable variation in experience. To begin, a comparison of Beth and Rose's experiences will in a sense anchor the ends of a continuum and reiterate the role of economic politics in care and identity.

Rose was injured quite young. There may have been several incidents, but a blow from a baseball when she was sixteen years old seems to have precipitated the onset of noticeable difficulties. She never received treatment for the injury and didn't enter any kind of meaningful rehabilitation until she was in her forties, four years before I met her:

> ROSE: It was twenty-four years from the time I had the trauma until I got the diagnosis. It was a nightmare, trapped inside invisible walls. I just couldn't make sense around it. [*Six-second pause*] The jobs I've lost, relationships—I can see why people commit suicide, just become drug addicts. I don't know what kept me from doing it. I remember thinking a lot that if I could just talk to God, if I could just make my case. If some doctor had just said, "describe what happens, when did it start?" Instead of saying, "I don't see anything wrong." [*Four-second pause*] If people have known about head injury, if there

are people who are supposed to be trained to help people, then *what the hell has been going on* for all these years?!

Rose's account is largely about lack of access to services and the "people who are supposed to be trained to help people." Although head injury is often overlooked as a diagnostic possibility, being a working-class Black teenager and living in a very small town would probably overdetermine the problems she discusses, particularly never being given a chance to make her case. What was going on in those twenty-four years is that beginning in school she was diagnosed as learning disabled and/or behaviorally disordered and later went on to receive various psychiatric diagnoses. She faced many barriers to obtaining a meaningful diagnosis, information, or help, but she didn't actually escape "the system." The ways her impairments—and her frustrations—were diagnosed and treated only further disqualified her:

ROSE: I flipped out and I ended up in a psych ward a year after my mother died. I thought it was my last chance.
ES: Last chance in what way?
ROSE: I know. It sounds crazy. I know they wanted to diagnose me as like bipolar or schizophrenic or something. But I felt like this was my chance to actually get somebody, you know, to, for me to get some-body to actually pay attention. [ES: Okay] Someone there suggested that I see a speech therapist at the university, but they were closing for the semester, so he suggested I contact Dr. Inaka, who was doing some research. But then the psych ward nurse called his office—out of pure mean-spiritedness—to tell them I wasn't "the kind of person they want." She wanted to queer the connection. It was only because I and my psychiatrist were persistent that it worked out and I got to see him. Dr. Inaka. A miraculous person, a neuropsychologist with specialization in right brain trauma, *finally*. It was fortuitous that I hooked up with Dr. Inaka. It's the fourth year I've been working with him. We spent three years undoing the damage done by the psych profession and by my own perceptions of myself.

It may be hard to relate to Rose's experience of her mother's death and subsequent stay in a psychiatric ward as a "chance." But she says it represented the possibility of finally getting to make her case. The account puts some of the criticism of brain injury treatment and rehabilitation in perspective. As objectifying and deficit-focused as it may be, *not* having access to expert discourse and services represents a significant and significantly more difficult problem; it means your problems will be interpreted and "treated" by other authorities, like the "psych profession," with all the iatrogenic damages that ensue. The lack of meaningful diagnosis and treatment damaged Rose's self-perceptions, damage that she and her doctor spent years undoing. It bears note that Rose connected and worked with Dr. Inaka in the context of his research. That is, she gained and maintained access to this care as a (grant-funded) research participant, not through obtaining actual access to formal rehabilitation facilities or services.

I want to bring attention to Rose's persistence, including the battle with her own Nurse Ratched here, in continuing to push for attention, understanding and appropriate services. She did locate allies, but the "happy ending" can't be attributed to the beneficence of the mental health professions. Things "worked out" only after a long series of fights against various classifications and misclassifications of her, her problems, and her resistance. Rose had to continue to refuse classifications even as she had no idea what would be the thing to say yes to. These were not just problems inherent in the medical and psychiatric field but also of cultural discourses and practices related to race, class, age, and probably gender that transect and also partially structure health care and mental health services. Furthermore, the experience of wanting to tell their story but of not being invited to or heard is an experience identified as ubiquitous among people with disabilities (St. Claire & Clucas, 2012; Zola, 1994).

Beth, by contrast, identifies a number of positive aspects in her rehabilitation experience, including being heard:

BETH: I got a lot of good therapy, and support. Good, good doctors. And therapy was nothing I would have sought, if I hadn't been injured. And, in fact, I am more content now than I was pre-injury. [ES: Huh] Um, and it was, that was partly the Elavil, too, but I mean it's not just drugs. I've been given some tools to work with. Um, and some insight, through the various professionals. But being financially

secure helps when you're in this situation. Fortunately I had taken
out disability insurance, so I've had that on top of my Social Security.
I've been able to afford a good HMO plan that covers these things.
That's very important. If you don't already have it, get disability
insurance.

Beth, then, feels that she gained from the therapy, support, and
insight that she received, and can claim a gain in terms of greater
contentment. She is very clear about how her financial security was
determinative in that experience. Beth, though, also possessed cultural capital; the outcome, and probably the quality of interactions
with her caregivers, may relate to the fact Beth had established herself as a professional with a family and many other accomplishments
before she was injured. An enforced slowdown means something different in your forties than it would in your twenties. Having accomplished these things, having known herself in these ways, made the
adjustment to disability easier to negotiate, made it easier to appreciate what slowing down, doing less, and relaxing more had to
offer. Being a socially secure professional who could speak medical
language and pharmacology also probably enabled her to evade or
resist some of the more objectifying and mystifying practices associated with brain injury and rehab and affected the expectations of her
caregivers.

Expectations are a recurrent theme in these rehab accounts, both
those that the women had for themselves and those communicated by
others. These expectations and the categorizations involved with them
derived from and shaped interactions with their caregivers and had significant impact on the women's experiences and outcomes (see Clucas
& St. Claire, 2010; Kumar & Clark, 2005;Lalljee, Laham & Tam, 2007).
The expectations of others obviously shaped Rose's experience, and
Beth's expectations of others and of herself influenced her rehab experiences. Both kinds of expectation connect the accounts of most of the
women, how they negotiated care and how they came to conceptualize
post-injury possibilities.

Nancy is younger than Beth, but she had achieved a measure of
occupational success before her injury. She was diagnosed with an arteriovenous malformation in her late twenties, though her actual injury

was the result of complications during surgery (about a year before this interview). In this passage, Nancy talks about discussing risk and outcomes with her neurosurgeon—before the injury—and the difference between expectations and the actual outcome:

> NANCY: So, my neurosurgeon, he said, you know, "I do these about once a week and they're fairly common." So I trusted him on that. Um, I knew I was going in for surgery, so I wrapped up projects at work, left notes on everything, but I was planning on being back in like three weeks. Um, completely did not expect anything to go wrong. Had no, um, warning from my neurosurgeon that there was risk at all. He had said there was, maybe a 5 percent chance of "extreme neurological damage." Now, to a lay person [*both laugh*] that doesn't mean anything, you know? And, looking back, obviously I should have asked, well, what does that mean, you know? But, that's a small percentage, and he knows what he's doing, he's really good at it, and I'm just not going to worry about it. Um, I went in for my first surgery and um, he tried this one procedure that essentially didn't work. Um, so they had to do it again. And um, in the second surgery he actually took the whole mass out and um, it cut off the circulation to, um, a portion of my brain that controls, obviously the motor activity in the left side of my body. The thing is, I woke up and I couldn't move half my body. I woke up and there were all these deficits and I was really blown away by it.

In retrospect, Nancy should have asked (readers take note). She accepted her doctor's confidence and framing and was just not going to worry about it, even though his conceptualization of risk or "extreme neurological damage" didn't actually mean anything to her. This mismatch of meanings between doctors and patients is a recurrent theme in research on doctor/patient interactions (Brody, 1987; Hunter, 1991; G. Miller, 1997). Nancy's experience confirms Hunter's (1991) findings that the terms and content of professional medical narratives often have little connection to the patient's experience, and so they can at best only be partly taken up and used in meaningful ways. Her neurosurgeon sees the procedure as fairly common, something he does routinely and well: Nancy is an interchangeable biological case. He sees the risks in terms of statistical probabilities, and when one is doing brain surgery 5 percent probably seems like good odds. For Nancy, of course, there's nothing routine at all about her brain surgery, and she takes her cues for how to conceptualize the risks involved from her doctor's confidence and minimization of concern, which to a layperson may not actually mean anything.

The common wisdom among the patients and rehab professionals I talked to is that doctors, but especially surgeons, don't want to make too much of possible complications, let alone catastrophes. Instead, the intention is to inspire confidence and faith, to reduce worry. Because her doctor didn't seem worried, Nancy wasn't going to worry, even when she had to go back in for a second surgery. About to have brain surgery, she'd need to trust her doctor. Interestingly, a while after the surgery Nancy did confront her doctor, asking him why he hadn't told her that things might happen the way they did. He replied that he "had told her all about" the risks involved and that "all in all, things didn't turn out too badly."

But Nancy was not happy when she woke up with left hemiplegia, no less so for being completely unprepared for the outcome. Even though her medical records clearly indicated a history of clinical depression, there seemed to be no anticipation of, let alone concern or attention for, her reaction:

> NANCY: Um, I was pretty severely depressed about it. Um, I have
> a history of clinical depression. I've been treated a few times for it,
> various antidepressants, mostly Zoloft. And, um, I was very bummed
> out about this. [*Both laugh*] And, uh, I mean sometimes I wonder,
> you know, why didn't the doctors put, figure out that I would be very
> upset about this. [*ES laughs*] "She has a history of depression, get her
> on antidepressants right away." Because they work for me. Um, but
> it got to the point where, you know, before I was transferred to the
> Rehab Center, I told one of my nurses, look, if you leave a syringe
> around, I'm going to use it. I'm going to carve up my wrists. I want
> to die. This is ridiculous! I hate it. Um, fortunately she picked up
> the sign [*both laugh*] and, um, flagged down a psychiatrist and they
> intervened and got me on medication and, um, came into see me a
> lot and that sort of thing.

Nancy was so severely depressed that the psychologist had to contract with her not to attempt suicide without first talking to her. It's hard not to wonder, along with Nancy, what kind of attention she was getting in recovery when she could lie in bed sobbing and screaming for weeks without somebody realizing there might be something wrong. It was only after threatening to carve up her wrists that somebody picked up on "the sign" and began to come into see her a lot, "and that sort of thing." Like Rose, Nancy wonders what it takes to get somebody to pay attention to or figure out what ought to be obvious to professionals. (Nurses are often mentioned as attentive allies in the women's accounts, but as may be apparent here, nurses are also less than empowered to intervene or cross the lines of professional authority.) This is something of an extreme example, but the same kind of frustration with not having one's experience or one's emotional response to the injury acknowledged, let alone validated, is fairly common in the women's accounts (and others; see Lalljee, Laham & Tam, 2007; Clucas & St. Claire, 2010).

Elise also encountered problems with getting useful information and having her experience acknowledged. In her case though, the problems were less (but not un-) related to professional disconnect and more related to the variation in outcomes and difficulties in prognosis with brain injury. As with Nancy, though, the kind of information she received seems related to keeping morale high and anxiety low. Post-injury, Elise was having difficulty determining exactly what her deficits were and their extent, and she was getting very mixed messages from professionals, family, and friends about how well she was doing. The result was a lot of confusion and self-blame:

ELISE: I started seeing a neuropsychologist, that's something that
I had been in for, a few evals while I was in the hospital. But I had
opted out of seeing the counselor because I didn't feel like there was
anything wrong with me, you know? [ES: Right] I hadn't made any
connection with him at all. But, once I—I wasn't cognizant of any difficulties, you know, they hadn't surfaced yet, for me. Once they did,
I started seeing somebody. And that, too, is something, in looking at
the rehab system, um, that I think could have been handled differently. [ES then Elise laugh] You know, there are a lot of things, a lot
of misinformation, that we were given. Another thing, another part

of the misinformation was, um, I'm not sure I can call it misinformation, but maybe just not clearly articulated? [ES: Uh huh] That my doctors would, um, they never, how do I say it—they kind of said, she can, we're not sure how much she'll recover, you know, she may very well become that "straight A" student again. She may very well be this, you know? [ES: Mhm] No realistic information coming back, about what it would take for her to be that "straight A" student again. [ES: Uh huh] And, you know, is that a reasonable or even necessary goal to have? You know, should I have to be that "straight A student" again. No one ever said to me, "Yes, you have limitations." People said to me, "You can do it! Keep trying!" And that just kind of left me feeling like, well if I can't do it then I'm a failure. If I can't do this that means I haven't done something right. Instead of, if I can't do it that means I have limitations; that's something I'll have to struggle with. And, you know, it would have been better for me to learn to adapt as someone who's got a few limitations rather than constantly being told that I can do anything. No, I can't. I can try anything I wanna try. I can't do anything I wanna do. Something more realistic would have helped a lot. I mean, I was still waiting for my voice to come back, years later. Because, you know, "nerve damage can regenerate, we don't know enough about it so there's nothing to say that it won't." So keep trying until you kill yourself!

Elise brings up a number of important and recurring issues in this passage; I'll take them in the order she presents them. First, Elise didn't feel as if there was anything wrong with her, even after leaving inpatient rehab. It took a while for her difficulties to surface. This is not uncommon, and it has a technical designation: *anosagnosia*, not knowing you don't know. It is a common characteristic of certain right-brain injuries, often transient but sometimes not. Most of the women mentioned the same experience. It often takes some time to get a handle on the nature and extent of one's deficits, particularly cognitive deficits; some people may never become fully aware of their impairments or their effects, or they have to infer them from the responses of others. Elise had just graduated from high school prior to her injury and was prepared to start college just months after leaving the hospital. To her dismay, she flunked out her first semester. That she was getting mixed, even conflicting messages from doctors, friends, and family about how well she was doing was made still more confusing by continuing difficulty with social perception. Social perception is also common problem after a serious head injury—a difficulty getting a handle on whether it's you that's behaving strangely and misinterpreting other's cues, or whether others are, in fact, behaving strangely toward you; often it's both.

The second issue raised in the passage is still more difficult. On the one hand rehabilitation professionals have to contend with the fact that it is often difficult or impossible to predict the extent of recovery. As Dr. Larsen says, "Patients defy our knowledge all the time." As an uncanny example, Elise's injuries were nearly identical to those of her friend Stephanie who was injured in a bicycle accident: trauma to and swelling of the brain stem causing loss of consciousness and interruption of cardiopulmonary function. Both women were in intensive care for weeks and in the hospital for months. Stephanie, though, never went through rehab at all, returned to college soon after release from the hospital, and has few residual deficits. Elise had serious problems early in recovery and still has residual motor deficits and cognitive difficulties. It *is* difficult to predict outcomes. The power of "positive thinking" is frequently emphasized (Doidge, 2007), and there is a desire in rehab to keep optimism and motivation alive, if only to keep patients engaged and to stave off demoralization.

But this is tricky, as Elise's account demonstrates: "It would have been better for me to learn to adapt as someone who's got a few limitations rather than constantly being told that I can do anything." When progress didn't occur as quickly or fully as she had been led to anticipate, she could only interpret it as her failure. The result was real demoralization, further distrust of herself and her perceptions, and a long stretch of depression.

The third issue Elise brings up is the haunting specter that the premorbid self can become. Having memory of prior performance and often still thinking of one's self in those same terms can make coping with impairments more difficult. The problem is not just psychological. Rehabilitation practices engender comparisons to the premorbid self and to prior functioning; one can't escape attention to functional deficits and to reclaiming what was lost. As Elise herself points out, telling her that she could be a "straight A" student again only fed the sense of comparison and failure. It also fed into her own tendency to beat herself up for not achieving perfection; every B was a sign that she wasn't working hard enough. And finally, whether implied or inferred, the prognoses also fed the tendency to disdain and fight herself.

Susan's account presents a different set of problems related to the expectations of rehab professionals in relation to the expectations of patients. As with Elise, Susan's account also implicates a lack of real and realistic information about the nature and extent of limitations, and a fixation on deficits. But Susan's injuries were more severe and more pervasive than were Elise's, and instead of unrealistically high expectations Susan had to deal with extremely low expectations from rehab professionals. She was also in rehab for much longer, her physical rehab alone extended over years and to several facilities. Her account also illustrates the variation in approach and services across rehab settings:

> SUSAN: I did my rehab at Wealthy Suburb University Hospital, for about a year, I graduated from their "reentry program." Then I went to Big State Medical. Then I went to Pastoral State University, for their Neuromuscular Retraining Program. And then the biofeedback program. And, it used to be this side of my face, it didn't move. I could only talk with one side. [ES: Mmm] They taught me to use my entire mouth. Yeah. I was very happy with that. Um, and they also, well, it was also the process of learning to walk, but they helped me learn the correct ways. They wouldn't let me do—to start with in therapy, at Big State they just let you walk any way you walk. They didn't care if you were hunched over, or leaning back, they didn't correct you. They said just do it. They figured you would figure it out eventually. So, Pastoral State, they straightened me out. They said you'll learn how to walk correctly now. That helped a lot. I was very thankful for them. I've never actually seen somebody try to learn how to walk leaning real far back, but I was afraid of falling forward. [ES: Ah, I see] And, so it was my perception. [ES: Uh huh] Why didn't anyone correct it? I have no idea. Made me angry. Angry when I realized. I could have done so much better, and learned so much quicker if somebody had corrected me. [ES: Mhm] I was just really pissed.
>
> ES: Do you think their expectations were just low, like—

SUSAN: Yeah, low. Whatever she can do. And, uh, the first doctor prognosed that I might be able to be at a first-grade level. [ES: Uh huh] Or elementary school? Then I, as time went on, I got to high school, and then I went on to college. And, um, now I'll read everything and anything, I can't stop reading. They tried to put me in jobs, um, they put me in remedial jobs: "Put this piece on eight pieces of paper and stack it." And I'm like, agh! Come on! [*ES laughs*] I don't think so. And, also, when you have ataxia, you can't work with paper so well. [ES: Uh huh. *ES laughs.*] So, they were thinking less of me, so I wanted to prove there's more to me than that, and I can't do a remedial job, I have to do a real job. And they just wouldn't give me a chance, and so I proved I could do it.

Here is the other side of expectations and prognosis: "whatever she can do." In not trying to correct her gait, and in setting the bar very low, Susan's doctors and therapists—across several facilities—left it pretty much to her to push herself and determine her goals. Low expectations don't seem to have had obvious long-term ill effects on Susan, partly because of her own tenacity and partly because her self-perceptions didn't match her doctors' perceptions of her. Susan was subjected to the kind of remedial tasks that are reserved for people with the most severe cognitive and motor difficulties and she found that boring and insulting. Susan, though, never questioned herself or saw herself as the problem. She had to do a "real job" and proved she could. She takes great pride in having made it to college-level education and that she reads so much and so widely.

Susan has had to do the lion's share of this self-authoring without much help from those around her, arguably in spite of them. Her motor, speech, and social-perception problems are the kind that often lead to being "treated as an object" (in Cindy's terms) or as "stupid" (Lydia's term) by others. A neuropsychologist might point out that Susan's "don't give a damn" attitude might be related to the damage to her frontal lobe; that may be a factor, but it also seems to be characteristic of her pre-injury self, something that was true of her pre-injury attitude or personality. Symptom or trait, it seems to have helped her fight for what she wanted and resist what she didn't.

Lydia, like Susan, had more severe and obvious cognitive and motor impairments, and she also was slotted into repetitive vocational therapy in the interest of helping her become a productive person. Lydia brings attention to how speech impairments relate to estimations of intelligence. She wants to separate herself from, and worries about being taken for, the "mentally handicapped":

> LYDIA: Did I tell you that when I, right after my car accident, my first job was in a shelter workshop. Did I tell you that?
> ES: No.
> LYDIA: That was hard. That was really distressing to me. I went to work there because of the factory work, and the fine motor coordination was very beneficial to me. In these, um, workshops, shelter workshops, all the people that work there are mentally handicapped. [ES: Oh] And, I had this speech impediment and I sounded just like them. Aah! It was such a, I felt like I was retarded, I felt stupid. And that's with this whole thing, I was stupid. Well, I really felt stupid. And it was really hard, hard for me. It worked. My coordination improved. I worked there for a little longer than a year. But it was hard, I felt like I was retarded.

Like all of the women, Lydia found it hard and distressing to have her judgment and abilities questioned, by others and by herself. She "really felt stupid," and felt she sounded just like the "mentally handicapped" people she was working with. In fact, throughout the interview and in other interactions Lydia kept returning to the topic of her intelligence, and questions of "smart" and "stupid." The interview took place almost thirty years post-injury, but Lydia returned several times to the topic of her recent performance on aptitude and intelligence tests. She had been a registered nurse before her accident, and she could tell me all about anatomy, pharmacology, and physiology; her long-term memory is intact. However, her short-term memory has been severely impaired and she has tremendous difficulty learning new information, which, along with some motor difficulties and balance problems, precludes a return to nursing. Also, as she indicates, her speech is impaired by some facial paralysis and motor impairments. She "feels smart but acts dumb." That feeling wasn't helped by her rehabilitation experience. She didn't feel that she had gone as far as she could go with recovery when she was "turned out" of rehab. In fact, she spent another twelve years rehabilitating herself: physically through relentless exercise, stretching, swimming, and various martial arts and cognitively through a variety of classes, exercises, and memory aids.

Lydia has been successful in many ways, improving her gait and speech for example, even if I couldn't help feeling that there was something punishing about the way she drove herself. As for being productive, she is still trying to find well-paid work, hoping for a full-time job at the Rehab Center. She does have a small clientele for her massage and physical therapy work, which she enjoys very much, but it does not provide enough income to support her. A "real job" is as much of a preoccupation—and as elusive—for her as it is still for Susan.

It is probable that many of Lydia's problems do, as she herself suspects, have a lot to do with her speech difficulties. By the time I interviewed her, I had talked to quite a few people with brain injuries, and I had learned (but not that quickly) how much speech performance is tied to my assessment of intelligence, and how disqualifying (and mistaken) that connection can be. But identity is at least partly performative. I remember lapsing into impatience and an internal (but no doubt leaky) patronizing posture with Lydia. That is until she would say something or ask a question that made clear not only her intelligence but also her full awareness of the dynamics of our particular interactions. I noticed the same dynamic in interactions between Lydia and other women at the Women's Center. The problem is further complicated by Lydia's own frustration and impatience with not being fully understood or validated in conversation, which can add a certain edge and volume to conversations. It's an interesting question, from a narrative perspective, how speech production relates to or constrains the authoring of identity. The women in this study seemed to have relatively little trouble with "internal" language practices, knowing what they are thinking, the story they wanted to tell, or relationships between things and people. The problems here are mainly motoric, affecting performance more than content (but occasionally there are problems with word finding, memory, or digressions).

It seems that the issue is how one is perceived by others as a narrator of one's self and one's experience, and one's chance at "storytelling rights." That is, "audience" affects the authoring of identity narratives, so how do you handle the gap, which both Susan and Lydia experience and discuss, between self-perceptions and the perceptions others have of you? Understandably, both women are somewhat preoccupied with signifiers of intelligence: Susan with being well-read and her college credits, Lydia with her intelligence tests and medical knowledge. Both are also fairly assertive and tenacious in conversation. Both women also seem to hold fairly developed and generally positive narratives for themselves, but both also seem fully aware of the problem of getting others to share them.

Tracy presents a different experience of and relationship to the expectations and contradictory perspectives of her rehab professionals, and a different handling of how she was being perceived by and perceiving others. She was seventeen at the time of her car accident, and at the time of the interview six months later. Her main preoccupation was getting back into high school sports and her social relationships. But she felt she was being treated differently by some of her peers, deciding if they may not be worth her time anymore:

> TRACY: Yeah, I thought it was because of the accident, I had been seeing them differently. Come to find out it wasn't. Everybody else was seeing them the same way. I was having a real big problem with just one of 'em, and that's the one that everyone else at school was having a real big problem with. Of course, I would tell Dr. Austerlitz about her, how she has been treating me differently, and kind of rude like. And he's like, well, yeah, of course, that's probably because—he thought it was just because of my accident also. So did my mom whenever I told her about all these things.
> ES: You mean, they thought it was *you*, how you perceived people because of your injury?
> TRACY: Yeah. It was me. And then I went and, um, mom was really good friends with one of my good friend's mom, and so they got to talking about us kids and she found that Nick—he's my really good friend—that he had been seeing 'em the same way. So, like they *were* different.

Tracy seems remarkably able to selectively draw the information from her doctor's and parent's accounts that she wants to use to her own ends. She also marshals counterevidence to their suggestions that her social perceptions are probably faulty, enlisting her friends to make her case, to validate her perceptions and counter the interpretations of her doctor and mother. She may have been different after her injuries, but she could still demonstrate to others that people at school were behaving differently toward her. Tracy also found ways to work the system and play staff against each other in order to get permission to participate in sports again:

> TRACY: They said, um, if I hit my head like really hard or something, it could kill me. I believe because of the concussion. So, uh, they didn't want me playing basketball. But my neurosurgeon told me I could go ahead. So, my physiatrist, she didn't argue with that, even though she didn't like it. And, um, she didn't want me playing softball. But she decided—because they let me play more for my mental well-being than my physical, because they were afraid my depression would get worse if I couldn't. Because I'm active in sports. So I kinda kept bugging them, trying to get them to let me play either track or softball, so finally they said okay, softball.

As a seventeen-year-old high school student living with divorced parents, Tracy's experience of and strategies for asserting agency, even when her judgment is called into question, no doubt differ from the other women's. She may in fact have had some advantages in that she was accustomed to having her judgment and perceptions doubted (by parents and teachers, as well as some of her peers), to finding ways to manipulate and play authority against itself, persistently "bugging" people for what she wants, and employing indirect resistance. Having to confront the infantilizing tendencies of rehab probably didn't represent an unusual experience for her. Moreover, Tracy indicates here that she is aware of the inconsistencies in expert opinions, and of the hierarchies at work: her physiatrist didn't argue with the neurosurgeon, even though she didn't like his decision. She seems aware of a certain logic at work that she could participate in—as the "patient"—by capitalizing on her doctors' concerns about her when they suited her goals: "they let me play more for my mental well-being than my physical, because they were afraid my depression would get worse." So, many of the elements that figured in other women's accounts here—inconsistent or

contradictory information, problems with social perception and determining if one's judgments are accurate and legitimate, reclaiming prior
roles and relationships—also figure in Tracy's experience, yet Tracy
appeared to handle them as a matter of the routine course of events.

Sarah provides another example of resistance through always returning interactions and expectations back to one's own terms; in Sarah's
case it was invoking a higher Authority. For her and her husband, Gary,
the car accident in which she was injured, the subsequent coma, and
even her injuries and recovery are a miraculous part of Spirit's plan for
her transformation. Sarah is therefore only conditionally receptive to
the framings and prognoses of her doctors and therapists:

ES: It seems like there really isn't a contradiction—for you—between
sort of competing belief systems, or ways of conceptualizing all that's
going on. You never had a problem integrating sort of materialistic,
medical information with—
SARAH: No, because I, we, knew the doctors were serving God in
their work. It all worked as a whole. We needed them to perform the
physical procedures that would enable my body to sustain my life,
while Gary and thousands of others worked with God—God was
working with us. Let's get the hierarchy, how it works, right. God was
working with everyone on my care. So it's part of a whole. And the
nurses and the staff, they were very receptive to Gary being there, at
my bedside so many hours praying.
GARY: If they had something to do and I was deep in prayer, they'd
work around me. Without exception they all said Sarah was a
miracle. One doctor said he'd never seen anything like it.
SARAH: And they regretted when we left, there were some tears.
And it's really fun going back when we have the time. The doctor's
appointments have gotten more sparse as time has gone along. But,
to your question and to how medicine and prayer work together, the
eye doctor, who put this eye back together as best he could, he would
say, "I don't expect any use of vision in that eye, ever." And, he's a
really good doctor, very succinct and very honest, he doesn't pad his
opinion at all, which we appreciate. But we talked to him and asked,
"Would you be open to a miracle?" [All laugh] And he said, "Well,
yes, I'm open to a miracle." He said, "from my point of view, I don't

expect any usable vision *and* I'm open to a miracle." So he was able to embrace both perspectives as well.

If some of her doctors interpret Sarah's optimism as symptomatic of her brain injury—which would make her husband's complicity something of a shared folly—others were willing to be open to a miracle. A kind of blissful indifference is characteristic of certain severe types of right brain injury, especially in the early, acute stages of recovery. (This interview took place just six months after Sarah's release from the hospital and a year after the accident. Sarah's awareness did change over the three years we met). I can, however, validate Sarah and her husband's experience: many of her doctors and attending staff did consider her recovery a miracle and were deeply affected by their interactions with her. However the reader may feel about this mystical accounting and the expectation of miracles, it did provide a counter to the more objectifying and pathologizing tendencies of medical discourse and practices. The doctors did what they do, God and prayer did what they do, no contradiction. And, again, while some readers may take this as a problematic lack of awareness or "organic affective disorder," it is also perfectly aligned with Sarah's pre-injury practices and perspectives. Here, though, the point is that Sarah and her husband's narrative—a narrative one can only believe—was less affected by than it was affecting of her rehabilitation experience and interactions.

As with Tracy, there were different framings and expectations for Sarah's condition and prognosis. There is, in fact, frequent inconsistency in expectations and the ways neurosurgeons, psychologists, physiatrists, and other rehabilitation professionals characterize risk, progress, and outcomes. Neurologists and surgeons have a different perspective on and metric for "success" than do the other professionals who are involved in rehab and "putting things back together." They are doing brain surgery, so survival of the patient, getting "most of the brain back in place," is success. If the patient can talk afterward, that's a great outcome. (These are not my characterizations, but those of various rehab professionals, patients, and family members.) Neurosurgeons often tell patients and family members that everything went great, raising expectations and ultimately increasing frustrations. Those doctors and therapists who have to work with patients through rehabilitation and help them adjust to impairments generally

have a very different perspective and metric, and may be much less san-
guine when discussing outcomes and expectations.

In those cases where I had access to medical charts, there were
remarkable inconsistencies in chart notes depending on who was
reporting. Sarah's chart is a fine example in that it would appear to refer
to several different people. Her neurologist notes:

> I would strongly encourage her to be optimistic. I think that very likely
> she will continue to improve. I would like to see her back in six months,
> just to follow up, but I think we will be impressed by how much better
> she is by then.

Six months later, her neurologist concurs with himself:

> Her mood is wonderfully optimistic. I am very impressed with her prog-
> ress and see her recovery as open.

By contrast, here is an excerpt from the assessment summary performed by her clinical neuropsychologist at around the same time:

> Mood was somewhat euthymic most of the time, and in conjunction with
> the racing thoughts, was indicative of an organic affective syndrome.

In general, neurologists and neurosurgeons appear to be considered the
"action stars" (to quote one speech therapist) of the brain injury world.
They tend to give their own work high approval ratings, but they don't
have to stick around to "clean up the mess" (in the words of a neuropsychologist who, by the way, wore a "do not resuscitate" bracelet because
he did not want ever to "wake up with serious neurological damage").
The point, and result, is that they're often speaking in terms incommensurate with patients' understanding of risk, success, and outcome. For
Sarah the terms were particularly incommensurate, which may have
contributed to the content and contradictions in her chart notes, but
it enabled her to define the terms and quality of most of her interactions with her caregivers. In a context of conflicting messages, interpretations, and authorities, and no real way to sort those out, it's not clear
what a better approach would be.

It is also likely that few rehab professionals are seriously concerned with your meaning-making systems or questions about why what happened to you happened, at least not in the acute stage—even if you are brain-injured, best to assert those for yourself. Even before her head wounds had been closed, Cindy was already preoccupied with meaning, but questions about who she was, what had happened to her, and why got little attention or interest:

> CINDY: See, my docs, some of my docs were really very good here, when they didn't talk over me, you know, they included me. And, this was years ago. Um, I don't know what the experience is like in other hospitals, in other settings. But, *but,* this is a research hospital, okay? And when I was, um, first injured I can remember my physician agreeing to allow me to have pins stuck in me for some kind of neural thing, and this or that, you know, all this other stuff. And, I would be outraged because most people who were testing me had very little concern for who I was, what happened to me, why it happened to me.

Except for Sarah, for whom every day in rehab was a "beautiful new miracle," the accounts of all of the women include some variant of this experience; and, they all had different strategies for contending with or ignoring them. Cindy goes on to explicate how and why this kind of objectification is all the more galling when you're confronted with cognitive and physical deficits that may be permanent and life altering, and when you're trying to figure out exactly what's happened to you and why:

> CINDY: You're constantly being reminded how poor your judgment is. [*Laughs*] It is a hell of a thing to, you know, keep being reminded of. So how do you get confidence about your judgment? Ya know? It's real serious, because you're, you know what I mean? [ES: Yeah, I think so] You, you just, you—it's everywhere. Um, so, I mean, I always felt like I was dealing with this *One Flew Over the Cuckoo's Nest* kind of thing, of sanity, of like "well, how much can you really trust?" I mean, whatever I said I always felt like people were gonna kind of turn against me. 'Cause they would say "she doesn't really

know what she's talking about, she's got unrealistic expectations. [ES: Uh huh] She's got an unrealistic vision of what the world is 'cause she's brain damaged." [ES: Uh huh] And, you know? [*Three-second pause*] So it was hard.

ES: You're disqualified. And you disqualify yourself sometimes?

CINDY: Yeah. And I, I always felt there was that. I think that brain injured people have a real hard time with that. It's real hard, 'cause you—and plus, to talk about, you get a real validation that you know things are different for you. The world is presenting itself differently to you and you are having a harder time making sense of things, and coping. And, yet, on the other time, there—on the other hand—there are times when there is this legitimate thing like: "I really *didn't* want to work at that job, and I really was trying to pursue something new. And I want you to respect that and I don't want you to just take that as some kind of effect of my injury and having poor judgment." It's tricky. *Or*, I prefer to work with a woman—I think people should be given a choice of psychologists, or, you know, who they want to work with. That's another thing that came up with me. I mean I had never worked with a man, in therapy, I wasn't, I mean the man was okay, he gave me a few things I remembered but, by and large, I was pretty uncomfortable talking to him.

Cindy appears to have been clear about, and glad to be clear about, what she wanted in terms of attention and recognition. She also seemed to draw on her pre-injury self and plans as a resource for resistance, even as she was figuring out exactly what the differences might be. But, even for Cindy it was hard dealing with the construals of others that she didn't really "know what she's talking about" or that she had "unrealistic visions." Knowing that she was seeing things differently, having a harder time "making sense of things, and coping," made it hard to fight for legitimate things, like respecting her career goals (and choice of therapist). Many of her early struggles were over her assertions about what she should do next, particularly regarding vocational and job issues:

CINDY: I think a real frustration for me, which I've talked about publicly here, and I think it's an issue, you know, you might find interesting, is that health care providers, particularly after an injury like this one, in a rehab setting are often so obsessed with this idea of you taking control over your life, and becoming quote unquote a productive person. [ES: Uh huh] I feel they often have a hard time understanding that there is a context that you came from. So when I got hurt, there was this big push to get me back into my job. They [*her former employers*] kept saying, 'Cindy, come on back to work.' And the vocational person and the psychologist, and my family, were pushing me to take this job back. And I was really upset because nobody wanted to really, because they hadn't been working with me they didn't really understand that I had *chosen* to leave this job. That, you know, this was something I had chosen to do prior to my injury and now because of my brain injury, because employment, and because being a brain injured person was such a hard thing, I should just go back into this environment. And I kept saying, "I didn't want to be there before I was brain injured, I didn't want to be there before I was disabled, I didn't want to be there before I was handicapped, and I *really* [*laughing*] don't want to be there *being* brain injured and handicapped and disabled." And it took a while to convince the health care providers here that it was okay not to force me back into that environment, even though they were welcoming me with a brain injury; that I had chosen to, you know, to go. They were so caught up with "you gotta get these people employed."

Back to economic narratives. Cindy illustrates how a discourse of productivity—productive lives, productive citizens, gainful employment, independent living, returning to the tax rolls—is pervasive in rehabilitation (and in culture more generally): "you gotta get these people employed," even if they "don't want to be there." The context Cindy is referring to is the particular career decisions she had made just prior to her injury, decisions she didn't feel were being acknowledged or respected in the crush to get her back in the work force. It's interesting, however, that while Cindy is critical of this preoccupation with employment in rehab it was her professional identity that occupied her most in those early days as well as for many years after. By her own account, it was as if she had to have that professional identity and role nailed down before she could go on to deal with other strands of her identity narrative. In fact, much of Cindy's account, and the context for many of her observations and stories, related to her professional identity, particularly the identity she has developed as a women's and disability rights advocate and activist. So it is not, for Cindy, the emphasis on work and career that was problematic in her rehab experience, but the fact that *her* goals, aspirations, and ascriptions of meaning in this domain were often discounted or invalidated. She was being denied authorship in a domain with which she strongly identified and where she valued her authority.

Welcome to brain injury rehabilitation: A new and compromised social position; the effects of new and of culturally embedded social categorizations; difficulties with awareness and social perception that are complicated by having to sort out what's "real" and related to one's injuries versus the objectifying and infantilizing way one is being treated; variable or conflicting expectations about progress and outcomes—among caregivers, between one and one's caregivers, and within oneself; a necessary yet maddening fixation on deficits, and the attendant comparisons to "normal," to the prior self, and what one ought to be; fighting against oneself and body, against managed care or insurance companies, and against the framings and disqualifications of others—oppositions that are likely to be construed as symptoms. It is a complex struggle with the question, "who am I?" in a context that perpetually reinvokes the "wounding process as the source of one's psychic organization" (Snyder & Mitchell, 2006, 8).

Yet it helps. All of the women pointed out good doctors and therapists, important reclamations of functioning, and useful tools, and Rose made clear what *not* going to rehab can mean. Rehab is a period of identifying and overcoming limitations, fighting for maximum recovery. One may be told that anything is possible—or find that what one is told is possible is unacceptable. Obviously, there is room for improvement in the rehabilitation experience; it is often fragmented, incomplete, objectifying, uneven in quality and availability, sometimes dehumanizing and, paradoxically, too brief.

In relation to the specific interests of this study, though, the array of cultural and local narratives and practices—obvious and cryptic, enabling and disabling—that the women confront and have to negotiate in rehabilitation have consequences for the reauthoring of identity, meaning, and relationships. The many comparative, classificatory, and divisive dynamics of rehab, and the ways in which one's identity is nailed to one's deficits configure the relationship of self to self. As discussed in the introduction, this is increasingly framed as a problem of relationship between the pre-injury and post-injury selves: The burgeoning awareness of impairments "precipitates dilemmas and yearnings over the loss of purpose and identity (the 'old me'), compounded by disdain for the 'new me'" (Klonoff, 2010, 75). The dilemma, the loss, and yearning are often taken and treated as psychological problems. No doubt they are *also* psychological dilemmas, but it is the case that nearly every message, ambient or direct, and many practices of rehab and of culture configure and reinforce precisely such a disdainful relationship to one's post-injury self—a nostalgia for prior functioning and a holding out for the immanent, restored self. Awareness *is* a problem, but it is important to attend to an awareness of the many disabling and disqualifying narratives that surround and define disability, the practices that maneuver one into an objectifying relationship to oneself, that deny one's individuality while forcing one back on oneself and tying one to a constrained and constraining identity (Corker & French, 1999; Foucault, 1983; Siebers, 2008).

3

Oneself as Another

I have already drawn attention to ways in which the pre-injury self figures into the women's accounts and in their experiences in rehabilitation. This presence, and the kinds of opposition or breach it may configure between the post-injury experience and pre-injury self, can play
out in varying ways. The pre-injury self may also loom as a desired once
and future self—the "nostalgia for a return to prior functionality" that
structures the rehabilitation experience (Snyder & Mitchell, 2006). This
is a haunting, mournful presence that continually invokes loss, tragedy,
and abjection. But the prior self also references a lifetime of experiences
and relationships, ways of knowing oneself apart from or other than
"disabled," and so can also serve as a resource, as grounds for refusing
objectifying and disqualifying treatment and relationships.

The pre-injury self is itself heterogeneous and constituted in terms of
contradictory cultural discourses and subjectifications. It is not surprising, then, that in the women's accounts the pre-injury self can, by turns
and simultaneously, be a resource and an impediment, opponent and
ally, an effect of rehabilitation practices and grounds for resisting them.
This is a relationship *and* a breach that plays out in and is constituted
by complex and shifting interpersonal and cultural contexts and narratives. It plays out over time and in strategies for finding or creating a

place in communities and in a reauthoring of metaphysical meanings of self and world. It is in recovery and rehabilitation that one "meets" the post-injury self and in that meeting one also "meets" the pre-injury self on new terms and from a new position. But because it clings to the acute medical phase, the "rehabilitation regimen becomes little more than a return to the site of the wound that disability has become" (Snyder and Mitchell, 2006, 8). A central challenge for learning how to live with brain injury and making the transition from rehab to living, then, is overcoming the division from oneself: working out how and when to stop fighting one's body and brain, disdaining one's "new self," and leaving the "site of the wound" and nostalgia for prior functionality.

One is confronted with a different self, especially early in recovery when deficits are new and/or most pronounced. This is also the time when important others are responding to the changes, amplifying the effects of difference. There may be contradictory information (and wishes) about how much one will "get back." Tracy was only six months post-injury at the time of our interview. She was aware of deficits and changes but still anticipating a complete or nearly complete recovery. But the major topic of discussion with Tracy was her relationships with her friends—and her "not so much" friends—at school. She has had some difficulty with her judgment, particularly in relation to social perceptions and the extent to which she may be misreading other people, or whether other people have themselves been behaving differently toward her. These discussions also involved questions about how Tracy might or might not be a different person after her accident:

> TRACY: Um, I've changed, like I said. I'm a lot easier going *and* I'm
> a little more cautious about some things. And, um, I don't get out as
> much. And they said my old person, my old personality is not exactly
> what it used to be. So they said it might be a year, two or three years
> before I'm back to my old self. And, so, I used to get really hyper a *lot*
> of the time, constantly smiling and that kind of thing. Now I notice
> that I hardly ever smile, like only occasionally will I catch myself smil-
> ing or laughing, and I remember how I used to do that all the time.

Tracy is aware of changes in her "old personality" resulting from the injuries, and she does give them some thought in relation to implications for relationships and her life. Only occasionally will she catch herself laughing and remember how she used to do that all the time. For her the car accident was "just one of those things," but she was very interested in showing me photos of the dramatically totaled car and getting me to agree how "amazing" it is that she came out of it okay. She was also intent on convincing me that she "really *was* wearing a seat belt"; the ER staff had written in her file that she was "unrestrained," something she hotly contests. But she has the expectation that she will eventually fully recover her "old self" in a year or three. The interview took place just a few months after the accident; much of what the injuries will mean in the long run remains to be seen and is not a worry at the moment.

As discussed in chapter 1, I began this study with the belief that a central part of the story of brain injury recovery is the problem of a "break" or discontinuity in identity, a before-and-after experience of self that would have to somehow be reconciled. Cindy corrected that as a misconception of the long-term reauthoring process, but she did go on to elaborate how the pre-injury self figures into post-injury life:

CINDY: I would think that one is always kind of living with this burden of the pre-injured self over one's—or the perception of the pre-injured self over your shoulder. And, it's you know, very nagging, and you know it's quite frustrating. And I think that a lot of the way it manifests itself as being frustrating is when one is involved in activities that you had been involved in pre-injury and realized all of a sudden you're confronted with the reality that you're limited by virtue of your physical impairment, or cognitive impairment, *or* that you're being perceived differently. And, you know both of those, we feel and, I believe, react to really create this new sense of who you are and what you're capable of doing. But I'll just give you a little story that was told to me by a friend of mine, who had a left hemisphere injury. He, like I did, had to relearn to tie his shoes. It's very difficult to tie shoes with one hand, um, and it's just an activity of daily life that one relearns, in occupational therapy for example. I don't tie shoes, I use Velcro on my shoes, it's just too hard. Now my friend, who I will call Joe, um, he said to me that he feels everyday since his injury when he got up to tie his shoes, he was always reminded of how he used to tie his shoes, you know, prior to the injury. And it was just this constant nagging feeling that he had this self or this way of life, um, that existed before this event. But, what he said to me is: "Then one day, *one day!* [*laughing*] it occurred to him that he wasn't thinking about the way he used to tie his shoes—the old way, anymore?—and that this is just the way he tied his shoes.

The pre-injured self then remains, for Cindy and for others like Joe, a salient, haunting presence during and beyond rehabilitation. The difference is experienced—and reconciled—in the details of everyday life like tying shoes—or deciding not to. A key point for Cindy was when she had her son (and had to fight for accessible OB/GYN services):

CINDY: I mean, you try to kind of achieve things post-injury that you maybe wouldn't have thought about pre-injury. And once you start building these new experiences for yourself—and they're not necessarily dissociated from your pre-injured life—but they're, they're, you know, they're age-appropriate, like having a baby. I got married and had a baby, and I had never had a baby before in my life. And this was all within the context of being disabled. I mean it's like such a major thing that after a while the injury itself recedes to the background. It gets to a point where it's not like *the injury,* even though it's been this *massive thing.* I mean you just get so caught up with living. [*Laughs*] Like getting involved in supportive relationships, interpersonal relationships, and achieving some successes, in an environment where one can make a contribution and be appreciated. There's this kind of thrill of doing something new, and different, that helps to add more meaning to the experience, more dimension. But, it's hard, being disabled is hard.

For Cindy, it was having *new* and different experiences, accomplishments, and relationships post-injury "within the context of being disabled" that allowed her to give up preoccupation with "the injury" and the comparison to her pre-injured self. It was also, and this is an important theme throughout the rest of this book, finding environments "where one can make a contribution and be appreciated." She did, though, think it was important to remind me that "being disabled *is hard.*"

While new experiences were important for Cindy, there were also elements of the "pre-injury Cindy" that were critical for moving past the rehab regimen and on to a post-injury identity. She was almost thirty at the time of her injury and had already achieved considerable professional success. For her, this served as evidence that she could do it again. She mainly just had to be "reminded":

> CINDY: I, it was like I completely forgot about the fact—I was talking
> to my psychotherapist and I *reconnected* that I had had this *quest*,
> this *quest* that I was shaping, you know, pursuing at the time of my
> injury. I completely forgot about that! I had gotten so railroaded to,
> you know, learning how to get dressed, and to read, and to write, to
> be appropriate, and to be on my own, and to cross a street, and get on
> a bus, and do shopping, and cook, that I had completely lost touch
> with all this growth that I had kind of worked up to. Um, the enthu-
> siasm and everything that I felt before I, um, the excitement I felt in
> leaving my job, and the excitement I had in shaping something new,
> before I could do something post-injury. And it was a real revelation,
> you know. But it had all gotten kind of pushed aside.

Cindy underscores how the rehabilitation regimen can push aside the long-term goals of value to people living with disabilities. When she does reconnect, experiences of the pre-injury self and of her "quest" are a *re*discovered resource. For others, however, prior accomplishments and competencies can remain tainted, and the gap between pre- and post-injury selves remains persistently preoccupying. Abby was in her senior year of college when she had a stroke. She had been a high school debater, was a communications major and popular public speaker at her prestigious college, and looking toward a career in politics. She had always taken pride in her voice and verbal skills, and these were the issues that concerned her most in rehab:

> ABBY: I was always thinking that everything would be okay, that I
> would be just like I was before the stroke. And I never really cared
> much about physical therapy or vocational therapy, but I wanted a

really good speech therapist—I wanted my *speech*. Language was very important to me. So I really made them work.

Clearly Abby is wed to a scenario of being just as she was before the stroke. Ten years after the stroke, it was difficult escaping invidious comparisons to who she was and, significantly, who she might have been if not for the injury:

ABBY: I would just prefer, you know, if I didn't have the stroke. I would prefer, um, and it took me a long time to say that you know? Because I remember I would always tell people, "Oh, I'm glad I had a stroke," you know? [ES: Really?] Yeah! And, um, "I've learned so much from it," and duh duh duh. Oh, no, I didn't learn anything from it. [*Laughs*] Well, I probably did learn stuff from it but probably I would have learned as much if I didn't have a stroke. Anyway, but, um, I think having a stroke is, it *sucks*. See, even *now,* even now I feel like I'm kind of like playing the violin, you know? "Oh woe is me." You know, that's not how I want you to see me, but, I mean it's the truth. But, it's like, since I can't have all the marbles anymore, I don't want to play. I can't recapture my past performance and the future that was based on them, and I can't settle. So I don't know what I'll do. I make life hard for myself, and um, I'm kind of tired of making it as hard for myself as I do. Um, I'm hoping that, I don't know, I'm kind of hoping that I'll, that something will give. I don't know though. It's hard.

The comparisons Abby makes to who she was before—and maybe more importantly to who she might have become if not for—the stroke are apparently compounded by her own impatience with her post-injury unhappiness and feelings of being stuck. She can't settle for anything less than the "marbles" she *would have had*. She knows this makes life hard for herself, and she's tired of it. She is hoping that something will give. It isn't clear, though, what that something should be.

It was hard to understand what Abby meant when she said that she told people she was glad to have had a stroke and that she had learned so much from it. Only as she began to tell me more about her religious affiliations and beliefs did it begin to come into focus. It reflects an interpretive strategy for making sense of *why* the stroke happened to *her*, one very clearly derived from the interpretations of members of her church. It was a rhetorical strategy that was, in a real sense, for *them*, but it also had complex and complicating effects on Abby's relationship to the stroke, to God, herself, and to that community (see chapters 5 and 6 for extended consideration). A lot of parties, then, were implicated in the something that she hoped would give. (I should also include mention of the possibility that Abby's preoccupation with her deficits may reflect the fact that she had injuries to her *left* hemisphere, which, in contrast to RBI, has been related to greater distress in response to being confronted with deficits; Lezak, Howeisen, and Loring, 2004.)

As discussed in the preceding chapter, Sarah and her husband, Greg, were entirely convinced by and evangelical about Sarah's vision and narrative of not just a recovery but a complete transformation. At times in our conversations, especially by the third interview eighteen months after the collision, Sarah would show signs of impatience and distress with the pace of her recovery, yet she never gave me any indication that she was wavering in her faith. That Sarah was both aware of the scope and effect of her impairments *and* strong in her faith in being "well restored" is evident in her recounting of a conversation with her adult son:

> SARAH: My son, over the holidays, was, *very,* it was like he was irritated with me. I couldn't quite figure out what I had done or not done that caused him to be grumpy with me. So, finally on my birthday I set him down and said: "I don't know what your perception is, mine is that you're grumpy with me and I don't know why. What's going on?" He started crying. [*Sarah begins to cry; four-second pause.*] He said that always before, he had depended on me for, it was just part of what I was about: "You just spilled over all this beauty and goodness on me." And he said ever since the collision, "You've been different, it's like you're so limited, [*crying; five-second pause*] in many ways, that it irritates me. Not because you're not giving anymore, but because you, you have the limitations now." He said I really hope you get compensated for this, this, obstruction in your life. So, I said to him, I said, "Well, there's no amount of money that could repay me for what I've lost." [*Sarah sobs, then stops crying; four-second pause.*]

It's really a matter of opening my heart to what's in it for me, what I can learn from all this that can assist not only me but the people around me. How to develop, or redevelop or expand, or whatever word you use.

Following upon the last quote from Abby, Sarah's story provides a further explication of the ways that the intentions—and needs—of others relate to the experience and framing of injuries and impairments. In no small way they influence one's sense of and relationship to the post-injury self. Sarah's son was the only person up to that point to have directly confronted Sarah about how she's "been different," that she is "so limited in many ways." Further, it irritates him. Not because she's not giving anymore, but because she has the limitations now. While the exchange can be partly understood as the youthful and self-centered response of a child "irritated" by the ways that his mother is no longer fully available to attend to *his* needs, that would be only one aspect of a complex of relationships and ascriptions. First, it is probably fair to also say that her son is upset by an injustice done to his mother, not only to himself; he does hope she gets "compensated for this, this, obstruction." But he is not the only person in Sarah's life who is dependent on her and on the "beauty and goodness" she "spilled over" on them (or, apparently, *used* to spill over). Her husband and her many friends and followers were also quite clearly invested in the return of that bounty, in being able to again depend on her for that beauty and goodness, along with the meaning that her faith ascribed to their lives. Greg, along with friends who visited while I was talking to Sarah, seemed dependent on her vision, her faith in a complete transformation, being maintained because it forestalled any sense of tragedy and any challenge to the spiritual narratives they had coauthored with Sarah. Not to mention that these were people who in many ways had become accustomed to Sarah taking care of them. In different but comparable ways Sarah and Abby both carried a burden of the (religious) needs and expectations of others. In both cases a lot is at stake in the interpretation of catastrophic events and about responsibility. Neither woman is willing to give up the spiritual beliefs and community that define so much of their identity, even if a durable fit and resolution with them is bound up with a full recovery.

The effects on Sarah of the expectations—and likely of the doubts—of others are apparent in the emotion she displayed in recounting this interaction with her son; this was the only time in many hours of conversation with her that she cried, let alone sobbed. This was the first time, too, that Sarah acknowledged anything like a loss: "Well, there's no amount of money that could repay me for what I've lost." But, after a brief pause in which she stopped crying, she went on: "It's really a matter of opening my heart to what's in it for me, what I can learn from all of this that can assist not only me but the people around me." This is a reaffirmation of faith, of opening her heart, along with a concern with how "all of this" can assist those around her. Sarah's faith, then, is entwined with her recovery and with her identity and role in the context of some complex social and interpersonal negotiations.

There is arguably a kind of metaphysics involved in "old selves" and "recovered selves" and how they haunt or perplex the experience of brain injury and recovery. But, there is a kind of collusion between medico-rehabilitation and religious perspectives here in that they share a central preoccupation with restoration and cure. Sarah's anticipation of miraculous transubstantiation is an example of how a cure is not just a medical preoccupation. If some of the women are having difficulty reconciling themselves to significant and enduring disabilities, it is a difficulty they share with, and arguably derive from, central cultural discourses. The medical profession has difficulty with chronic illness and disability (Ingstad & Whyte, 1995; Williams, 1991), and most people have difficulty reconciling themselves to catastrophic events or illness—when it happens to others and when it happens to themselves (Sontag, 2001; Whyte, 1995). Recovery from and learning to live with brain injury, then, is densely overpopulated with the intentions of others, including one's own other, and that is aside from—and complicatedly configures—the other of one's impairments.

Shifting the Fight

This problem of acceptance and of making a livable story and relationships of and for one's body, brain, and disability is sooner or later encountered, though not necessarily resolved once and for all. It also seems to recur, because the impairments don't go away and in fact will become more pronounced with age and related complications. Brain injury does create problems. But there is a difference between having problems and seeing one's self as a problem. Spending one's energy, time, money, and psychological and spiritual resources fighting being disabled, not to mention all of the punitive and pejorative narratives bought into doing so, only alienates one further from self and from community. But, as Cindy points out, that's often very difficult to see when you're "in it."

Rehabilitation professionals, disability theorists, and activists seem to agree that there needs to come a point when gears and metaphors shift from the fight against or resistance to one's disabled body and brain. The shift is a shift in focus from the body or brain as the problem, as the other, the not self, to an acceptance and incorporation of disability into one's life. By extension, there has to be a shift from the relatively individual struggle—and treatment programs tend to treat every disability as completely individual, if also and paradoxically impersonal—to a shared and social experience, or to membership in a community or set of communities. The "fight" of early recovery, against one's impairments and self, becomes the "fight" against the physical and discursive barriers and assertions of the culture: from fighting identification as disabled to the labor of reauthoring an affirmative identity. That reauthoring will depend less on the physical and cognitive measurements and procedures of rehab than on reemplotting or rememorializing of biographical elements of the previous identity, the new actions and stories of actions with others, and the retrieved or created richness, insight, emotional weight, and point of view that enable narratives of identity to "disrupt normalizing closure" (Venn, 2000, 101).

This is a difficult shift to make, particularly during the acute stage of brain injury recovery. It is hard to give up on the hope of further or even complete recovery, and hard to know when you've gone as far as you can go. It's difficult to embrace an identity that is so devalued and marginalized in our culture. How one navigates—and when—the transition from fighting being disabled to "accepting" it, from waiting for the cure to constructing a life and narrative that incorporates the disabilities, is a central and vexing question. But what biomedical narratives of impairments communicate is very different from the kinds of narratives that go along with day-to-day living with a disability.

In the passage that follows, Dr. Larsen is responding to my question about how she facilitates the process of connecting patients to a community of other people who share their experience. She tells me a story to illustrate one of the stages many of her patients hit, one that may be relatively brief or quite protracted:

DR. LARSEN: I have had some patients who get stuck in the angry stage [ES: Yeah] and who don't want to identify themselves as disabled, for years. I've got one woman I can think of off the top of my head who, who is probably four or five years out now and I would say she's just finally made that transition to where being disabled is okay. And she's gone on to living despite it, she's not continually fighting it, not looking for cures, not looking for magic answers, but it's okay now. And she can go on and, she's happiest at this point that I've ever seen her. Um, it's been pretty impressive to me how that change finally occurred.

ES: And, uh, I don't know if you can answer this, but how did she, what were critical components of that process, of that change? I mean is it a matter of time, or..?

DR. LARSEN: I think it was having to fight really, really hard and realize no matter how hard you wanted it and how hard you fought, things weren't going to happen the way you wanted. Uh, and the amount of her life, and energy, and time or money that was being expended, I think finally came to a head, um, when she hit a crisis medically. Um, some of the things she had been pursuing didn't work out. She ended up having a decision forced upon her that she had been resisting, and which would have made her life a whole lot easier. It was a colostomy. Because she would spend three to four hours a day doing bowel programs, because she had a terrible bowel problem. And she didn't want to do anything surgical because that would, um, cut into her dream that eventually there was going to be a magical cure. And then she had a perforation and an emergency situation, um, had the surgery and it was so much easier. You know, it simplified her life so much. I think that she could begin, I mean having had that crisis and then having seen how much better it was to accept it, and how much that opened up for her, there was a transition there.

Although it didn't always involve this kind of crisis, or a period of years coming to it, many of the women here have gone through, or are going through, a similar transition. For the woman in Dr. Larsen's story, fighting really, really hard might have been a necessary part of the process. It seems to have been very important for Lydia and Susan. Many women want to be sure the inevitable *is* inevitable. It may be that there is something helpful, perhaps necessary, about fighting when you've been injured, despite the "energy, and time or money" being expended. When something like brain injury has happened to you, with the sort of helplessness and vulnerability that it invoked for most of the women (not to mention what it suggests about the world, justice, and order), fighting might feel good, or at least like something one *can* do in the circumstances. Most women here also report having some anger, sometimes a lot of anger, to deal with, and often no place to direct it. Again, fighting might help. Lydia could only manage her intense anger through a grinding exercise regimen and her self-administered physical rehabilitation program. Eventually she had to find another strategy because the intensity of her exertion was causing severe pain problems. In the interim, it helped her recover a sense of agency and efficacy that had been compromised by her injuries.

This is not simply a matter of personality or individual differences, or even the effects of brain injury. I'm sure these play a role, but you don't have to be Susan Sontag to recognize that many metaphors and cultural narratives surround and inform the perception and experience of disability. "Handicaps" are something to be "overcome." The appearance and condition of the body are somehow reflections of character and/or intelligence or soul (Ingstad & Whyte, 1995; Sontag, 2001). A just-world assumption tells us and others that bad things only happen to those who deserve them, and that belief colludes with related beliefs that with more faith and better living (or harder work, more science, or greater political consciousness) the disability would go away (and that it *should* go away). In sum, illness and disability are equated with weakness, ignorance, or evil; at best, illness and disability will be understood, on some level or by some others, as a test or trial that one must "pass" (see, for example Davis, 1997; Fries, 1997; Goffman, 1963; Ingstad & Whyte, 1995; Shakespeare, 1996; Sontag, 2001; Zola, 1994).

Furthermore, as disability studies have explicated, we have few narratives for living with disability or chronic illness (and few structures and resources for it). Both medicine and religion tend to be "cure-focused"; cure (or disappearance) is the optimal and sensible outcome (James, 2011). Sarah continues to decline a surgery that would allow her to breathe and speak without a tracheotomy tube because she is expecting a complete and miraculous transformation. The surgery would be less than a perfect outcome for her, as well as a betrayal of faith. Cure is the only acceptable resolution:

> DR. LARSEN: But, patients defy our knowledge all the time. So, I
> think it's a good thing to have people uh, who are highly motivated,
> who want to work very hard towards their goals, um, as long as they
> can also live in the present. I mean hope is a good thing. It's just a
> problem when hope interferes with your ability to live. And for some
> people, I mean actually Christopher Reeve again was a person who
> was certainly an issue because he was talking about cure, cure, cure.
> By the year two thousand he was going to be walking again.

Hope is a good thing, except when it's not. It's not clear how one knows when hope becomes that kind of problem, when to let it go or at least place it elsewhere. Christopher Reeve took a lot of heat from the disability community in the 1990s for his very public emphasis on money for research on spinal cord regeneration and his relative silence about difficulties with access, personal care assistance, discrimination, quality and availability of care—the "real" issues for (non–movie star) people with disabilities (see McRuer, 2002). It is hard not to want to fight to be "abled," or just less disabled. But the fight can easily become a fight against one's self, and it may mean an ultimate isolation. It can also be exhausting.

Snyder and Mitchell (2006) argue for the importance of the particular emphases of the cultural model of disability because they do not "assume an absent relationship between therapeutic beliefs about disability and disabled people's experience. The two inform each other, for better or worse, and consequently we must begin to theorize the degree to which a dominant discourse such as rehabilitation science comes to be internalized by disabled people" (7). Ignoring this relationship, they argue, allows "rehabilitation providers and researchers to justify their own practices without acknowledging that they capitalize on a transitional phase of impairment inevitably subject to change" (8). What would it mean, they ask, if rehabilitation decided to "base its intervention strategies on long-term goals of value to people living with disabilities, developed after the primary period of adjustment?" (9).

Rehabilitation, perhaps necessarily, in its rituals and repetitions, incessantly returns attention to one's limitations, to elusive principles of normalcy and "prior functioning that by definition of one's impairment, cannot be regained" (Snyder & Mitchell, 2006, 9). There is support in the preceding accounts for the assertion that while one is working to renegotiate identity and relationship to one's injured body and brain, one is also invited to an opposition or a tragic relationship to them. And it is fair to say that medical culture in general seems preoccupied with a certain if tacit metaphysics of restoration or perfectibility, so it often has relatively little to offer by way of helping people live with disability (Garland-Thomson, 2011; Lorenz, 2010; Williams, 1991; Zola, 1994).

However, even those facilities like the Rehab Center that want and try to provide greater attention to and resources for living with disability and facilitating greater peer and community participation in the rehabilitation process are increasingly less able to do so. There is alongside the metaphysics of perfectibility the metaphysics (if you will) of scarcity and the market economy. Dr. Larsen indicates that a restricted focus on acute and corrective care has become more and more the only allowable focus of rehabilitation under current public policy and managed care practices.

A cultural model of disability requires consideration of the ways that culture more broadly is the site, source, and effect of these dominant discourses that play out in therapeutic settings, and certainly not only in therapeutic settings. Political economy and neoliberalism structure and perpetuate ideologies in human sciences and services, ideologies about perfectibility, about productivity and what qualifies as productive expenditure, and a quantifiable, dollars-and-cents metric for the quality and value of bodies, lives, and living. And, again, the same political economy determines access to, the range of, and the social valuation of medical and rehabilitation services.

Medicine and rehabilitation, furthermore, cannot be said to have invented normalization practices and discourses, the cult of perfectibility or restoration or of illness and disability as a failure and disappointment, as a cause for shame; a cursory review of the Bible should make that clear. "Communities" also do more than a fair share in supporting or inscribing the less than constructive blaming and shaming narratives that some women already have been recruited into (either implicitly or explicitly) before their encounter with rehab and afterward.

It isn't clear that it is reasonable or even strategic to make rehabilitation *the*, at least the primary, target of cultural critique. In asking what would happen if rehabilitation science decided to base its intervention strategies on long-term goals of value to people living with disabilities, developed after the acute stage of brain injury recovery, Snyder and Mitchell (2006) seem to be assuming that: (1) rehabilitation possesses an independent agency and freedom to "decide"; and, (2) that it would in fact be desirable for these settings to take on responsibility and procedures for identifying and addressing those long-term goals of value. It is not apparent that rehabilitation—inpatient or outpatient, as a physical site or as a set of discourses—is the best or even a good location to try to address questions about identity and identification, ethics and aesthetics, meaning and value, or life's destinations. I'm not sure that these are matters that ought to be professionalized or commoditized (and I say that as a clinical psychologist). Rather than seeking to "resolve" the future, the "coming-towards" of the who one might become, during the acute, making-present moment of rehab—because it will invariably be bound by the past and by the cognitivist and instrumentalist framings, the "normalizing closures," of rehab and economics—it may be better to preserve the open if enigmatic temporality of the future, of being "prepared to receive what thought is not prepared to think" (Lyotard, 1989, 17).

More prosaically, and perhaps more appropriately within the domain of rehabilitation science, Tobin Siebers argues that "people with disabilities usually realize that they must learn to live with their disability, if they are to live as a human being. The challenge is not to adapt their disability into an extraordinary power or an alternative image of ability. The challenge is to function. . . . People with disabilities want to be able to function: to live with their disability, to come to know their body, to accept what it can do, and to keep doing what they can for as long as they can. They do not want to feel dominated by the people on whom they depend for help, and they want to be able to imagine themselves in the world without feeling ashamed" (2008, 69).

This seems to align, though not without various qualifications, with many of the women's accounts. These are realizations and challenges that begin to crystallize in formal rehab, and the rehab setting can have real influences on how they are met (or not). But, as should become clear in the chapters that follow, this process extends well beyond rehab and best takes place outside Sontag's "kingdom of the sick" (2001). It seems to require support, resources, and audiences in relationship to people and communities. It requires escaping disability as something private or individual, refusing being forced back on oneself and "tied to one's identity in a constraining way" (Foucault, 1983, 212). It also involves locating contexts and relationships that allow disability—and one's self—to be defined outside of an exclusive relationship to medical and rehabilitation practices and discourses. Why those communities are crucial, how they are negotiated, and their bases in complex identifications and personal relationships, pragmatic problem solving, and information sharing, are the topics of the next chapters.

4

Fighting

The fight in recovery and rehabilitation is the fight to recover prior functioning. The self or identity that figures prominently is that of the pre-injury person, along with the even more supernatural future fully restored person. What formal rehabilitation often doesn't offer or support in clear or consistent ways are strategies for living with disability, which is not something that is cured or overcome but that must be incorporated somehow with one's whole life (Zola, 1994).

The struggle has to shift from a fight against one's body and self to a resistance against experiencing oneself as isolated and embarrassed in the world. This involves a shift from viewing disability as something personal or private to a set of practices and discourses experienced and shared by a group, class, coalition, or community of people. Finding or creating "places in the world" involves contexts and relationships for the development of strategies and narratives that illuminate the means of marginalization and provide meaningful, livable responses and alternatives to them. Disability has to shift from being an individual's (medical or psychological) problem to a relational concern shared by people—the disabled and the currently nondisabled alike. That means that the complaints and critiques of people with disabilities have to shift from being perceived as selfish or narcissistic to being understood as matters of critical and ethical concern for every fragile and vulnerable person (which would be all of us).

This is a chapter of extended passages and complicated stories, mainly of accounts from four of the women—Cindy, Nancy, Elise, and Abby—who discussed direct fights against specific barriers or forms of discrimination at some length. It begins with Cindy's story of how she came to identify, politically and personally, with the disability rights community and with "other disabled people," more than a decade before the interview (and prior to the passage of the ADA).

Cindy: "On my own"

My first interview with Cindy took place about fifteen years after the violent criminal assault that had left her fiancé dead and Cindy with extensive, open-head injuries to much of the right side of her brain. In recovery and in coming to live with disability, she had had to deal with the effects of injuries, but also the traumatic way they had been incurred. In telling me what had been important or helpful for her in those years she mentioned a number of factors. *Time* was central, and something she feels is not sufficiently recognized by those negotiating recovery or by those around them. She also cited her "loving family and my wonderful husband, and that kind of thing," though she didn't go on to elaborate on those relationships. Cindy also highly valued psychotherapy with "a compassionate and *extremely* knowledgeable" clinical neuropsychologist, Glynnis, who was well-informed about brain injury and the effects of trauma (and also a committed feminist). From a "technical point of view," that therapy was "number one." Cindy then went on to talk at length about coming to be involved in the disability rights community:

> CINDY: The other thing that has helped me personally, uh, reauthor, has been my involvement in the disability rights community, which is very interesting. I did not seek to get involved in that community. What happened was, Glynnis and I were confronting issues that came up in therapy that she didn't know how to resolve. She simply didn't know. And I didn't know. And they were environmental, they were, you know, they were very bureaucratic. I mean they were, like

I needed to get to the hospital. I couldn't drive. I couldn't walk. I
couldn't get service. I couldn't get on and off a bus. I couldn't, you
know—we were just dealing with a very basic, you know core issues,
like how I could get to therapy. And, I started off being entitled to,
uh, certain services from the transit authority, and somewhere in
the midst of my therapy they just cut us all off—anybody that wasn't
using a wheelchair. [ES: Really?] Well, it was just like a bomb. In
a way, you know, Glynnis and I look back at it and we—and you
know I had written to all my congressmen. I had, you know, you do
all the things that you try to do. [*Three-second pause*] It happens all
the time. And you know that, you're involved in community work.
I mean it *happens all the time.* So, I, you know, I was just astounded.
And I got very frightened when I found out. This was in the context
of my therapy, which I had found quite helpful up to that point, that
my therapist didn't have a clue where to go.

ES: It's not a psychotherapy problem.

CINDY: Yeah, and yet it was a therapy problem because I couldn't get
to therapy. [*ES laughs*] And, you know, it was real important. So, um,
I started making phone calls to people at the Rehab Center, who gave
me the names of people at the Center for Independent Living here in
the city. And they said, oh, well we've got a few people who are starting to work on this aspect of transit and that aspect of transit. And,
and, I kind of knew that was going on, but in the past I really didn't
have a need for it, and I didn't identify myself as being quote unquote
disabled.

ES: Ahhh. Huh.

CINDY: But once I started realizing that my services were being
threatened, and my ability to do what I wanted was being threatened
by decisions that were completely out of my control. And, you know,
just huge stuff, you know, like who controls the resources. [ES: Uh
huh] I started letting down my guard and allowing myself to start
working with other disabled people. It was very scary. It was very
hard for me to do that.

ES: It was?

CINDY: It was very hard. That's not true for all people but it was very
hard for me, especially in the beginning. Very, very hard. It was
hard. Because the leaders of the disability rights here in the city, as

other places, were very radical from my point of view. Um, they were chaining themselves to buses and that kind of thing. And I simply, at that time, I didn't understand it, I didn't need it, and it wasn't my personality, you know? [ES: Uh huh, yeah] But, once I got fucked over *big time*—I mean it was horrible because I had just moved to the suburbs and I was trying to get down to the university, which is, you know, it was like thirty miles away. And I had signed a contract on my house, with the understanding that I had transportation services into the city. And when I called, and when I protested, and whatever, all I was told was that they had made a unitary decision to just stop giving services to people that were disabled that didn't have wheelchairs. And, so when I started allowing myself to realize that, uh, the senators and the congressmen, and the mayor, and the head of the transit authority, that *nobody's* really going to listen to me unless I start working with other people. You know that ended up being a gigantic turning point for me, because I got to a point where I would allow myself to identify with a larger community, you know. It was really hard. But it worked, and you know, I've been working in it ever since. So that's my, in addition to personal and family relationships, having a very supportive, and proactive, community that I could feel safe in, and um, work in, to work collectively to help get some of the things that I needed personally, that's been very important to me.

ES: So, I'm not sure what I'm about to ask, [*Cindy laughs*] I take it that this was a major shift for you personally, [Cindy: Yes] and in terms of how you thought of yourself, and so, but, was there a political change in that?

CINDY: Sure! *Big time*. Well. I mean, see, we started going to Transit Authority board meetings, and they're very big. [*Five-second pause*] Keep in mind I come from a professional business background, so you know I was thinking this is just a group of business people and I'll just use logic [*ES laughs*] with them, like I did when. But I forgot one thing, and that was that I wasn't an insider. [ES: Ahh, uh huh] Whereas in business I was an insider, I was one of the players. And that being an outsider trying to go to something like the Transit Authority, which really saw itself as servicing the quote unquote northern suburbs, you know—[*laughing*] where I live now—but refused to believe that people with disabilities, even though we were

taxpayers, really had entitlements to use public transportation. And
we were pretty much told that—I was told actually in a letter from
the executive director at the time—that they were not a social service
agency and they weren't required to provide services to disabled
people, that I should start talking to social workers to find ways to
get around. Um, so all of a sudden I'm like dealing with the reality of
what it means. And I'm not, you know, I'm a person that has some
money, not a lot. I have a lot of family support. And I'm like *wow!* If
it's this hard for me, think how hard it is for all those other people
that have access to even fewer resources, that don't have a husband,
or a father or a mother to drive them around, you know. Or, that
can't talk. My speech is intact, um, you know, I mean a lot of people
have a very difficult time communicating, and have an even harder
time dealing with the same issues, for the same reasons, but have
speech impairments and disabilities, uh, coupled. So. [*Six-second
pause*] It was major. It wasn't just a matter of theory or a choice to be
a liberal or progressive person, it was out of necessity, to get services.

A lot happens in this passage. It is obviously an account of Cindy's
coming to be involved in the disability rights community and of identifying herself "as quote unquote disabled." It is an account of the difficulties that precipitated that identification, but also the difficulties that
attended accepting the identity. Cindy uses the word "hard" six times
and "scary" once in one short part of that discussion. This is a powerful, even emblematic, account of coming to political consciousness, to
collective identification, and to a change in identity (see Linton, 2007;
Torrell, 2011); so, the points Cindy raises here are considered at some
length.

Cindy did not set out to become involved in "that community," referring to the disability rights community. But, when the transit authority
"cut us all off"—there is a shift there from me to we—the experience
was like a "bomb." As discussed later, she had resisted using a wheelchair, which would have made transit more accessible, because she
didn't want to give into it and sacrifice being "ambulatory." (At the time,
Cindy used a leg brace and cane for her left hemiplegia and balance difficulties.) Apparently, her resistance to a wheelchair was stronger than
her resistance to the disability rights community. When Cindy—and

her therapist—are confronted with issues that were "environmental" and "very bureaucratic," problems her therapist "didn't know how to resolve," she first wrote to all her congressmen, her senator, the mayor, and the transit authority, who told her they weren't a social service agency, "you know, all the things you try to do." Cindy was astounded and frightened and her therapist didn't have a clue of where to go.

The experience precipitates a turning point in Cindy's relationship to a disability and to identification with other people with disabilities. Cindy was referred to the Center for Independent Living, who told her about a "few people" starting to work on transit-access issues. She had kind of known things were going on, but in the past really didn't have a need for involvement, and didn't identify herself "as being quote unquote disabled." Given that Cindy was clearly aware of her injuries and their effects on her mobility, and that a lot of what she working on in therapy was the effects of her brain injuries, not identifying as disabled here seems to refer to identifying *with* people with disabilities, a distinction that is clarified—and shifts—as she continues.

The problem of confronting structural forces and the inadequacy of individual tactics in that confrontation is fairly clear here. But I want to bring attention to how that dilemma led Cindy to let down her guard and allow herself to start working with other disabled people. This is an account of a shift from not identifying as "quote unquote disabled" to including herself with "other disabled people"; what had been *the* other for Cindy becomes *her* others, others *like* her, or at least sharing the same problems of access and discrimination.

What she was guarding against becomes clearer as she continues: "It was very scary. It was very hard for me to do that. It was very hard. That's not true for all people but it was very hard for me, especially in the beginning. Very, very hard. It was hard." Part of what made it scary and hard for Cindy to allow herself to work with other disabled people was that the leaders of the disability rights movement "were very radical" and she didn't understand it, didn't need it, and it wasn't her "personality." Until she "got fucked over *big time*," and realized, after trying to play it as an "insider" that nobody was going to listen unless she started working with other people.

It is an emblematic account of embracing a marginalized identity or becoming involved with an identity-based movement that carries a stigma or a characterization of gratuitous radicalism. It is hard because these identities are devalued, even embarrassing, something anyway that one would not want to actually foreground in or about oneself, let alone rally behind. Cindy's characterization of disability rights activists and of her response to them underscores something about discourses of individualism, particularly in tandem with marginalization, that make collective identification seem immature, narcissistic, or just, well, *lame*. These cultural pressures work, in varying combinations, to allow people with disabilities (and many others) to be danced into a corner of isolation, quietism, and self-devaluation. As Olkin (2009) points out the disabled should be plucky but mournful, never angry.

The experience "ended up being a gigantic turning point," because she got to where she could allow herself to "identify with a larger community," and become aware that what was happening to her happens all the time. It was hard, but it worked, and Cindy's "been working in it ever since." Having "a very supportive and, proactive, community" that she could feel *safe* in and work in collectively to help get some of the things that she personally needed has been very important to her. Things working is important here. Participation in a disability community wasn't a matter of "theory or a choice to be a liberal or progressive person, it was out of necessity, to get services."

Cindy describes something beyond a pragmatic affiliation of necessity, however. She goes on to the realization that if the experience of confronting structural barriers was hard for her, it must be even more difficult for people without her resources: "I'm like *wow!* If it's this hard for me, think how hard it is for all those other people that have access to even fewer resources . . . Or, that can't talk." It was, as she says, *major*. There is a suggestion of what she can offer to a community, a realization of resources she can bring and a role she can play. Cindy went on to make a career in disability rights and activism, especially for women, and working and career are quite important to her. She cites the value of a supportive community where she feels safe and where she can work. Cindy describes political coalition here, but she also describes mattering and reciprocity, and emotional identification with a community of people—a sense of community.

Cindy switched topics after that passage, but I had some persistent questions or a lack of clarity about Cindy's initial reluctance to identify as disabled and with the disability rights community. I wanted her to

explicate further why that was so difficult and to say more about what
identifying as disabled meant for her at that time. That is, I was interested in her critical analysis of that process. This took what felt like per-
severation on my part and, in that first interview, it wasn't clear if it was
going to be appropriate or effective:

ES: Something you said a little while ago that I wanted to get back to
because I'm not sure I was completely clear on, was your reluctance
to sort of identify yourself with disabled [*three-second pause*] *people*?
[Cindy: Mm. Hmm] And I wasn't sure if it was just with the *movement*, because of the, of the, sort of the, the—

CINDY: It was both. It was both.

ES: —because of, sort of, the *tenor* of it?

CINDY: It was both, it was both.

ES: —or to embrace that *identity*?

CINDY: It was both, you know. [*Five-second pause*] Um. It's going to
get louder here, I should tell you. [ES: Okay] And we can move to my
office, which is smaller, and not as pretty. But that's your choice. I'll
stay as long as you want because it's pleasant here.

ES: Okay. Also, if you want to have lunch, we can stop and have
lunch.

CINDY: Okay. [*Six-second pause*]

ES: Uh, so. Well, I realize that now you'll be talking about *that* in
terms of—you know—your present experience, but, I mean, what do
you think it was? I mean, I'd like to hear a little more about why you
were reluctant to, to embrace that—

CINDY: Oh. Well. I felt that I could do mostly what I needed on my
own.

ES: Uh huh. Okay.

CINDY: I thought I could, up until I hit this, this brick wall in, in
Glynnis's office. "Ugh! I can't do this on my own!" [*Laughs*] Um,
there was that. But probably larger than that, I was buying into this
[*four-second pause*] stigma, and, uh, the stereotypes that the medical
model sets up for people that have disabilities as being abnormal. I
mean it's yeah, it probably had more of a fear of being stigmatized,
losing some respectability, um, and, um, seeing myself as an outsider
to humanity. That's not seeing myself as a person.

ES: Uh huh, and, do you think that there was a paradoxical outcome [*Cindy laughs*] in that by embracing that—

CINDY: Yeah! Oh, yeah. *Yeah.* Yeah, I work through that with people all the time. It takes a long time, you know. A turning point for me was when I met this woman accountant who was—at the time she was ambulatory, she now uses a chair full time—but she and I were like fighting these transportation battles at the same time, and she was working downtown and she lived in the suburbs also, and had to have her husband physically carry her off the train, and have the conductors carry her on and off the train, to use the damn train to get to work. [ES: Yeah. *God*] And, I mean, you know. I mean it was just, it was just, it was—and she was a professional. And I looked at her, and I really liked her, and she was smart, and she, uh, and she could break all this disability stuff down into dollars and cents and like still show them that it would be in their interests—dollars-and-cents-wise—to put lifts on the trains. And, you know, they wouldn't do it [*laughs*], you know.

ES: As if it was really about rationality.

CINDY: Yeah, of course, right. *But,* I, she, once I, you know, I think I had to see somebody. I had to eventually connect with somebody that was working in this, and struggling with the same issues, that I could see somebody like me. You know? And it was interesting because she ended up going on to become a lot more disabled. I mean she kept falling a lot, and was wearing leg braces on both legs, and finally just had to start using a wheelchair all the time. And I originally started identifying with her because she was ambulatory, and yet she was still having severe problems, as I was, just taking part in society. And her balance was an ongoing issue for her, as it was for me. So, when she got her wheelchair, she called me up and said, "Oh, Cindy, I'm just *so* much more *relaxed.*" [*Both laugh*] And, *then,* it's what actually allowed me to get my wheelchair and I've been using it since, um, because I've since developed rheumatoid arthritis on both sides of my body, which makes the effects of the brain injury all that much *more* difficult, because I have pain now. Um, and there was her, and there were women that I knew, on the board here, that were postpolio, that were saying "once you get your wheelchair you're never gonna regret it. You're just gonna not have to worry about

trying to find chairs to sit down in or about getting pushed over."
And, [*three-second pause*] it was just, like, *it took a while.* But, I, I
[*four-second pause*] Yeah! It seems paradoxical, but you don't see it
right away. There's no way, there's *no way* you can embrace the totality of that at one time or in one encounter. It just doesn't work like
that. It's impossible.

Cindy did try to change topics in response to my question, and there
were a couple of pauses that felt very long to me, before she decided to
elaborate. I was curious if it was about the movement and its tactics, or
if it was something about being a disabled person that accounted for
her difficulty with becoming involved in "that community." She knew
where I was going with the question; before I could even manage to
formulate the question she told me four times that "it was both." Cindy
wanted to do what she needed mostly on her own, up until she hit a
brick wall in her therapist's office: "Ugh! I can't do this on my own!"
Probably larger than that, though, was buying into the "*stigma* and, uh,
the stereotypes that the medical model sets up for people that have disabilities as being abnormal." Cindy didn't want to be stigmatized, lose
respectability, or see herself as an outsider to humanity. Who does? She
wanted to see herself "as a person."

The paradox that Cindy understood before I articulated it is of
becoming less of an "outsider to humanity" by embracing identification
with other misfits, other "outsiders." It's a switch that Cindy now works
through with people all the time: "It takes a long time, you know." An
array of discursive pressures overdetermines the difficulties involved in
authoring identity post-injury and in identifying with other disabled
people. In both passages Cindy articulates well the workings of the discourses of individualism and of ableism. In fact, both the political right
and a critical left frame such collective identifications as a "politics of
resentment," as politically and socially regressive, a politics "invested in
its own subjection" or based on "a narcissistic wound" (Brown, 1995).
There is additionally the critique that identity-based movements serve
to reinscribe or reify the margins and categories they (should) aim to
contest (for example, Butler, 1997) and lead to conformity (within the
group), intolerance (within and across groups), and political divisive-
ness (across the "serious" body politic) (Fraser, 2000). And, not so very

different, there is the feeling that people asking for help, people who are dependent on others for services or "accommodations"—that is, people who are a burden—should not make trouble, should not behave, in Lester's terms, as a "privileged and growing interest group of oppressors of more ordinary people" (Lester, 2002, quoted in Siebers, 2008). This last characterization is reflected, albeit in quite different terms, in Cindy's own initial perspective on the disability rights community. In addition to (and related to) these problems of political collation formation and action, there is also the stigma and pathologization of disabilities offered by the medical model and many other quarters that the disabled are abnormal, and "less than human." It is little wonder that it's hard to identify with the disability rights community or to embrace a disability identity.

What is omitted from those analyses is any consideration of the value of cooperation, trust, caring and, as Cindy mentions, safety in the relationships built and supported within such communities or coalitions. I think there is a further failure to recognize how the work and support within a disability community can enhance relationships and common interests between the disabled and the nondisabled.

Cindy had to see somebody, to eventually connect with somebody struggling with the same issues, somebody like her. Somebody who was smart, a professional, and that Cindy "really liked." A woman who was, like Cindy, fighting the transit authority and breaking down "disability stuff into dollars and cents," but who was also, like Cindy, "having severe problems just taking part in society." This identification allowed Cindy to get her wheelchair, be "more relaxed" with her post-injury body. (Paradoxically, it was Cindy's resistance to a wheelchair that initiated her fight with the transit authority, and to her meeting someone like her.)

"*It took a while.*" Time is a crucial factor in the process: "You don't see it right away. There's no way, there's *no way* you can embrace the totality of that at one time or in one encounter. It just doesn't work like that. It's impossible." That point is important in relation to the accounts that follow, accounts of other women, like Nancy and Elise who seemed to have less difficulty (more than a decade later, and after the passage of the ADA) framing and confronting their battles as social battles, as well as to Abby's continuing difficulties with that embrace.

Return Trip

Before moving to those accounts, though, I take up Cindy's account of a reprise of her initial battle for transit access, over ten years after the initial struggle, and how some things don't really change that much over time. In an account from another interview four years after that first one, instead of fighting the transit authority for public transportation access, Cindy discusses finding herself having to fight with the *Rehab Center* for access to the employee shuttle service. In the first passage of this (long) account Cindy establishes the context, her initial attempt to redress the problem, and the Center's response:

> CINDY: I'm using the train. I have to use the train. The trains are
> wheelchair equipped, lift equipped now, for wheelchairs, so there's,
> you know, the transit services are saying, "We don't want to pay for
> special vans to transit people back and forth from the city to the
> suburbs, we want you to use the train." [ES: Uh huh] And we say *fine*.
> Now, most employees of the Rehab Center, or the medical center,
> that use the train use a shuttle bus to get back and forth from the sta-
> tion. If you use city buses, um, just mainline services, you're taking
> at least two buses, possibly three, *and* you walk. And, so, I thought I
> should have the same option [ES: Uh huh] to use the shuttle ser-
> vice as my nondisabled colleagues, both here at the Center and at
> the other hospitals. Now, I knew all along that the shuttle was not a
> Rehab Center service, but a courtesy extended to our employees by
> the Memorial Medical Center. And I brought this to the attention of
> the people here a long time ago. Put in a memo to the attorney here,
> a very nice woman, and basically heard *zero*, even though I asked—I
> very politely asked people to work with me on solving, you know, the
> problem. And, um, heard *zero*, until one of my colleagues, Pepper,
> who's also a board member, kind of nudged the medical director and
> the CEO into at least *talking* to me, *calling* me. And they basically
> kept saying to her, "Well, what's Cindy going to do?" [*ES laughs*]
> That was their response. [ES: Right] "Well, what's she going to do?"
> As opposed to, "What are *we* going to do, collectively?" [ES: Right]
> Which would have been the appropriate response, mostly given for
> whom I work. So, that was when the medical director called me

and basically said to me, this is not a Rehabilitation Center benefit, transportation, you know, it's not an employee benefit. It's not in the handbook. [*ES laughs*] You know, I knew right away he was taking this hardcore legalistic line. [ES: *Really?*] Yes! And, never, you know, thinking about what their mission is, who they think they are, and what their priorities should be. And, what *I* do here, I mean I—of course my center lives up to *their* mission, it's not my mission; it's their mission. *I* go that extra step, *we*, you know—we pull money out of our pockets to get people to and from an event here. [ES: Uh huh] Rather than any of us saying, "Well, that's not my responsibility."

I want to attend first to the rather complex back and forth in Cindy's use of "we" and "I" in this passage (and those to follow). In relation to Cindy's first story about becoming involved in disability rights, she begins here with an uncomplicated inclusion of herself in that community: "And we say *fine*." But as this account continues, it is often Cindy alone, as an *I*, that is taking on this problem with the shuttle service; in fact, part of the practical and ideological struggle here is over the framing of the problem as *hers* versus, as Cindy points out, a collective problem of *we*: "'What's Cindy going to do?' As opposed to, 'Well, what are we going to do, collectively?'" Then in talking about what she does there, she contrasts the Center's position, and their positioning of her, to what she and *her* center does for *their* mission. But, as if to underscore the dilemma in such a framing, Cindy has to shift again in discussing the Women's Center's work: "*I* go that extra step, *we*, you know—we pull money out of our pockets . . . rather than any of us saying 'Well, that's not my responsibility.'" That I/we (or them/us and my/our) construction figures recurrently in struggles over disability rights and the accounts of other women here; it figured, in a different way, in Cindy's initial difficulties with identifying as "quote unquote disabled." It is also a key and strategic aspect of the Rehab Center's maneuvering of the problem and who has it.

Cindy thought she should have the same option to use the shuttle service as her nondisabled colleagues and "very politely" brought the problem to the attention of administration, and "heard zero." Zero, that is, until another of Cindy's colleagues, who also uses a wheelchair and is on the boards of both the Rehab Center and the Center for Independent

Living, "nudged" the CEO and medical directors. Despite a powerful ally, it is still framed as Cindy's problem, individualized in the way difficulties with discrimination and marginalization (like racism, sexism, heterosexism) are often framed as individual or interpersonal problems. The concern over what she is going to do is whether she might make legal and/or publicity trouble; not, as Cindy points out, taking the position of collective problem solving of a collective problem. The latter would be seem to be the appropriate response, given the Rehab Center's progressive rhetoric of advocacy and accessibility, which, as Cindy points out, her Women's Center helps to legitimate. But it's "not in the handbook."

The strategy of personalizing this issue is a double hit for Cindy. First, making the issue of accessible employee transportation a personal one is, as mentioned, a classic strategy for shifting the problem, minimizing it, and silencing troublemakers by making them seem (or even feel) selfish, demanding, overly sensitive or neurotic—whether it is an employee shuttle, a flight of stairs, boardroom full of misogynists, or a whites-only country club (Garland-Thomson, 2011). When you are disabled, as Cindy points out below, part of what disables you is the feeling of being a burden or a lot of trouble, a feeling reinforced in countless ways by implicit and explicit material and discursive messages. Second, the Center's response shifts Cindy from insider to outsider, a distinction to which Cindy is very sensitive. Her problem is not their problem, except that Cindy herself may become identified *as* a problem. This puts Cindy in an unstable and uncomfortable subject position because she has to fight and be fought by people she has known for a decade and that she sees on a regular basis, people she thought she was friendly with, that she has conscientiously tried to be friendly with. Especially around issues of marginalized identities, this can be an extremely chilling and isolating experience, involving a real sense of betrayal. Her work in building the Women's Center is a major part of her identity narrative and her day-to-day life; Cindy's professional identity and personal identity don't separate cleanly. The "we" that Cindy often speaks from refers to the Rehab Center as often as it does to disabled women. So, finding herself alone with a problem like accessibility to her work, finding herself at odds with and othered by people and an institution she identifies with and promotes, is particularly alienating and disappointing; one might say paralyzing.

Her effort to pose and hold on to counternarratives is evident as she continues the account, as is the continuing insider/outsider and I/we dilemma, and the now troubled interconnection between Cindy's personal identity and her public and professional role:

> CINDY: I almost didn't want to come in here anymore. [ES: Mhm] Because I felt like, oh, Lori [the Women's Center intern] and I kill ourselves here and, and I get paid part-time, I raise basically all my funds here. And our job is to work with people that have problems like I have. And they have such disregard, not to mention *pure stupidity*! Having no idea of what it really—I kept explaining to them—this is the other part—I kept explaining what it took for us to just even get lifts on the MTA buses. And all he kept saying was "*We* supported that." And I said, "*No*! No, no, there were *protests*, there was media stuff." And he still didn't get it. He still didn't get that I was not threatening him, I was just simply saying that you really don't want to deny me service, because of all the stuff that I've done since ten years ago. I'm known and respected and people will back me up. [ES: Right] And it won't look good for you. And, it, it wasn't, it didn't even—still—*get in*. So, I, I don't know. So, um, Glynnis just said, "I really think we're about to move to another level. You're headed for another growth spurt here." [ES, *laughing*: What?] Kind of, because I'd already made the move into the community-minded thing. [ES: Okay] And, um, taking this place on, on, on more visible and policy-level *as an employee, on the inside*, I mean really butting heads with it directly, was really, really hard. [ES: Yeah, of course] Because I think I've had a pretty friendly relationship, and, um, I, I don't think I'm really finished. [*Both laugh*] I feel like I'm still at the kind of beginning of it, from a personal growth standpoint. Um, I guess I, I um, um, I have since gotten a call from them to say, that they, um, would accommodate me.

Cindy here continues her discussion of the work that she and others do at the Women's Center and sets it in contrast to the Rehab Center's "disregard." This discussion makes clear Cindy's disappointment and disillusionment, not just with the Rehab Center administration's lack of recognition and consideration but also with their "*pure stupidity*." Not only are they resisting doing what would be the right thing from a personal and moral perspective, but the right thing in terms of the kind of public image trouble they're courting: "He still didn't get that I was not threatening him, I was just simply saying that you really don't want to deny me service . . . I'm known and respected and people will back me up. And it won't look good for you." Cindy shifts back and forth from speaking as an experienced and well-connected disability rights activist to speaking as Cindy who is hurt, sick and tired and working through this in therapy as a personal growth issue. Of course, it *is* personal, in that it is happening to Cindy and that she is having to marshal the personal resources to mount and persist in the fight, a fight against people with whom she has personal relationships. These two perspectives are also at play in her discussion of the Women's Center. She is protesting that her work and commitment there aren't recognized and appropriately valued (nor are the hours of her day spent just dealing with transportation problems). She is at the same time deliberately contrasting the ethos of her Center with that of the Rehab Center. What may not be as obvious is that she is also pointing out that the Rehab Center owes more to her and the Women's Center than vice versa: *her* Center advances *their* mission. They are putting her loyalty to the Rehab Center at odds with her loyalty to herself and the disability community, and that seems to be as galling to her as the transportation problem. But, it is also that she is disappointed—as an insider and a businesswoman—that the administration is being "stupid" about their policy and public image.

This is a complicated insider/outsider dilemma. Cindy is speaking by turns as disability rights insider, as a Rehab Center insider concerned about their image and mission, as one placed outside by their institutional response, and personally as someone just tired of having to deal with it. She is also framing the confrontation as a matter of "personal growth." Exactly how this is a matter of personal growth is more fully explicated in the next passage. Cindy does get a call telling her that they would accommodate *her* (again the use of the singular pronoun), but the story behind getting the call involves some friends in high places, more personal growth, some foot dragging and qualifiers, and more fighting:

CINDY: Now the only reason I got that call was because I accidentally ran into Cara in the lobby here. Which was meant to be. She

was waiting to see one of our gynecologists, who was delivering a
baby. You deliver a baby, you don't come back right away. So, all of a
sudden, here's Cara, sitting there. I'm like talking to her for an hour
straight. She said—she's had cabinet positions, she's on the Center's
board of directors, and she's the head of the Center for Independent
Living. So I tell her the whole story. And her words were "Unfuckingbelievable." [*Both laugh*] She says I can't believe you're going through
this. And then she says, "Would you be willing for everybody else
to lose the shuttle? Because you know that's probably what they're
going to threaten you with." Because they've already used everything
else in the book. They used, "Cindy's the only one"; "The shuttle's
already going bankrupt, to make an accommodation would put it out
of business." Now, this is a hospital that's raising millions of dollars
quarterly, you know. [*Both laugh*] You know, a judge is not going to
look at what's going to happen to the shuttle, he's going to look at
what's going to happen to Memorial Hospital. That's the last thing
that's going to happen to Memorial Hospital is bankruptcy putting a
lift on a school bus. [*Both laugh*] You know? Um, so, so at first—Now
this is interesting Eric, when she said to me, are you willing to allow,
seriously, your coworkers and everybody else at Memorial to lose
their shuttle services, first I said *No!* Because [*both laugh*] you know,
I mean *that's where my mind was.* This is the growth spurt thing. And
then she said, "Yes! You are!" You know, "Cindy! I mean the more
pressure there is, I mean how else are you, *how else*?" You know? [ES:
Uh huh] She said, "This place, I mean of all places, should, even if
they don't have responsibility for the shuttle, they should at least be
going out there and advocating for it." [ES: Right] There are disabled,
you know, employees over there, even though we don't know who
they are, but, you know. The other argument they use, which is a cir-
cular one, is, well, you know there's nobody that's disabled that ever
wants to use it. [*Both laugh*] Well, it's like, this is like well how, why is
somebody in a wheelchair gonna come and say—other than me, who
happens to push—say I wanna use your shuttle, when they *know* it
obviously doesn't accommodate a wheelchair.

ES: I really don't understand how they can be so, um, you should
pardon the expression I guess, *blind* [*Cindy laughs*] I mean—

CINDY: It's, see—

ES: I mean, [*Cindy laughs*] we're in the Rehab Center!
CINDY: I know! I know! *And*, I mean, I don't think they're blind at all, you know, that whole thing. They *know*.

This passage provides further demonstration of some of the complicated lack of clear boundaries between the personal and the political, the bodily and the cultural. The context and relationship involved in the conversation Cindy recounts indicate something about how and where some of the important transactions of community and coalition work transpire. In community psychology it is almost axiomatic that many critical developments and strategic insights of community organizing occur in interactions that take place in informal settings like this one. That is, attending only to public policy statements or official board meetings misses much of the real action and many of the real processes of and opportunities for change. The conversation that Cindy describes here is one that takes place "accidentally," in a lobby between two friends. Cara is waiting for a delayed appointment with her gynecologist and Cindy is about to start her long wait for her paratransit ride. Cindy describes it as a "meant to be" encounter. Cindy could have *called* Cara, who is a major player on several counts, and enlisted her support and advice. But the impromptu conversation described here seems less about asking Cara to use her influence, and rather more about Cindy wanting a sounding board and some informed understanding from somebody she identifies with as a friend and as another accomplished, professional, disabled woman. There is also an indication here of the role of settings where paths are likely to cross for people with disabilities as well as how *waiting* operates in the lives of people like Cindy who are dependent on services like paratransit or personal care assistants for many day to day tasks.

The conversation and its context points to at least one of the ways community works, in terms of networking of course but also in the possibility and practice of conversations in which a background of experience and knowingness already exists: Cara can remind or support Cindy in how "unfuckingbelievable" it is that the Rehabilitation Center, "of all places," is the antagonist here. Cara can also, in the way a friend and someone with shared experience and perspective does, remind Cindy of the necessity for creative maladjustment. Cara asks the strategic question, "Would you be willing for everybody else to lose the shuttle?" Cindy first says "No!" Because *that's where her mind was.* This is part of Cindy's personal "growth spurt thing" and it is also something Cara can remind Cindy about: "'Cindy!' I mean the more pressure there is, I mean how else are you, *how else?*" It is worth comparing this transaction with Cindy's account of her first battle for transit access over a decade earlier, when the idea of "working with other disabled people" was "very hard" and "very scary": community and identity.

The fight is still personal in that it challenges some of Cindy's reluctance to make trouble for other people, at least people she knows or works with. There may be something gendered about this, about Cindy's general desire to be "friendly" and "polite" in this circumstance, and Cindy and her therapist both identify this struggle and her response as involving or necessitating personal growth. I'm saying that it may be gendered because it's not clear that this is unique to women, as compared to say, disabled men or anyone in a marginalized identity category. And Cindy does identify herself as someone who "happens to push." The dilemma is definitely something related to being disabled and the looming sense that you are or will be tagged a burden or troublesome. It requires a constant reframing of the narrative to keep it from slipping back to being a personal, individual problem, when every response, from "you're the only one" to bankrupt shuttles, casts you as unreasonable and alone. Cara here helps in keeping that dynamic in clear focus. As Cindy points out, it does involve personal growth to put herself out there in that kind of position and resist the impulse to "be nice." But it is also, of course, political or cultural work insofar as it involves identifying and resisting the discursive formations of others. And, as this conversation with Cara illustrates, resisting that discourse and posing a counternarrative requires the support of community and the willingness to be a member and representative of a class of people: "*How else?*"

If anyone entertains the idea that fighting or activism are dramatic and exciting, Cindy's account illustrates how much of it is sheer persistence, of acting in ways you'd often rather not, of rehearsing or reflecting on conversations, and of an ennui-inspiring kind of sameness and repetition to the things you have to contend with (even if Cindy does, maybe must, view it as part of a process of personal growth). Despite the muscle flexing of board members (with disabilities), she was still waiting for a decision, and a lift. She was still contending with arranging and waiting hours for transportation and being forced to reconsider her relationship to her employer, or her employer's estimation of her and other disabled employees (let me re-reiterate, this is the Rehab Center). The final passage of Cindy's account further explicates that throughout the process she is trying to reconcile her natural tendency to be nice with the sense that she has to keep pushing on the issue of "accommodation":

CINDY: Um, I've been still in the meantime trying to work things out with paratransit. So, but the big thing is, is that when I saw Jim [a Rehab Center board member] last week, he said, "Cindy, have you pushed 'em on their willingness to make an accommodation for you?" I said "Not yet." And he said, "Well, you really have to do that." So, I'm at this point where, I mean, it's *hard* when you're on the inside, and you're working inside of a place and you gotta see these people everyday. And you're already a person, or you belong to a class of people that already struggles with this issue of being a burden, and an inconvenience, and a costly one at that. [ES: Uh huh] You know, I have to take on another level of troublemaker. So, I, I'm like gonna have to do this, and it's not easy for me. I mean it's really hard for me. I mean it's really hard, you know. [ES: Uh huh] I keep trying to be nice. [ES: Right] And, um, in the meantime, I'm sitting out in the lobby for two hours, you know, waiting for rides that they're lying to me about. Not, not getting to go two miles, when the shuttle drives by [*laughs*] that I can't get on. You know? I was in a, you know, in trying to deal with this and probably other things, revolving around not only my relationship with this place, but my sense of who I am as an advocate, as a professional [ES: Right] and, you know, who I am. [ES: Uh huh] You know, because these are not easy for me; well, at this time in my life and career it's not any easier for me to take on my employer, particularly this one, than it was for me to take on the transit authority so many years ago. [ES: Uh huh] You know, but, and it's different. I will say ADAPT has already offered to come in and stage demonstrations. I've had to kind of quiet them down. [*ES laughs*] They're pretty radical. They're a national group, they're fairly aggressive. They're the ones who like chain themselves to MTA buses. I've been kind of stalling them. But George Bush, senior, was coming to town, and I knew ADAPT could really capitalize on it. And I kept thinking how stupid the Rehab Center was that they didn't even know that potential was even there. So that's where I am. [*Both laugh*] In the meantime, I'm still trying to get to work everyday! I'm not sure, uh, it's a very confusing time because, *again*, like the last time, a decade ago, so much of it is the sheer energy of just *struggling* to get to and from work, [ES: Right] and to try to get my work done in between time. You know, because I end up spending so much of my work time, um, to just take care of the problems I need to get here and back. Which is *stupid*! Another stupid bottom line thing.

It is striking that even though she has some support from board members, some of them personal friends, this battle keeps coming back to being *hers*. Jim asks, "Cindy, have you pushed 'em yet on their willingness to make an accommodation for you?" She's not exactly alone in this battle, but it is nonetheless Cindy who has to push them for *her* accommodation. *She* really has to do that. As she continues, though, it becomes apparent that there are differences between this fight and the one a decade earlier, including her relationship to ADAPT, to which I return shortly. One key difference is that Cindy is fighting this fight from the inside, which makes it harder because she has to see these people everyday. Despite being the director and fund-raiser for a key program for the Rehab Center and its image, and having known most of the people involved for a long time, Cindy still has to grapple with the problem of being seen as a burden: "And you're already a person, or you belong to a class of people that already struggles with this issue of being a burden, and an inconvenience, and a costly one at that." She has to take it to another level of being a troublemaker, and she has to stop trying to be nice. This is personal work and it is emotional labor.

Meanwhile, Cindy sits in the lobby for two hours waiting, and being lied to by paratransit about when the van will arrive. *And*, it's ten years later and she finds she's still having to fight essentially the same fight, but against friends and colleagues she thought knew better. Cindy also indicates again that the Rehab Center is stupid in underestimating the kind of trouble she *could* make for them, in fact the kind of trouble she is staving off, in her relationship to the "pretty radical" and "fairly aggressive" ADAPT. George H. W. Bush (the senior) who signed the ADA into law, was coming to town and to the Rehab Center in honor of the retirement of the Rehab Center's previous CEO; ADAPT is ready to come and "capitalize on it" by staging protests. Cindy has to kind of quiet them down so as not to embarrass (her friend) the retiring CEO.

So, while there is a kind of recurrent sameness to the battle for transit—Cindy says elsewhere in the interview that she knew "disability transit was always going to be fucked up"—there is something Cindy can now appreciate about the prospect of making real trouble, and an enjoyment of the power she does hold, even if the Rehab Center underestimates it, and even if she is too "nice" to deploy it. The changes between the two battles involve changes in Cindy's relationship to disability community and other disabled people, her new "community-minded thing," along with and as part of her process of "personal growth." There have also been changes in culture that include several disabled board members at the Rehab Center, the passage of the ADA, and the development of a constituency of people with disabilities. But as Cindy's account makes clear, there remain questions about what a difference a decade makes.

Nancy and the Corporate Body

Four months after she left for her surgery, Nancy was ready to return to her position with a prominent financial services and consulting firm. Things didn't go as smoothly as she anticipated:

> NANCY: About four months ago is when I went back. But I was part-time for a month, so like three months, really, is when I went back full-time. Full-time, supposedly forty hours a week, it's more like sixty. I felt like, I don't know, I had, well, I still feel like I have something to prove. Not so much prove, I just, it's extremely important to me to make myself invaluable, even though [*ES laughs*] in the grand scheme of things, it really doesn't amount, you know, in the words of Humphrey Bogart, to a hill of beans. But there's a history. Um, I was getting ready, I was about to be released to go back to work. I

was actually released at the beginning of October and for about a
month prior to that I had been in contact with human resources and,
telling them I was about to come back and everything. They were
pretty, I don't know, *distant*. Weird things, like they wouldn't return
phone calls and, um, strange things like that, so it got me a little bit
suspicious. And then I went once to visit people in the department
and there were new faces with *my* title. And I was the only one when
I left. The job was created and I filled it. Um, so that made me even
more suspicious. So, I got the Rehab Center's um, their employment
people, um, involved, the job counselor involved and uh, what it
came down to, and they finally called the head of human resources
and said, look, you know, you've got the doctor's release, she's ready
to come back. What's the deal? And, uh, he said, "It's my understanding that her position's been filled and there's nothing available for
her." So, I was given thirty days to find another position within the
firm. Um, if I didn't I'd be terminated. Yeah. *Very illegal*. [*Laughs*]
But, nonetheless, that's what they said. Um, so the first thing we did
was make an appointment with the EEOC, um, but then after that
I met with some of the HR people there who took different placements, internal placements and that sort of thing. I had maybe two
interviews in a one month period, and I only got those after I called
and said, "Look!" you know, "I'm about to be *fired*!" You know,
"Get on it!" Um, and then I got those two interviews, which went
well, I got called to come back for second interviews. Um, then
two days later I guess, I got a call saying, "A job's opened up in your
old department! We want to offer it to you. No questions asked, it's
yours." Um, same salary, you know, just come back. The catch was
that it was a lower position. Ouch. And so, I raised my concerns
about the legality of that because that's also very illegal. Um, but in
the end I took it, just because I had no other option. But my first
day back, my boss leaves his office and says, "If anyone asks you, you
have your old title, you're doing your old job. If anyone asks in the
elevator, that's what you're doing." So I said, "Yeah? Let's see how this
goes, let's see what he's up to." And immediately I was doing my old
job, it's not like I was doing anything lesser than I was doing before.
I finally went over to HR and said look there's a discrepancy here
between what I'm doing and my actual title, as well as things like

benefits, vacation time, stuff like that, and the difference needs to be rectified. So they did, they changed it, gave me my old title and a nice little raise too. Which inclines me to think that perhaps they were beginning to smell that she, she knows what she's doing and we're doing something wrong and I bet we better get out of this right away, you know. Um, that's the kind of feeling that I have. Um, I think that they probably weren't aware they were doing anything wrong until I told them. So, it wasn't out of maliciousness, it was just ignorance. I think once they did learn they immediately backpedaled to try and get out of it. Uh, I have friends in the firm who are partners and I told them what was going on, and so I wonder if there was a little bit of pressure put on that way. So, in any case, long story short, um, I feel like, "Okay, I'm back. I wasn't invited back, I had to fight my way back." I'm gonna do the best job they've ever seen, you know. And I'm going to be absolutely indispensible.

ES: And then quit.

NANCY [BOTH LAUGHING]: Exactly! I hadn't thought about it, but you're right! I hadn't thought about that, but you're right. That will be a few years from now, Bill's just starting his dissertation, but yeah, essentially.

Nancy had always been planning to leave this job and go into teaching high school as soon as it was practical, so she didn't have the same kind of career investment that Cindy has in her work with the Women's Center. That didn't make this entirely a fight on principles however, as she did need to maintain the insurance benefits and salary this job provided. It also doesn't mean that matters of identity and identification weren't factors in this struggle: Nancy clearly wanted to "prove" herself to be an "invaluable" and "absolutely indispensible" employee, even if she would then be leaving.

It is noteworthy that she had no problem with jumping right into the fight without hesitation, and no worry about being thought of as a troublemaker or about alienating anybody. That may have something to do with her perceptions of her employer and the context of corporate culture. In contrast to Cindy's account, there is no indication here that Nancy held any idealized beliefs about her boss or the firm (something that becomes much more obvious in the next passage). It did have something to do with Nancy's awareness of her legal rights in the situation and how to assert them. That awareness was arguably facilitated by having come of age in the era of the ADA and taking for granted that she would be protected from discrimination. It was also—ironically, in relation to Cindy's account—facilitated by the support of the Rehab Center's "employment people," who made calls on her behalf and provided referral to the EEOC (Equal Employment Opportunity Commission).

There is in Nancy's account a similarly vague and evasive nonresponsiveness that Cindy encountered, and the waiting to see what "they" would do. Waiting, it seems, until Nancy suggested the possibility of legal action and visited the EEOC office. Something also seems to have changed at the company when after the threat of legal action, Nancy had two interviews in other departments in which she must have made a favorable (that is, non–brain damaged) impression. It may also be that Nancy's friends, partners in the firm, brought some pressure to bear on her behalf, another factor echoing Cindy's account and underscoring how much of this kind of fight takes place behind the scenes and how much can rest on personal relationships.

Nancy, at least as she recounts it now, dealt with the process in a fairly distanced and strategic way—"Let's see how this goes, let's see what he's up to"—and doesn't seem to have personalized it in the ways Cindy did. In fact, Nancy assumes here that her company wasn't aware they were doing anything wrong, that it was "ignorance" rather than "maliciousness" that drove their response. It wasn't until they began to "smell" that she knew they were doing something wrong that they "immediately backpedaled." In talking with the women here and with other people involved in disability rights, I was told several times that if the threat of an ADA suit doesn't work, you're probably out of luck; court battles are costly and are far from guaranteed to be effective (see Krieger, 2003). Fortunately for Nancy, the threat—or maybe just the awareness she raised, it's hard to say from her account—worked. Nancy also suggests that the impression she made in interviews—the fact that she wasn't too obviously brain damaged—had a lot to do with the change of response.

Actually, in Nancy's account so far it isn't entirely clear that her disabilities *were* the problem with reclaiming her position. It seems from her telling and her interpretations of the corporate response that they

just "weren't aware." (Another interesting contrast to Cindy's assertion that her employers were fully aware and strategic: "They know.")
In this next passage, Nancy makes it obvious that her disabilities and
her departure from the perfect image the company seeks to project had
everything to do with what happened:

NANCY: I think, um, the majority of it was my boss's call. He makes
the hiring and firing decisions, so it came from him. Um, HR, I think
was in on it in the fact that they didn't know and therefore they didn't
tell him, you can't do that. Um, but he is, he's not comfortable with
people who aren't perfect, beautiful, you know, it's the corporation.
I mean there's a *standard*, you know. Everyone who works there,
you know, perfect, beautiful, and this and that and the other thing.
[ES: Yikes] Yeah! [*laughing*] They don't call us Arthur's Androids for
nothing. It's disgusting, I mean, you know that in the world, we have
firmwide globally, we have three thousand partners, or something
like that. Maybe five hundred are what we call minority, and they're
probably in like French Guiana offices, or African offices, you know.
We certainly don't have any African American partners or Hispanic
partners or anybody "like that" here in this city. Um, and this is one
of the largest offices in the world, and, uh, I haven't seen anyone with
a disability. There's a standard, I guess, *culture* of what the firm is,
what it's about. Um, and I don't fit that any longer and I think my
boss is very uncomfortable with my disability, I think he was very
uncomfortable with the fact that, "Okay, she's disabled. She doesn't
fit into what I want to create, you know, in terms of my department."
Um, I think there was also some concern that she's just had brain
surgery: *can* she do the job? You know, regardless of the fact that,
you know, letters from my doctor and my employment counselor
at the Rehab Center, and she's tested well above normal, she's good
to go as far as cognitive issues go. I think he was still uncomfortable
and needed some proof. So, that's, that's why I, I want to make myself
completely indispensable. It's my revenge [*laughing*]. I'll show them!
And that's pretty much the source of my unrest at this point. Feeling
like this is, this is really sick, you know, this isn't me, this isn't really
what I want to be doing. If I was really strong, if I was really great,
I'd just up and say forget it, I'm going back to school and becoming a

teacher. Um, however that would mean giving up my health insurance, which is not an option at this point.

So it *is* the "culture of what the firm is," a "*standard*, you know. Everyone who works there, you know, perfect and beautiful." Nancy describes it first as her boss's call; he's not *comfortable* with people who aren't perfect and beautiful. He is *very uncomfortable* with Nancy's disability. But she goes on to explain that this is also the *corporate* standard. While the firm may not be "malicious" in their treatment of her, it is *sick* (which I suppose doesn't preclude ignorance) and "disgusting" in its practices of racism and ableism, apparently its beautyism, in the service of a perfect corporate image. It is, then, difficult to say what Nancy thinks they were "not aware" of in their handling of her and her reinstatement. Nancy's perspective and analysis shifts in the course of her account, from the first passage, where the problem seems to be one of corporate bureaucracy, to this passage, where it is clearly about corporate beauty. It would be unfair to ask whether she was uncomfortable with that culture of discrimination before this experience, but she has obviously had her consciousness raised by the experience. That she and her coworkers were aware of the "culture of what the firm is about" doesn't disqualify Nancy's position here at all. Rather, it points to the ways that this struggle was cultural and structural and economic and discursive, and therefore hard to step outside of. It was also unrelentingly and complicatedly personal: Nancy is who had to take up this fight here, in day-to-day skirmishes while she had to worry about her health insurance and rent.

Nancy can see the problem as a sick corporatism and an obvious manifestation of discrimination based on able-bodiedness, which she can relate to racism. She can place the problem outside of herself in the sense that she appears from the beginning to see it not as problem of her "deficits" or abnormality but as the company doing something wrong. But only sort of or unstably: she does feel the need to "do the best job they've ever seen," and make herself "completely indispensable." Nancy also makes reference to her above-normal certification on "cognitive issues." Maybe it is partly a plan for revenge, but it seems from the words and the telling that despite resenting the job and what the company stands for, Nancy has something to prove—to them and to herself. It is partly to prove something about the wrongheadedness of their assumptions about brain injury and disability in general, but it is also about proving herself.

As in Cindy's account, this is a battle on (at least) two fronts in that Nancy also has to struggle with the ways she has been recruited into ways of relating to disability, brain injury in particular, but also of relating to being the antagonist in a discrimination battle that implicitly calls into question her abilities, her appearance, and her value. Nancy's fight is extremely personal because it is about maintaining health insurance and her livelihood. It is extremely personal because it is about her *as a person*: about her appearance and how comfortable or uncomfortable people are with disability, and how she physically aligns with the image valued by the company. She struggles because she also knows that the culture is sick, and that if she "was really strong" she'd leave. But that would mean losing health insurance—for a preexisting condition, by the way—which was simply not an option. Far from the kind of narcissistic, self-indulgently angry and self-righteous fighting that discrimination battles—maybe especially disability battles—are frequently characterized as, Nancy and Cindy, in fact all the women with whom I talked, are fighting to be allowed to get on with their work and their "productive" lives. They would rather be doing something else.

Elise: "A good quality to have given my condition"

Elise, as she describes herself in the passages to follow, is a happy fighter, but not so easily or happily on behalf of her own rights. Part of that problem has been a lack of information about her condition and having to, like Rose, somehow articulate a need for services as well as figure out just what those services should be:

> ELISE: I didn't actually know that Traumatic Brain Injury was my diagnosis, or that it was a disability, legally. I didn't know there was a name for what I was experiencing. I went through the whole system, and went through all kinds of therapy at the hospital, and no one ever told me there was a name for what I went through. I mean, I did have neuropsych evaluations done, but nowhere in these evaluations did it say, was traumatic brain injury capitalized? Or, was the TBI acronym anywhere? Um, *and*, not only that, those weren't things that they sat down

and discussed with me. I didn't read them until years later, and said, "I want this." [*Laughs*] You know? "I'm in college now, and they want it at college so they know how to help me." You know? Um, so I was left with the challenge to somehow articulate to Disabled Student Services what brain injury was. They didn't want to give me any services as a disabled student. But when I was studying to be an interpreter, one of the things we studied was, um, the other forms of disability that we might run into with our clients. Um, and reading through this information I discovered that a traumatic brain injury before age nineteen makes one developmentally disabled. I'm developmentally disabled. [*Laughs*] Um, I didn't know that TBI *was* a disability, legally, until I somehow came across that. I was furious that I had gone through all of that and nobody told me, that you know, ADA could have been helping me get services, people could have gotten information on what kinds of help would be appropriate. You know?

For Elise, *not* being apparently disabled proved to be a problem, in contrast to Nancy who had to demonstrate that she wasn't *too* disabled, and to Cindy for whom mobility is the primary problem and the one she feels most constrained by. The difference complicated dealing with barriers and services, and she was "left with the challenge to somehow articulate to disabled student services what brain injury was. They didn't want to give me any services as disabled student." Elise had to demonstrate that she was disabled enough to warrant services. She had to try to obtain services without knowing what kinds of help would be appropriate. That's a really hard fight to fight.

Ironically, it was because of her injury and its effect on her vocal cord—also never explained to her—that she put her vocal performance education on hold and took up sign language interpreting as a career. That's how she came across the fact that she had a "disability, legally," by studying how to be helpful to other people with disabilities: "I'm developmentally disabled."

That sequence of events had the effect of shaping the nature and context of Elise's identification with disability rights. She first learned about and became an activist for disability rights in the context of the deaf and hard-of-hearing community, and in that context learned about her own legal status as a member of the disability community. Those factors, along with the relative invisibility of her own problems, led to a complicated relationship to fighting for her own rights:

ELISE: But, um, most of the speaking up that I do, about disability rights generally relates to deaf and hard of hearing, the deaf and hard-of-hearing community. Um, but I'm full of spit and vinegar, I think that's the southern phrase. I bring it up every chance that I get. I bring it into a conversation. I make it something visible. Um, I'm not afraid to say, to identify myself as a person with a disability in front of a crowd of people. Especially if they're hostile, then I'm even more willing to, [laughs] you know, be in their face, which I suppose is a good quality to have given my condition. I'm very protective of the rights of my blind friends, friends in wheelchairs, you know? Their rights, boy, you better not even put a toe on top of their rights because I'll be right there, you know? [ES laughs: Yeah] Um, for my own rights, it's really harder to fight because the more articulate and convincing I can be defending my rights, the less it appears that I need them. [ES laughs] And I've had people say that, if you can make this argument, if you can speak this prolifically about this subject, why do you need a note taker in your class? You're pulling a fast one on us here. [ES laughs] You know, and I get that all the time. I think that's one of the hardest that, um, that makes it hardest for me to feel a kinship with the disabled rights movement. Aside from, you know, I involve myself in the disabled rights movement by volunteering to interpret for grassroots meetings, you know? [Laughs] That's not allowing me to have my own voice as a disabled person. Mine are such fine motor things, memory things, input things, nobody notices these things in general. They don't impede too much of my daily living, of what other people see. So much of it happens in here [points to her head] that, it's not, um—so when it comes to feeling part of the disabled community, I do and I don't. I do when I'm not with them, when I'm with nondisabled people I'm disabled. And I'm fine with that. When I'm with disabled people, it's a little more iffy.

The company of other people with disabilities has the effect of making Elise feel *less* disabled, even *not* disabled. Elise makes clear her sense of political or activist solidarity with the disability community is mainly on

the behalf of others. It's hard to feel kinship in the disabled rights movement because she is articulate and convincing in defending rights and so
appears not to need them: "You're pulling a fast one here." For the rights
of her blind friends or friends in wheelchairs, she'll be right there, full
of spit and vinegar, but it is hard to fight for her own rights. Elise is in
the difficult position of having either to prove or to set aside the fact of
her disabilities, and that makes it hard to feel like a part of the disabled
community: "I do when I'm not with them, when I'm with nondisabled
people, I'm disabled . . . When I'm with disabled people, it's a little iffy."

I return to this problem in the next chapter to discuss some of the
dilemmas of fitting in the disability community, but here Elise articulates an interesting kind of identification and kind of fighting: She can
and does "speak up" quite a bit on behalf the deaf and hard-of-hearing
community, partly as vocation, partly as what seems to be a principled
commitment, but there is also an expressed sense of identification.
Especially if they're hostile, she's not afraid to identify as a person with
a disability in front of a crowd of people. She's not afraid to make it
visible and to be in people's faces, which she identifies as "a good quality to have given my condition." Yet, it is difficult to fight for her own
rights in the specific contexts of student services and the company of
other people with disabilities. As in Abby's account, which follows, how
disabled Elise "feels" often has less to do with the actual effects of the
injury than it does with how she is received, with context and audience factors, which can shift the meanings and significations related to
"being disabled." In Elise's case, there is even the experience that people
think she's trying to *pass* as disabled. Consider this experience in comparison to Cindy's initial aversion to identifying with disabled people
and Nancy's need to prove how undisabled she is at work. Disability is
relative and a function of fitting or misfitting, and identity is relational
and contextual. It also has something to do with the "visibility," or more
accurately the *perception,* of dis/ability. But the shifting value and desir-
ability of being seen and seeing oneself as disabled makes things tricky.

Abby: "I just get tired of asking people to help me"

The perception of dis/ability is also a problem for Abby in obtaining
recognition and services for her cognitive difficulties at school, but it

operates in a countervalent way in her church, an important site and interpretive community for her. Abby does have visible physical disabilities: she walks with a leg brace and cane for some right hemiplegia that affects her arm and leg. But at school, it is her difficulties with things like reading and note taking, along with some concentration problems, that she needs help with. Yet these are the problems she has difficulty getting recognition and help for. In the following passage notice how, like and unlike Elise, this affects her relationship to other disabled students:

ABBY: I was thinking about, um, thinking about, going to school, while I'm on campus, you know? [ES: Uh huh] And going in that, um, the SSA [student services] building, and there's also, there's another girl who has a disability, she's um, she uses a wheelchair. [ES: Mhm] So, I don't know, but I don't really like her that much. [*Laughs*] You know what I mean?

ES [*LAUGHING*]: No, I mean I'm not sure. All disabled people like each other.

ABBY [*LAUGHING*]: Ohhhh! Noo! No! Aaagh! Well, you know what's really funny is that, um, yeah, I knew her before, before we started school. As a matter of fact, we did our, um, admissions essays together. We did all that stuff together. And, um, but I don't feel like I should have to be like, I don't like her much because I believe that she, she's able to get, um, a lot of attention? [ES: Uh huh] And, um, she's able to, um—see, I don't know if she's—this is really, really horrible, I mean I'm saying it and it sounds really horrible. And, so she's, ugh! Yeah. The problem with me, or that I had, is like when you're thinking about someone who has a disability, you don't think of someone who's like walking around, you know? You think of, well, of someone in a wheelchair. But, um, cognitively, you know, um, I don't know if she's ever, if she has, I don't know if she has the same problems that I have cognitively. [ES: Right] You know? And, um, and that's where, that's why I have a big problem with it. Because, um, because I could be walking, I could be doing everything that I'm doing now, and, um, people who are "normal" or people who don't have a disability, um, and go to school with me would think that I was doing okay. You know? Would think that, um, you know? [ES: Uh huh, sure] But then they don't know. They don't know at all. You

know? They don't. [ES: Right] And, um, and it's harder for me to
explain to them, um, my cognitive problems.

ES: You mean other students, or like student services and teachers?

ABBY: Yeah, student services. Like they don't really pay attention. To
me. But, yeah, both, like everybody. And it's not, it's not, I don't think
it would be hard at all to say, well, if I was in a wheelchair. [ES: Right]
You know, they'd have that always reminding them. So, I don't know.

ES: So, you don't feel, you don't feel like your difficulties get recognition, so much as if—[Abby: Right] Because there, there are other
people with disabilities, and people have seen other people with disabilities before, they have an idea of what disabilities like, "look like"?
So you don't get much recognized?

ABBY: Mhm, yeah.

ES: But, you've said that you feel *very* marked other places, like at
your church.

ABBY: Yeah, see, it's really funny because, um, as I listen to what I
just said, um, and I compare it to, um, to what I was saying before, it
totally goes against, it goes the other way. I should be happy that, um,
that there are no people who have disabilities, no people who require
a wheelchair, in my church. You know I should be happy.

ES: Um, but you've mentioned that you don't feel very, like, supported, in your church?

ABBY: No. I don't feel supported. There's nobody there, yeah, there's
nobody there that supports me. You know? [ES: Uh huh] Although
I'm sure there would be if I, if I were to let myself ask for help, or ask
for, um you know? [ES: Uh huh] I'm sure there would be somebody
there. [ES: Yeah] But, um, it's, um, *sometimes* I, well, sometimes I,
something happens, let's say I fall down and I need someone to help
me up? [ES: Uh huh] Well, then, that means I have to ask someone,
you know what I mean? And, um, so I like put all these high goals on
myself, and I wish I could do this, and that and that, aside from asking somebody to help me up. Um, maybe going into church I would
also, as another institution where I would have to ask people to help
me, you know?

ES: Like at school, at SSA?

ABBY: Yeah! And, um, I guess, I don't know, I guess I just get tired
of asking people to help me. But I have these high goals for myself,

and um, it's just really hard for me to lower them? [ES: Right] Like for instance, I know I could get a bus pass, that you know, I would receive money off of?

ES: You mean like a "disabled pass"?

ABBY [*LAUGHING*]: Yeah. But, why bother? You know what I mean? It's hard for me even to do that, because that's saying that I have a disability. And I feel like, you know what? I don't feel like doing that. And so, so I don't know where I was going with that.

ES: So you make life hard for yourself.

[*ABBY LAUGHS*]

ES: I'm teasing, but *is* that where you were going with that?

ABBY [*LAUGHING*]: Whoa! Yeah, yeah. Yeah, I do. I do, I make life hard for myself, and, um, I'm kind of tired of making it as hard for myself as I do. Um, I'm hoping that, I don't know, that I can let go, or other people could let go of it? [ES: Yeah] I don't know, though. It's hard.

ES: Well, you probably must become just totally exhausted and have, I don't know, [*Abby laughs*] to stop.

ABBY: Yeah, well, I'm like that. Like, it's like in the morning I get up and I have so much energy, so much, you know, I'm doing every-thing, doing everything. And then, I can't rest, you know, take a rest during the day. I have to just work, work, work until I'm just completely tired. [ES: Mmm] And then I can just fall asleep, without thinking. So I just have to, I don't know.

Some contextualization for that passage is probably necessary because a number of dynamics are operative and a few of them may be obscure without some additional reference. First, this was my fourth interview with Abby, and we had known each other for several years by this point. If it seems that my questions or interjections included an unusual amount of explication or recapitulation (and teasing) it is because I was both trying to check my interpretations and also to fill in, for the record of this interview, some points that had become taken for granted or implicit in our conversations. Second, and part of that implicit background in the conversation, is Abby's strong if complicated identification with her hometown African American church and com-munity. That relationship will get extensive discussion in chapters 5 and

6, but it is worth pointing out here that her Southern Baptist Christian faith is very strong, and also anchored to this particular church and community.

Abby's struggle for recognition of her disabilities at school is similar to Elise's in that her difficulties there are cognitive, and it's harder to explain her cognitive problems to student services. The problem Abby has with getting attention is that when you think about someone who has a disability, you think of someone in a wheelchair. People "who are 'normal' or people who don't have a disability" would think that Abby was doing okay. They don't know, because Abby, like Elise, doesn't fit the model of a person with disabilities. Because her difficulties—even though they are salient in a university context—have to be explained, she is in the position not just of having to prove her disabilities but also of competing for attention with other students whose disabilities are "what people think of." Bear in mind that Abby is in a graduate program in rehabilitation services.

Lennard Davis (2001) has noted that the "universal sign for disability—the wheelchair—is the most profound example of the difficulty of categorizing disability because only a small minority of people with disabilities use that aid" (544). As Abby says, "I don't think it would be hard at all to say, well, if I was in a wheelchair, you know, they'd have that always reminding them." The double bind here is obvious, as it was in Elise's account: both women have to demonstrate that they are actually disabled, or disabled enough, to merit disability services and support. They don't "look" disabled (on the demand to perform disability for gatekeepers, see Ghai, 2006; Marks, 1999; Shildrick, 2007).

This, however, is more treacherous than it might at first seem; the other way we "see" or think of disability categorization is in terms of "mental defect" or "mental retardation." People with brain injury or cognitive impairments are in a difficult position already, in that they feel the need to demonstrate their competency and intelligence so as not to be classified as "stupid" or "retarded." When Abby and Elise have to make a case for being disabled enough to obtain services—particularly in a university setting—because of cognitive difficulties, there is then a line they have to worry about: the line beyond which they become perhaps too disabled to be in that setting, at least legitimately. This is an especially hard fight to win if those who keep the gates of services are largely ignorant of the kinds of problems brain injury can create and so require they be explained and defended; the explaining must be done very precisely so as not create the wrong impression (of mental defect). No wonder, then, that Abby is reluctant to "bother." It is hard for her even to get a bus pass "because that's saying I have a disability. And I feel like, you know what? I don't feel like doing that." For context, Abby devotes time and energy to the Women's Center and working with disabled women and, again, she is in a graduate program in rehabilitation services. Elise finds it easier to fight for other disabled people's rights than her own; that's also the case for Abby.

If the bind of invisible disabilities creates a problematic relationship to service providers, it leads also to difficulties relating to and feeling solidarity with other people with disabilities. These are related dynamics. Abby's account addresses a problem with identification, though her example may be tempered with some personal antipathy. She begins this passage talking about another girl who uses a wheelchair. In the context of SSA, Abby doesn't like her much because she's able to get a lot of attention. Part of the story may be attributable to personality factors or differences, but the system is implicated. If a wheelchair is an instant, no explanation necessary signifier of disability and need for clearly understood services, Abby has to explain her cognitive problems to people who don't have a clue what her difficulties might be. The need to prove deservingness, to be legibly disabled, to have to compete for services that student services offices appear to view as limited and requiring rationing, would foster a sense of competitiveness—and militate against a sense of cooperation and caring—between these two women. That's not to mention the generally competitive or ranking atmosphere of academic settings. The same dynamics aggravate Elise's difficulties feeling "kinship" with disabled people. As may be clear from previous parts of Abby's account, she is herself pretty competitive, but I think that the climate of competition for recognition and services carries over and can affect relationships between people with disabilities. This is better understood as an effect of discourses of individualism, of scarcity and of competition on human relations generally, but particularly in the context of "helping." Disability, in the way it is culturally configured and in its entanglements in discourses of need and helping, can derail a sense of community even where it ought to be most on track.

Abby occupies more than one context, however, and so experiences different relationships to disability. If she finds that her difficulties are unrecognized and that she can't get attention on campus, at her church the problem is an opposite one. She is *the* disabled member of her congregation, and she feels that her disabilities are extremely visible and recognized. As she says elsewhere, at her church people are "always going to say, 'Oh, you know Abby, the girl who had the stroke.'" In this context having her disabilities recognized has the effect of making her *less* supported. The dynamics of her experience at church are complicated by some other factors, not least being that her stroke is frequently and overtly interpreted as a sign—a stigma, if you will—of her prodigality (see chapter 6). Another complication is that this church and its members represent an important and frankly unquittable part of her identity and identifications, but she is no more able to ask for help or support in this context than she is at school.

If Abby and Elise are averse to asking people for help, it may have something to do with personality and the high goals both women hold for themselves. But taken in the context of everything the women have recounted about contexts and responses, there is clearly something about the terms on which help will be provided, and the performative roles entailed in the relationships, that makes it tiresome. At school, Abby has to compete for and prove a need for help, which places her in a treacherous double bind; at church asking for help further defines her as "the disabled one" and makes her less of a full congregant and more an object of ministration.

Hard

The four women included in this chapter all made reference, implicitly and explicitly, to ways in which they had to prove or justify themselves— at work, at school, in relation to other people with and without disabilities, and in relation to themselves—as just disabled enough. None of them felt easy about asking for help, recognition, or accommodations, yet they were put in positions of having to do so. And none felt easy about making trouble, at least not on their own behalf. They also had the extra work of working against the cultural and interpellated discourses related to being a burden, to being a troublemaker, and to being "less than human."

What unites these battles is how much they were characterized by daily hassles, and how amorphous and shifting the battlegrounds were. These battles happened in phone calls, visits to offices, through misinformation, shifting accountabilities, subtle and not so subtle threats, excuses, silences, and sometimes trying to decide if it was worth bothering. Just about everybody here encounters barriers and has to struggle on a day-to-day basis with accessibility, getting places and information, denial of services, distorting and mystifying representations, and worrying about how to perform disability for others. Having a sense of community behind them was helpful, but those relationships were always complicated, and much still fell to individual combat:

DR. LARSEN: It's a philosophical fight. I mean *why* should Cindy, at a rehab hospital, have to be trying to convince people that this is the right thing to do? [ES: Right] It's infuriating. And a medical center that acts like the ADA doesn't exist. I think that sense of feeling discouraged after fighting *so long*, and still having people who you would expect to be, I guess above average in terms of knowledge and savvy, but you have, you know, some sense of relationship to. I mean it's extremely demoralizing for her. [ES: Uh huh] And for me. I mean I have to say, it's been very frustrating to feel like, "I can't believe [*laughs*] we're starting at this point again." Um, and having to make points like we're not talking about individuals, we're talking about a class of people. You know, this isn't about Cindy, this is about anyone with a disability who may want or need access to Memorial Med Center or work here at the Rehab Center. Um, and that's what disability burn out I think *is*. I mean, I think after a while of doing this. I mean, Cindy's been an activist for years, and she fought the transit battles, and she won. Uh, but I think after a while it just feels like, you know, how much energy and time do I really have to devote to fighting the barriers? [ES: Mhm] You know? I have so much I want and really need to do with the rest of my life.

It is a philosophical fight, but of course it is also not philosophical. It is relentlessly personal. It is embodied and physical. These are fights for things one *needs*, and others will perpetually frame the problem as yours, if not, in fact, *as you*. These are also fights about who one is, or will be allowed to be. And they are fights for full and meaningful participation, at work, school, church, or as part of the disability community. As Rose said about her difficulties getting a diagnosis and help, "nobody else should ever have to go through what I did, if I can help it." It may be that engaging in those fights, on behalf of oneself and on behalf others, is necessary for escaping isolation, and for incorporating disability into, in Zola's (1994) terms, "one's whole life."

5

Sense (and Sensibility) of Community

Tobin Siebers (2008) makes the point that "oppressed social locations create identities and perspectives, embodiments and feelings, histories and experiences that stand outside of and offer valuable knowledge about the powerful ideologies that seem to enclose us" (8). The cultural preference for able-bodiedness, along with cultural anxieties about disability, "affects nearly all of our judgments, definitions, and values about human beings, but because it is discriminatory and exclusionary, it creates social locations outside of and critical of its purview, most notably in this case, the perspective of disability" (8). Beginning by referencing her battles with the transit authority, Cindy discusses how she became involved in "women's stuff" within the disability community. Picking up the threads of her institutional battles from the last chapter, Cindy here talks about how working with disabled women helped her locate or develop needed resources as well as to escape feelings of dismemberment and isolation:

> CINDY: And like with the whole transit thing, how that wasn't about
> theory or a political choice but about getting services I needed, that's
> exactly how I got involved in women's stuff. It was the same thing
> only not as, not as [*two-second pause*] confrontational. I mean, when

I had my child, I was appalled at the lack of resources available to disabled women, to support pregnancy, and mothering, and parenting. And, when I came back to the Rehab Center to ask for help and resources, they, at the time—and this is going back some years—they didn't have any. Even the exam tables, I had to be lifted up on to the table for a GYN exam, because they didn't lower. They just really didn't work for many women with disabilities. And, they said that they'd be more than happy to use my book when I wrote it. [*Both laugh*] Or whatever I was going to do. I mean that's about the state they were in. And the people at the Women's Hospital didn't have any resources. And the women's movement—quote unquote—was not really incorporating the needs or the issues of disabled women at the time. So, I had another all-of-a-sudden realization that there was this real disenfranchisement.

ES: So you weren't getting any help from women's organizations, like the women's health movement?

CINDY: No, not at that time. It wasn't on the "agenda" I guess. But, you know, and that was part of—It takes a long time to really, to identify with any whole—W-H-O-L-E—you know? It's like you don't have this sense of wholeness in your own *body* from this kind of injury. And I had a really hard time when I was pregnant. I kind of had a hard time even thinking that I would give birth to whole baby. Like I had a hard time conceiving that, at that time in my life, I could produce something whole. And, I will say that after the injury, I feel like I was very lonely. Unusually lonely, even though I had lots of friends. And that I was, in the university I was very lonely, and I always say that it was when I got involved in disability rights that my loneliness ceased to be a problem. I mean I was lonely when I was married and I had a great marriage. You know, there was this consuming loneliness. And I had never experienced that in my life before. Yeah, it's um, see—I'll give you this article that I wrote for a women's journal. I think you'll like it 'cause you're a community person, because it actually starts off talking about the inability to, I mean the dissociation I experienced from my body, and the dissociation I experienced communally, in the women's community, I kind of use that as a parallel. And, then how I reclaimed, you know, a sense

of community and a sense of personal body and wholeness through
my work in disabled women's issues.

Cindy begins by saying that her involvement in disabled women's
health was not driven by a theoretical or political choice but by immediate and embodied need. As with the transit battles, there was an "all-of-
a-sudden realization" about an appalling lack of resources for disabled
women's sexual and reproductive health. Even if, as Cindy implies here,
there was a philosophical willingness, it was incumbent on disabled
women to articulate and develop the resources. And, it would have had
to be *disabled* women, because at the time the women's movement—
quote unquote—didn't have the needs or issues of disabled women on
the agenda.

Before moving on to the transitional moment in Cindy's account,
to which it is clearly related, it seems important to give some consideration to the women's movement in relation to disability. Until fairly
recently, the agenda within the disability rights movement was largely
defined by men (Lloyd, 2001). Long after the time Cindy is referencing
here, Susannah Mintz (2007) could still write that an emphasis on both
the subjective experience of femaleness and of disability, and cultural
constructions of that simultaneity, presents a challenge to feminist theory (4). Along with Rosemarie Garland Thomson (2002, 2011), Jenny
Morris (1996), and Margaret Lloyd (2001), Mintz argues that feminism
needs to "go beyond simply critiquing the able, male body of patriarchy
to confront feminism's presumption of certain types of female corpo-
reality, thereby rewriting the myths of self-control that problematically
exclude some women from feminism's theoretical and political agen-
das" (4). There has been a double exclusion of women with disabilities:
within the disability rights movement and within the women's movement. Historically, the women's movement, as Cindy indicates, has
not placed the experience of disabled women on the agenda, including experiences with physical limitations, sexuality, dependence, or the
pain and discomfort of many women who live with disability or chronic
illness. Jenny Morris (1996) has pointed to how the interests of women
with illness or disabilities are rarely incorporated in or are entirely
absent from feminist analyses of, for examples, job and economic

equality, health- and community-care access, domestic violence, and reproductive rights (5–8).

In relation to the specific dissociation that Cindy is referencing here, Deborah Kent (1988) identifies the ways that a disability perspective challenges feminism's "dismantling" of marriage and maternity because that project overlooks the kinds of stereotypes disabled women confront: that they are asexual and unfit for motherhood, essentially "incomplete" in the "basic expression of womanhood" (93). The struggle for women with disabilities, then, is the "entrance *into* such relationships, rather than freedom from them" (Mintz, 2007, 6). In a very short passage Cindy evokes this sense of both incompleteness and exclusion from the women's movement agenda and from reproductive health services.

As Cindy continues her account, she expands on the sense of not being whole and her difficulty in believing that she could even produce something whole. Relevant to the value of a sense of community, particularly a community of other disabled women, Cindy describes her experience of a new and consuming loneliness, even with a great marriage and a lot of friends. Cindy has done some literal authoring here, and sharing it as one community person to another she underscores the authoring process in relation to community and identity, connecting a sense of personal and bodily wholeness with coming to feel part of a community through her work in disabled women's issues.

In linking her personal identity and her personal body to her work in a community of disabled women, Cindy is describing something more than (yet not entirely other than) the kind of political coalition building aimed at rights and access. She came to identify with "women's stuff" as she came to be involved in the disability rights community more broadly, through firsthand experience of disenfranchisement and lack of resources. But Cindy uses language that evokes something more than a pragmatic, political relationship. Without eliding the complexities and the multiple axes of her identity, she clearly articulates the embodied and subjective value of community identification with, and the company of, other disabled women.

Elise also discusses the importance of a disabled *women's* community, and her involvement with the Women's Center. Although her experience is not uncomplicated she identifies her participation in the

Center's support groups as valuable for what she does *not* experience in that setting:

> ELISE: I guess my involvement with the Women's Center, to some extent, they have, um, um, support groups that meet that are only women with disabilities. And that helps a *lot*, because it gets rid of the misogyny [*laughs*] you know. What I felt often from male therapists that I saw for many years, you know just this sort of inability to relate, on his part, to what I was experiencing, or to how I interpreted things, or how I felt about things. And, often having sort of a, um, I won't say being shamed, that's a little too serious, but he would not, um, he would make a diagnosis of something that was really just a part of being a woman. [ES: Uh huh] And, uh, being aware of your status as a woman. Instead, it was being paranoid, or being, uh, [ES: Overly sensitive] yeah. You know. So, um, in that sense it's really nice to be around just women. And, also, women with disabilities are more inclined to believe me, believe what I have to say about my disability and not question it, and not ask me to prove it. And not look at me and go, "What do you mean, you don't seem like you have trouble with that." You know? You know, "Okay, thank you for rejecting me again. Thank you for marginalizing my experience. Thank you for pushing me away." So, yeah, women have been, um, far less apt to do that kind of thing.

For Elise, support groups for women help because women *get* her experiences as a woman and support her in an awareness of that status. Women are also more likely to believe what she has to say about her disability, without question and without proof. The invisibility of Elise's disabilities has been problematic not just for getting services at school but also for feeling fully part of the disability rights movement. In the company of women with disabilities her experience isn't marginalized. In a group of disabled women with a more or less implicit recognition of the cultural construction of those identities, the necessity of having to argue her case—as a woman and as disabled—is diminished if not entirely eliminated. The grounds for making one's case are provided.

Rose's work is also about increasing visibility and resources, but her constituency, so to speak, is different and more related to the specifics of her experience with traumatic brain injury:

ROSE: Well, you know before I got, you know, found somebody who diagnosed it correctly, I had some really hard times. It was really two people that got me through the University, two deans in the program. One, a guy in the EO office, who was African American and also from a small town, he believed in me. He really labored for me—*with* me. But it was completely an article of faith, because no one knew what was happening. It was like I was trapped inside these invisible walls. The effects of the trauma, and the cognitive and emotional problems, and I was blaming myself. And, you know, I couldn't make any sense of it, so it is amazing that somebody else really tried to. Plus, I was angry, really angry all the time. And, it was people who had no understanding at all who still believed in me, that kept me from just giving up. You know, and so many people do, they become total alcoholics or drug addicts. So, people with brain injury, and especially traumatic brain injury, need a *lot of support.* And, I've been trying to get more, you know regular support groups going. And some groups need a neuropsychologist who understands traumatic brain injury. Because it's just not recognized as a disability, people are totally ignorant about it. So, I've been doing community education on brain injuries, you know, because they're silent, brain injuries are silent. People just don't understand. Organizations like DORS [Department of Rehabilitation Services] need some kind of intensive community education process. I guess I'm using my anger in a good way now. [*Both laugh*] So, in my research I ask questions that are based on my experience, I ask them for the story of the trauma.
ES: Yeah, I was going to ask you, you feel like the trauma itself was a really big part of what made your experience so difficult?
ROSE: Oh, yeah. It's almost like PTSD, maybe it is PTSD. Any time I get near a baseball or softball field, anywhere balls are being thrown, I relive that horrible thud and the lights going out. Even riding in a car past the little park by my place. And, you know, when it happened, I just went home and went to sleep for like sixteen hours. [ES: Oh no] Nobody thought anything of it. So I always ask for the story of the trauma and how that's affected their lives. I don't think you're doing this, but I'm talking to family members, about how all the parties experienced the trauma, and about the setting *before* the

trauma. I want to know how each person *sees* what happened, and what happened after.

ES: Is that because nobody recognized that you had had a traumatic injury? Like other people's responses, or I guess their not responding, was part of what created trouble for you?

ROSE: Oh, yeah. Definitely. People around me made nothing of it. *I* never linked events after the trauma with the trauma. Nobody did, for like twenty-four years. It was like being locked inside this nightmare that I couldn't seem to wake up from. A psychologist diagnosed me with bipolar disorder and, you know, I bought it. It did get me Social Security disability support, so that was something. But, you know, it wasn't good. The psychiatric profession is like a meat grinder. Now, I can't stand being associated with the mental health profession. [*Both laugh*] No offense! There were some great psychologists, the ones that had a clue. [*Laughs*] But, that, that's, what I'm working on, with community education, and I hope with the research.

Her own and others' lack of awareness about brain injury and trauma was a source of Rose's difficulties post-injury: "invisible walls," "hard times," "nightmare," and "meat grinder." And she was really angry, all the time. The difficulties she was experiencing as result of her injury were compounded by misinterpretation and the iatrogenic effects of the treatment she received. Those experiences inform and drive her work as a community educator, as well as her course of study and research of the oral history of families of people who have had a traumatic brain injury; she's using her anger. She is committed to raising the general level of awareness about and support resources for brain injury in her community. But, and this is important, Rose is also interested in understanding the family and community context of and response to traumatic injuries.

In contrast to many of the mental health professionals she encountered, Rose points to the dean at her school, like her an African American from a small town, who seemed able to handle her anger and to labor *with* her. The cognitive and emotional problems she experienced, including anger, feeling trapped, and a nightmarish quality, can be linked to the effects of the injury coupled with the lack of recognition and response to her difficulties. She points to how drugs, alcohol, or giving up might be common outcomes. They also fit with the effects of trauma, posttraumatic stress disorder or chronic postconcussion syndrome: sensitivity to noises, anxiety, irritability, anger, and/or depression (Lezak, Howeisen & Loring, 2004). These are symptoms of any number of psychiatric disorders, and in the absence of thoughtful assessment could lead to the list of diagnoses Rose received over the years. My experience and a fair amount of anecdotal evidence suggest that anger does not evoke the most thoughtful responses from others, including (maybe especially) mental health professionals. Furthermore, the likelihood is slim that an angry young Black woman with slight economic means, in a highly segregated small town, especially many years after the injury happened, would activate consideration of PTSD as the problem.

Rose has made trauma and its sequelae a central focus of her research and community education. Her experience as related to and in response to trauma, and her framing of it as a contextual problem requiring community intervention are, I think, important and provocative. Her oral history research frames trauma as a familial and community concern, with a context, a history and an aftermath. As a historian, Rose's research views trauma as having a cultural and local context and history, as well as persistent effects in families and communities. She is working with a range of families and ethnicities, but her point of departure is the relationship between trauma, race, and class. I'm aware that I'm moving fairly far from Rose's on-the-record account here, but in those communities or populations that experience the highest rates of trauma (and TBI)—lower-income and minority communities, the young (age fifteen to twenty-four years), young men in particular, but also women who have experienced sexual and domestic violence and, of course, those in the armed forces—trauma (and TBI) often receive little more than epidemiological attention, at least absent some form of coalitional insistence. Perhaps it is the ubiquity of the problem that leads to the relatively slight amount of clinical or community response and resources, or perhaps it is because these are people in relatively powerless positions. There is, furthermore, often an element of victim blaming in relation to trauma. That is, violence and trauma simply mean something different (or less) and evoke different responses depending on where

they happen and to whom. These relationships and how they affect situated presentations and receptions of self are relationships that Rose
takes up in both personal and community terms. Her account points
to the variety of ways that people are disabled by culture and a range of
cultural discourses and practices. It also suggests something about the
definition of disability, in terms of class and race and of inclusion (see,
for example, Connor, 2008; Hughes et al., 2011; James, 2011; Sander et
al., 2009).

Nancy defines her "disability community" in very different terms
than do Rose, Cindy or Elise. Age is the primary axis, though class is
arguably of equal importance. This is partly due to the fact that during
her inpatient rehab Nancy was placed on a floor with stroke survivors,
most of them quite a bit older than she. She thought the older people
she met in rehab were "really wonderful," but she didn't find too much
in common with them because of the age difference, which changed
the implications of the injuries for thinking and talking about life post-
injury. It wasn't until outpatient rehab that she started meeting people
her own age:

NANCY: I made a lot of good friends through outpatient, the outpatient center that I was at. Um, a lot of young people, a lot of kids.
And a lot of people in their twenties and thirties. Um, and I guess in
that sense, definitely because a lot of them did go on, um, they have
moved on, and they have reclaimed their lives. And, um, and their
disabilities are still very different from mine, but nonetheless, they've
gotten their lives back. And, I occasionally go back to the outpatient
center where I was, to just kind of meet people, talk to people, and
stuff like that. Um, now that I'm back at work, full time, I have less
time to do that. Um, so what I've done to sort of make up for this,
I've joined the associates board at the Rehab Center. And what we
do is raise money. Just do fund-raising, for the Center. And, uh, the
Center has a center for health and fitness, where people with disabilities can go and work out, they have sports teams—really good sports
teams, actually. Patients and former patients can do this. They don't
charge, because that's what we raise money for, primarily. And to me
that's, I have a personal connection to that because on the eighteenth
I have an appointment with a trainer there, and I might be able to get

back to playing rugby again. That's very exciting to have that kind of connection. And I miss the interpersonal contact that volunteering has. Um, hopefully, um, I'm waiting at this point, they have a, they do have a primary peer support group at the Rehab Center, but they only do training once a year. Um, so I'm waiting for that training, hopefully I'll get more involved. Because the Center for Independent Living is sort of detached from the Rehab Center, so I'm not seeing that many, I'm not having the contact. Although I keep calling my old nurses and bugging them, you know, all the time, but they're good, they do call me. But it's very important to me to keep in touch with that because the people that I met through this, through this whole ordeal, have been the most incredible people I've ever met in my life. So *strong*. And it's like you have an experience like this and it *totally* changes your focus, your perspective. And you really get a sense of what's important and what's not. Um, I don't want to lose that. I think the best way for me not to lose that is to keep in touch with, with those people, keep in touch with what's going on up there, to help people through this, let them know they can get through it. And there are a few people that I've talked to, that I've met through this support group we have, and I've had this, this conversation with, the people in rehab, the friendships we've formed, the conversations that we had. And the *intimacy* of the conversations, it's just unlike anything I had ever experienced. I went back for a physical therapy recheck a few weeks ago, back to the outpatient clinic, and, uh, met with a few people there and I talked to the new patients and every-thing. And, in talking, just the instant rapport, while talking, there's intimacy and, like honesty and some level of trust and communica-tion that you don't, you don't achieve with the outside world. You don't, I, I've never had it.

It may not be apparent in the written transcript but this was a fairly emotional accounting, and it is the only point in the interview where she discusses involvement in disability community. It is a relatively compact accounting compared to the pages of transcript relating her inpatient experiences, her career concerns, and her church involvement. The con-tent clearly emphasizes the importance of the relationships and commit-ment she has found in working with other disabled young people.

First, Nancy pegs her community of reference here as "kids," people in their twenties and thirties. Nancy's emphasis on reclamation, on "getting back" one's life, on strength and transformation as she talks about the people she wants to be involved with, the people who are "the most incredible people she has met in her life," says something about what is important in her own narrative of recovery—and it is about *recovering*—and identity. That structuring of the narrative, and of her affinities, matches her experience just a year post-injury: she *has* in a fairly short time "reclaimed" her life. The total change in focus and perspective, as well as of the importance of strength, also aligns with her spiritual beliefs about things happening for a reason (see chapter 6). There is every reason for her to be interested in reclamation and transformation: this interview took place fairly soon after her injury, she is quite young and *is* reclaiming her life in the sense that she is recovering quite well and has returned to her former job and former relationships.

And yet I want to consider that there is something evocative of the "heroic overcoming" ideology that has been the object of critical scrutiny in disability studies and disability rights (see Klein, 1992; Siebers, 2008; Snyder & Mitchell, 2006; Wendell, 1996; Zola, 1994). Successfully dealing with disability, in that ideological framing, involves being "the image of strength, competence, and independence" (Klein, 1992, 72), of "turning" one's impairments into something special and inspiring—inspiring, particularly, for the nondisabled. The ideology of ability "requires any sign of disability be viewed exclusively as awakening new and magical opportunities for ability" (Siebers, 2008, 63). As discussed in chapter 3, the push toward overcoming, reclaiming, or transforming can present real problems for people's actual ability to "move on" *as* disabled. That is, there are in Nancy's narrative traces of an ideology about what would or could count as a satisfactory resolution to, and a satisfactory meaning for, brain injury and disability. In retrospect, I wish I had asked Nancy what she meant by "reclaiming" here, what was *re*claimed, and from what or whom, and about who she is *not* including here, who would be the people not moving on and reclaiming their lives—the people she does not seem to count here as the most incredible people and her good friends.

I realize that that's a heavy interpretive burden to put on Nancy, particularly based on one passage of a long interview. Frankly, as I was talking with Nancy this sounded to me like a perfectly reasonable, if not admirable, perspective and choice of affiliations. Not incidentally, it fits with Christian narratives of meaning and redemption that are so central to her authoring of the injury, her identity, and her community involvement. But this will be relevant to matters that come up in other accounts related to the ways the women draw lines of distinction or distance between themselves and others in "the disability community." The ways, for example, that Susan and Lydia distance themselves from the "mentally retarded" or the difficulties Elise and Cindy experience in some contexts within the disability community because they are "higher functioning." It also will relate to the ways that Abby and Sarah can see only a complete return to prior functioning as a satisfactory outcome for themselves. In a different and more complicated way, it also relates to the delineation of hierarchy in relation to a disabled *women's* community.

The point here is not an indictment but to point out another difficulty in narrating disability and disability identity. The recounting does seem to place Nancy on the "other side" of reclamation and moving on. But it is also about defining the relationships and contexts that hold personal relevance for her and for her authoring of post-injury identity. If there are discursive traces in this passage that do in some ways echo ableist, perhaps ageist, ideology, well, Nancy lives in the same cultural moment as the rest of us. In different ways or at other moments in their accounts most of the women here also grappled with positioning themselves in relation to those who are "more" or "less" disabled than themselves. Furthermore, a "how I got over" narrative is not idiosyncratic to any of the women; it is, in one form or another, an element of most liberationist narratives including those of disability rights and disability studies (not to mention every therapeutic enterprise).

To extend what may be a slightly grounded digression, there are implications about how well disability as an identity and/or as a political identification can draw on the theory and strategies of other identity-based (or identity-critical) analyses and movements. That is, it makes no sense to wish, let alone urge, that a person become *more* disabled. Nor, with the notable exception of the deaf community, would it make sense to view as politically suspect any relief or happiness that a person has become *less* disabled. But, there is a political and personal-identity logic to embracing, being free to discover, author, or express greater Blackness, or queerness, or woman-ness (though what these might mean invites questions). And any move to "escape" or minimize those identities would be suspect—except in the sense of shedding the effects of colonization, interpellation, and imposed meanings. Consider an exhortation or goal to overcome or move on from "Black" or "gay." But the problematic of wishing or working to be less impaired, to experience fewer cognitive or physical difficulties, to be less dependent on a personal care assistant, or to resist becoming more disabled, can pose problems in and for disability community in that it makes certain speech acts and relationships tricky. There is always the risk of the implication that one is saying that s/he wants to escape, in Cindy's words, "that community," to avoid identification with and as the "quote unquote disabled." There is no easy way, conceptually or practically, to separate disability as a political identity from *impairment*, such that a person could wish to minimize the latter without stigmatizing or disqualifying the former (see Garland-Thomson, 2011; Hughes, 2009; Siebers, 2008). There is an interpretive ambiguity to Nancy's valuation of people who have reclaimed their lives, moved on, have been strong and incredible. There *is* a form of overcoming in relation to brain injury that can't be assigned to political or relational benightedness or self-loathing; but there does remain a certain degree of ambivalence about it that presents a narrative challenge for some of these women, and for the reading of their accounts and interpretations.

Nancy talks about her experience with the injury and rehab as profoundly life changing, as something that totally changed her focus and perspective. The events of her injury and rehab, the relationships she made through them, shifted her sense of "what's important and what's not." In chapter 4 she discussed how these experiences have made her job and its corporate culture seem "sick" but also how they help her not get too caught up in it, to see her struggles there as a "game." The relationships she's formed, through rehab, the support groups, and people she meets through her current volunteer contacts, are clearly distinguished from "the outside world." In this context and among these people she experiences "instant rapport," an *intimacy* and level of honesty and trust unlike anything she had ever experienced in her life. Nancy wants to keep in touch and "help people through this, let them know they can get through it." It's clear enough from her own words, but I still want to underscore that Nancy is not talking about finding a rapport and intimacy that she hasn't found anywhere else *since the injury*, but that she never had before at all, this is completely new for her. Cindy makes similar and similarly strong statements; Elise does also, though with more qualifications and a greater attention to multiple identifications. Like those women, Nancy was interested in practical resources; for her it is the health center and sports, but she is very clear about a personal identification with people who link her to a community, to a *we*, and an intimacy she doesn't find anywhere else.

Nancy's discussion of volunteering—as well as the amount of work that Cindy and Elise (and Susan, Beth, Lydia, and Rose) do in their respective commitments—foregrounds matters that have been another point of contention between disability and feminist inquiry. There is an established feminist analysis of volunteerism that focuses on the fact that it is often these kinds of human services provided to the marginalized or powerless—most often by women—that are relegated to volunteers and the volunteer sector. This means that service providers—or carers—aren't paid and therefore, by implication and status, are not important. These services, therefore, may also be uneven in quality and availability. In short, it is yet another form of exploitation of women's labor and a form of marginalization of the people providing and receiving services, veiled in a cloak of altruism and "human spirit," not unlike the discursive and economic status of motherhood.

However, Mintz (2007) and others have written that feminist arguments about caring and "volunteering" need to be expanded and more fully articulated to include an awareness of the shifting and *reciprocal* roles of caretaker and cared for, doer and done for, a reciprocity and relevance of relationship important where disability is a factor. Disability scholars like Margaret Lloyd (2001), for example, reject the "feminist orthodoxy" that caretaking is merely "unpaid labor, performed out of duty, by women" (716). Recent scholarship within feminist disability studies has taken up (re)consideration of dependency and caring—and of vulnerability as a universal human experience—as matters of social justice and human rights (see, for example Fineman, 2005; Garland-Thomson, 2011; Lynch, Baker & Lyons, 2009; Scully, 2008; Siebers, 2008).

Obviously, the kinds of participation that Nancy discusses involve a reciprocity or mutuality, camaraderie in fact, that isn't captured by terms like "voluntarism" or "unpaid labor." There are, nonetheless, legitimate concerns to be raised in this context. One concern is about the effects of market ideology, effects that lead toward a commoditization of caring and the transformation of widely shared difficulties and vulnerabilities in life into "problems" requiring professional taxonomizing and expert services. At the same time, neoliberalism pushes for a relegation of (unprofitable) human services and care to the "personal sphere" or to un- and underpaid volunteer, charitable, or community service enterprises. There is merit to the critiques posed by feminists and analysts of political economy about the kinds of work that do and do not merit pay and direct economic valuation, as well as the amount of work that has been transferred from "employment" to volunteerism (or internships, service learning, and "participation"). Full and direct consideration of these points is beyond the scope of this book; it is, however, relevant to the experience of many of the women (and disability generally), so it merits a nod. Cindy's discussion in chapter 4 about the valuation of her work on behalf of the Rehab Center and the effects of managed care, Beth's experience with her professional colleagues about what she does with all of her time, and Susan and Lydia's difficulties finding paid work within the disability community all relate to the broader cultural and economic question, as well as to what being in community means.

In addition to those questions about the cultural framing, allocation, and valuation (not to mention gendering) of caring and participation, *working*, and working for pay, is a matter of concern for many of the women here. Working relates to concerns about identity and full participation in society, to the narratives of independence and productivity that pervade rehabilitation (and our culture), and to the disability community where many of the women here work or look to work. As Freud said, work and love define the healthy individual. Work also seems to define status as a full citizen. Much of the actual work done by several of the women I talked to is un- or underpaid work with or for other people with disabilities. It also often doesn't count as "real" work in the estimation of others and sometimes in the estimation of the women themselves.

I now turn to accounts of working and community, and working in
and as community.

Working

Beth's professional identity as an orthodontist and teacher was quite
central to her pre-injury life. She now has temporal lobe epilepsy as a
result of penetrating injuries to both of her temporal lobes; it was the
epilepsy, which took years to control, that ended up being the most
traumatic of her injury's effects. She has become an active volunteer
board member of the Epilepsy Foundation, helping to organize events,
rounding up donors and potential donors, and exploiting her social and
professional networks to do so:

> BETH: I've found the Rehab Center, um, the Women's Center, the
> support groups, to be a good resource. I still see my old friends, but
> I have some *new* friends. I had been, *have* been attending some of
> the support groups there. I tried different support groups. I tried the
> Epilepsy Foundation. I tried, um, the young stroke survivors group.
> You know, you kind of try 'em out until you find one that clicks.
> [*ES laughs*] And, um, that's been helpful, um, Pepper's group, at the
> Women's Center.
> ES: Yeah, Pepper told Cindy to have me contact you, I think. [Beth:
> Right] I've heard good things about her, about that group.
> BETH: Yeah, I learned about Pepper even before I met her. Her
> cousin was one of my orthodontics students. And after all of this
> happened I ran into him, and he said, "Beth, I didn't come see you
> in the hospital because it brought back such painful memories of
> my cousin Pepper." And I didn't know Pepper at the time, but since
> then I've learned who she is, and I've really enjoyed her company.
> So, that, Pepper and the group at the Women's Center, some new
> friends and, um, support. And, also through being a volunteer at the
> Epilepsy Foundation. [ES: Oh yeah] Yeah, you want to come to our
> fund-raiser?
> ES: Sure, as long as I don't need to have any funds. [*Both laugh*]
> BETH: Yeah, that's the problem. Well, you will have funds soon, then
> you can support these things. But, um, yeah, most of the people

I interact with there aren't people with epilepsy but people with money. [*Both laugh*] It's important, you know, but it's different.
ES: From the Women's Center? [Beth: Right] Because? It's more, like um, personal, like for you, rather than the work you do for the Epilepsy Foundation?
BETH: Yeah. Well, they're both important for me, both personal, as you say, but I guess in different ways. Um, I've also been taking some, a couple of adaptive courses. One is adaptive sailing? [ES: Yeah?] Uh, the parks department along with a private, I guess you'd say agency, the Adaptive Sailing Program, offers adaptive sailing lessons, so I took that last summer. This summer I'm doing horseback riding.
ES: Those both sound great.
BETH: Yeah! Things that I, ordinarily I wouldn't be doing. I'd have been working. [*Both laugh*] I still, there's a little bit of resentment when my colleagues say to me, "Well, what do you do all the time?" [ES: Really?] Um, it's a little difficult for me to get over. It's difficult not to be defensive. [ES: Uh huh] Because I worked. A lot.

Beth moves in this very brief passage from discussing her new friendships, the value of her participation in support groups at the Women's Center, and her fund-raising for the Epilepsy Foundation, to the resentment and defensiveness that she "can't get over" when her (orthodontist) colleagues ask her what she *does* all the time. My question had been about the kinds of things she has found helpful in recovery and living with brain injury, and she had already talked about how much she has gained from being able to slow down, spend time with her family, and do some personal and couples work in therapy (both of which have "greatly improved" her relationships). Finding a group that clicked for her and getting to know Pepper have also been important. But sailing and horseback riding, things she also enjoys, are—like the therapy and spending time with her family—things that she wouldn't ordinarily be doing; she'd have been working.

In fact, Beth is still active in her orthodontics practice. Her injuries have affected her motor control; she has hand tremors and uses a leg brace and cane. All of these limit her ability to perform the actual orthodontics, but she develops treatment plans and helps manage the practice. She is working. And I don't know what else one would call fund-raising if not work. She also lectures in orthodontics classes occasionally, and she is an active leader of her professional organization for women orthodontists. She also runs a household. (Not to mention sailing with a leg brace and cane and compromised balance and motor coordination.) Nonetheless, despite her connection to other women with disabilities, particularly here her relationship with Pepper, and her involvement with the Epilepsy Foundation, her professional colleagues remain a critical (in several senses of the term) community of reference for Beth. It is difficult to get over and difficult not to be defensive about the questions from those colleagues about what she does all the time. It's not a question she'd likely be asked by women with disabilities. For her professional colleagues, though, the work she does, volunteer and otherwise, doesn't quite account for "time." And Beth, who holds on to her professional identity, is defensive about the fact that she "worked" (note the past tense) "a lot." So her current work doesn't seem to fully count in her own estimation.

Despite Nancy and Cindy's professional post-injury accomplishments, their accounts in the previous chapter indicate how they can still be vulnerable to implicit or explicit questioning of their professional role and value. This is a problem of the cultural and rehabilitation discourse about being productive, "returning to the tax rolls." It also relates to pre-injury identity and to "reclaiming" (Cindy and Nancy both use that term) one's life and former level of functioning. It does relate to the things that are important to these women, like accomplishment and independence, and it is a function of reconciling pre- and post-injury identities and purpose. But as I said, it also relates to cultural ideologies about productivity and worth and, in that, becomes a concern for disability community as an oppressed social location from which to develop perspectives on and knowledge about those ideologies. Participation in disability community may also provide a position from which to resist recruitment into, or divest one's self of, beliefs about one's value and contributions.

Finding meaningful and paying jobs or careers is often a problem and preoccupation for women with brain injuries, and the disability community is a logical site or network in which to find jobs. For Lydia who is now several decades post-injury, working or looking for work, and being viewed as employable, is a constant preoccupation. It was the

direct or indirect topic of several hours of interview time. She has identified the disability community the key location for that quest:

> LYDIA: I had been coming here to the Women's Center. Um, my
> *mom* knew Cindy. [ES: Oh, yeah] And she was very impressed with
> Cindy. Cindy's a very impressive woman, because of what so many
> of us have learned here. You know? [ES: Um, maybe I know what—]
> My mom just thinks a *lot* of her. And Cindy is the one that got me
> in to be Dr. Larsen's patient, and it was Dr. Larsen who finally told
> me "no, no, no, you're not stupid." And she also really helped me
> with my pain. So, I was having a lot of therapy and I would get down
> here to the Rehab Center, and then work in the Women's Center, in
> the summer, after therapy. I'd come in and help them out with the
> paper work. I'm currently, now I'm coming in to work on my office
> skills and take some of the pressure off in the Women's Center. I do
> computer work, and some typing. That's getting me to use the big
> computer I have at home, that I'd been afraid to touch [*laughs*].
> ES: Yeah, Cindy told me you were really helping them catch up. And
> you're involved in some of the groups here, right?
> LYDIA: Well, I go to the one that Pepper leads. I like her. And, she's,
> well you know, she runs Access Living. She's wheelchair-bound, she's
> very athletic. She does ballet. You know she performs with ballet
> companies. And the groups are good, you know primarily for cama-
> raderie. I know *all* the support groups there are. [*ES laughs*] Because,
> you know, I've been in this since 1972 or '73. So I know them all. But
> I like Pepper, because she's athletic, like me. And she also knows, she
> knows the massage therapist here in the Center, so she's kind of help-
> ing me get connected, so I can build up my practice. I don't know, I
> just try not to be too aggressive about that, 'cause I'm kind of aggres-
> sive. But, I'm biding my time, and that may turn into something.

Lydia had been a registered nurse prior to her injury, but problems
with balance and motor control, along with pretty serious difficulties
with short-term memory, meant that she couldn't return to that work.
Decades after her accident, she is still looking to find ways to return to
work, and she has recently identified massage and physical therapy as
her course. She was in physical therapy for twelve years herself and she

has a firsthand understanding of coping with chronic physical pain, so she has something to bring to that work. Lydia likes the support groups and camaraderie she finds in them—and she knows them all because she's been involved for almost four decades. She has been coming to the Women's Center almost since it opened, and Cindy has connected her to helpful doctors like Dr. Larsen, who "finally" told her that she's not stupid and referred her to somebody who has helped with her pain. But here, Lydia is preoccupied with *working*. Networking and skills development are at least part of her interest in support groups and the Women's Center. Lydia's family is wealthy enough that she'll never have to worry about money, so her concern or insecurity about working is not about survival but about things like recognition and purpose.

As Cindy puts it, "We've got women with two or three degrees who still can't get a decent job. It doesn't matter how many degrees you've got, it's just not the same as working." It may not be surprising that many women end up working in disability services and/or advocacy organizations, which while not exactly a large or high-paying field, is generally more enlightened (and enlightening) on disability issues and access and offers a less marginalizing environment. That's not to minimize the desire to work with other disabled people, as coworkers and as "clients," to put one's experience and empathy to work, and/or to improve the lives and prospects for others. Cindy has made a career of advocacy, activism, and education, though she in many ways had to create her job. Abby is active at the Women's Center and is pursuing an advanced degree in rehabilitation services. Lydia is hoping to get into the Rehab Center as a massage therapist, particularly for people dealing with chronic pain. This kind of "vocational" involvement often starts out (or has to start out) as volunteer work. But it may never get past voluntary, unpaid labor because of limited resources and the increased tendency under managed care to move these unprofitable kinds of work to the "community." Yet there is at the same time an increasing professionalization and credentialing of many roles and services in rehabilitation and disability services.

Susan is currently working for pay as a clerical assistant at the Center for Independent Living (CIL). She also does a lot of peer support and family counseling there (not for pay). She is now hoping to "move up" to a better-paid and professionalized Employee Advocate Professional position, while also concerned that will mean that she will no longer be working just with *her* population:

> SUSAN: I trust my own judgment. I have to. And I think my own judgment comes from hearing a lot of other people that have been there, that know—along with my family, social workers, counselors. All point me in the right way. And, um, working at the Center for Independent Living, um, I connect with, well people who have been through, not the same—No, definitely no brain injury though. [ES: Really?] A few, I've had to counsel one family that had recently gone through brain injury, and the kid wanted to drop out of school. [ES: Uh huh] Because, um, they were putting him in remedial classes, because they didn't understand, after a brain injury, what he needed. [ES: Uh huh] And I'm like, well, he needs his parents to be the advocates, to promote him getting the hardest learning he can get, the hardest they can get him, um, for his grade level. Don't make him do stuff for the mentally retarded. After a brain injury, it doesn't mean you're stupid. He isn't retarded. It might mean you're a little slower, but you're not retarded. So, that was the one case I got to do. But, um, I would be glad to do many more, but they just don't always come in. Because a lot of parents, I think know how to handle brain injuries, because brain injuries have been going on for so long. [ES: Well, uhh—] And social workers, I would think people would know how to handle it.
>
> ES: I don't know, I mean lots of things have been happening for a long time that we don't really—
>
> SUSAN: And different people, and everything keeps changing, that's the way life is. Yeah. But, um, that's what I, I read an article in the, um, *Brain Injury Today*, a newsletter that goes out every couple months, about how they need more people out there that will promote, things like I was doing. [ES: Uh huh] But there isn't a job for that specific thing. I wish there was, I would do it. Because I love being able to give voice for survivors, who need it. And, I don't, I mean if I went into the Employee Advocacy Program, would I be dealing with those people? I mean, I don't want to deal with people doing the wrong things, the wrong path. I know, I know how to handle it. But I don't want to go get trained in the, quote, drug trade. I'd rather just deal with my population. I think that would be best.

Several different strands are woven together here, some of which, like the drug trade comment, require some explanation. First, however, throughout this passage (in fact throughout the entire interview) Susan fairly frequently revisits the topic of her own judgment, intelligence, and self-reliance. In discussing her job, Susan has the opportunity to present herself in the role of informed expert, something important for her and something her work at CIL allows her to do. To remind the reader, Susan's injuries were severe and fairly pervasive, and her cognitive difficulties are perhaps the most immediately apparent of the women I talked with for this study. She has some speech production problems, which are more motoric than cognitive. She has sensory and motor deficits that affect her face, meaning she has some speech impediments as well as a kind of not quite focused quality to her eyes. It is, I think, easy to misread Susan at first encounter and to assume that her cognitive problems are more limiting than they in fact are.

As with Lydia, these facts and responses, along with experiences in rehabilitation settings, keep the issue of intelligence and judgment foregrounded for Susan: "I trust my own judgment. I have to." She has acquired or refined her judgment from "people that have been there, that know," that is other people with brain injuries, but also from family and counselors. These remarks not only serve to validate her judgment but also to frame the following discussion of her own counseling work at CIL. In that discussion, she is also making a point about how to esteem people with brain injuries and, in that, how she wants to be estimated. The advice she provides draws on Susan's own frustrations with the very low expectations and incessant remedial work that she experienced in her own rehab. She echoes her own (and Lydia's) concerns: "It might mean you're a little slower, but you're not retarded." Susan is a believer in setting the bar high and in doing the hardest work one can. (In fact, all of the women in this study expressed a similar perspective, sometimes to their detriment.) Bringing her own experiences to bear in her counseling work allows her to provide an expertise, and working at CIL also provides a supportive context for her to take on the role of expert.

Susan would be glad to handle more cases of brain injury at CIL, but they apparently don't come in. She virtually quotes Rose (whom she's never met) in saying that because brain injuries have been going on for so long people ought to know how to handle them. But Susan then references *Brain Injury Today* about the need for more people out there to do exactly the work she was doing. There is a need for the kind of work she is particularly qualified to do, there just isn't a job for it. If there were a job giving voice for brain injury survivors—again, that is, a "real" paying job—Susan would love to do it. This is clearly who she defines as her population, and dealing with *her* population "would be best." Her reference to *Brain Injury Today,* along with the recounting of this specific case demonstrates that she takes pride in how well-informed she keeps herself, that she takes a lot of pride in her work at CIL, and that she has a clear expertise. But none of these qualities translate into paying work, at least not in specific relation to her population. The importance to Susan of the opportunity to assume the role of counselor and advocate is clear and it carries personal and relational meaning, but actually *getting paid* for it, in her estimation and the eyes of society, would make it more meaningful and legitimate.

While Susan is ambitious, and hopeful, about an EAP position, she has questions about the kinds of people she'd be dealing with. She's not sure she'd be dealing with people she'd love to advocate for. As an EAP, she'd deal with a full range of people with disabilities and those coming out of various kinds of rehab (including drug rehab) and returning to the workforce. Susan knows how to handle it, but she doesn't want to deal with people on the wrong path or get trained in the drug trade.

As an EAP, advocating for people in recovery from substance use problems *would* be part of her work. What is not included in this passage is that Susan's twin sister is a social worker, something Susan herself considered as a career path. Much of her sister's clientele is made up of drug users and former drug users, and Susan's sister describes the work as difficult and frustrating. Susan does not want to have that experience. That is, though, only one level of meaning here. Susan herself was a "wild" teenager who used "a lot of drugs and alcohol," and she believes the car accident that led to her injuries turned her life around, took her off the "wrong path." Susan's car accident occurred because she was behind the wheel and under the influence (see chapter 6 for the full account.) Shared experience is not necessarily a basis for community identification; in fact it may motivate a deliberate *dis*identification.

Distinctions

Susan draws another line of distinction between herself as a brain injury survivor and "the mentally retarded." She also cautions the parents she counsels to make that distinction; in fact, she seems to make it imperative that they do so. There are different prognostic expectations between those with an acquired brain injury and those with a lifelong developmental disability. There would also be meaningful experiential differences between people who have lifelong cognitive difficulties, like those with Down Syndrome for instance, and those who acquired their impairments as a result of injury later in life. One difference that is a central interest of this study is the need to *reauthor* identity *post*-injury. All of the women in this study were at one time on the "other side" of disability and its attendant marginalization. In other ways, too, the difference between the two forms of disability is qualitative, and most people want to be perceived in terms of their own experiences and qualities (or difficulties). Shared experience is obviously a basis for identifying with others. And in regard to that experience, it does seem to be the estimation of (nondisabled) others that makes the distinction important for people with acquired brain injury.

I find this implicit hierarchical distinction and the deliberate disidentification to be complicated—for purposes of interpreting Lydia and Susan's intentions in that disidentification as well as for understanding how boundaries or distances within disability community are drawn. This is not an indictment of Susan; it *is* complicated, it is something we are all recruited into, and it is not something one realizes or divests oneself of all at once. Also, as with Nancy, at least some of the need to reiterate the difference is based on the lack of distinctions experienced in rehab. And, of course, for purposes of relationship, it is also about wanting to be in the company of others that one can identify with on experiential and resonant terms. It is also just wrong to say that "they," meaning people with disabilities, "should know better" because they have experienced marginalization, as if the oppressed should be more enlightened than their oppressors—and by virtue of that oppression. Yet there does seem to be a "caste system" operative in relation to people with mental or cognitive disabilities, a caste system that influences the organization of the disability community itself (Siebers, 2008,

78–81). Of course, that caste system wasn't born in the disability community; it's an ideology that is part of the broader culture, and it affects how people with brain injury relate to themselves. It also is part of what propels the need to draw the lines.

Brain injury and cognitive difficulties generally have not been directly included or addressed in the broader disability studies and disability rights discussions. It would be hard to deny that the hierarchy attached to cognitive impairments is more vicious than those involved with physical disabilities, and that discrimination is present among people with disabilities (Chan et al., 2005; Rosenthal, Chan & Livneh, 2006). Level of post-injury functioning and cognitive or speech difficulties— whether one is "higher functioning" or not—play out in complicated and complicating ways among people with brain injuries. Brain injury also may or may not mean visible or "physical" disabilities like hemiplegia, motor difficulties, or loss of vision. Abby and Elise have already discussed the problem of "invisible" cognitive disabilities. Whether one's disabilities are primarily cognitive or primarily physical—in one's own estimation as well as in the estimation of others—affects the kind of recognition and services one can find or expect, and the kind of reception one will receive both inside and outside the disability community. There are tricky and often indefinite negotiations involved here, partly because these distinctions can be relative to context and referents:

CINDY: There's a real collegiality for many of us in the disability rights movement. But there's an issue that you and I need to talk about: I have not been very active in brain injury—I speak at conferences from time to time, and participate, but I'm higher level when it comes to brain injury, higher functioning. [ES: Right] I know you know that, but it's an important thing to talk about. I'm very empathetic, and I actually mentor several head-injured and brain-affected women, who have a very hard time. And, a lot of the people coming to the women's support group I started here, were dealing with issues that were maybe—well, certainly had a certain invisible degree—but maybe speech issues were a lot more telling that there were problems. So, I kind of got to the point where I couldn't derive a lot of benefit, um—see, I had to look at the functions of my life that meant something to me, like transportation, and I could easily relate

to the wheelchair users. Okay? [ES: Sure, uh huh] But when I would
sit in on brain injury support groups, I would realize that most of
what they were dealing with, I could deal with on my own or in my
therapy with Glynnis. That, being part of a group of people that were
just having a really hard time remembering where their keys were, or
being constantly treated as an object because they were not speaking clearly, um, I was sympathetic, but it got to be, my issues, when
I brought them out, they just seemed less serious. And they were
harder for some members in the group to relate to. When I made the
comment one time, in one of these groups, about my frustrations
with not being able to drive my child around, one of the women
in the group, who's head-injured but could drive, said to me, "Ah,
I know how that must feel because I know I would die if I couldn't
drive." I mean, it was like, it was more like "Yeah, I really feel sorry
for you." It wasn't "Let's see ways that we can help you get around
this." So, when it came to the social stuff and just basic services that I
needed, um, I had a lot better time relating to the Independent Living movement in general. Not everybody does that.

Cindy is not active in brain injury. Politically, as part of a movement, and professionally in starting groups, mentoring, and speaking at conferences, she is inclusive of and involved with head-injured
and "brain-affected women." She is empathetic and understands they
have a very hard time. But being "higher functioning" when it comes
to brain injury makes a difference in where and how she can benefit
in her relationships and involvements. In her support group involvement Cindy is primarily interested in practical support and strategiz-
ing day-to-day problems and frustrations, as well as finding some
solidarity in dealing with them. She finds more in common with the
Independent Living movement and the "wheelchair users." Most of
what came up in brain injury groups Cindy could deal with *on her
own*, or in therapy.

Cindy's unease in these support groups relates not only to her
problems not seeming serious enough but also to the ways that being
the higher-functioning member of the group put her in a different,
exterior, position. Cindy identifies a couple of boundaries here: the
"wheelchair users" and people who have "hard time remembering

where their keys were"; and the higher functioning versus those being treated as objects. I don't perceive her as making these distinctions in terms of "caste"; she is clearly sensitive to that problematic, which is why she says it's important to talk about. The point is about usefulness, along with the possibility, or impossibility, of reciprocal relationship and support: "Yeah, I really feel sorry for you" versus "Let's see ways that we can help you get around this." Cindy can inclusively place herself among women with brain injuries and other disabilities in a coalitional sense, acting as advocate and facilitator of resources and information, but personally she defines *her* community much more pragmatically and experientially, with the wheelchair users.

Because Elise is both high functioning *and* mobile, she gets little acknowledgement for her disability or her difficulties, and has a hard time feeling "kinship" among disabled women in general:

ELISE: As far as involvement in the disability community, one of the frustrations that I had is that I don't look disabled. [ES: Uh huh] And, so I've often met with, um, some suspicion. When I attend things with the Women's Center, at the Rehab Center? [ES: Yeah, uh huh] Um, I'm often in the position of—which I don't mind so much because, you know, because I care for these women and I generally don't mind reaching out to other women for any reason, when I can—but I'm often in the position of sort of the *aide*, sort of the help, because I'm the only one who can reach that? [ES: Right] I'm more ambulatory than most of them there. And, I'm really, really high-functioning, you know, I recognize that, I'm extremely high-functioning for someone with an injury as severe as mine was. Um, but I still consider myself disabled, I still went through it all, I still have residual effects. I still *am* disabled. That's never going to go away no matter how high-functioning I am. You know, I'm only high-functioning on a good day, and I worked my ass off for that. You know it's hard to get recognized for that. [ES: Right] It's tough, a lot of times, to feel a kinship, a sisterhood, with a movement when I'm sort of—I won't say I'm placed on the outside because I haven't had that feeling, especially at the Women's Center, but, you know, where I am, I'm asked to make something accessible, like in my role as an interpreter.

I'm not disabled when I'm interpreting, I'm the assistant, I'm what
makes the meeting accessible *to* the disabled. . . . I think *politically*
I feel entitled to services, but um, when, you know, I go to a political movement, or to anything with women and disabilities, uh, is
political—just us meeting together is, it's a political action. [ES: Yeah]
But, um, you know, when I get together with women at the Women's
Center and I am, you know, "Can you pull that chair out from back
there?" "Can you get the book off the shelf?" "Can you close the
door?" "Can you open the door?" [ES: Right] "Can you answer the
phone?" You know, I, I'm uh, you know, then I *wonder*, you know,
am I really entitled to this, these services, this classification?

Like Cindy, Elise finds both personal and principled value in being
politically committed to women with disabilities. She sees being in the
company of other women with disabilities to be politically important:
"anything with women and disabilities, uh, is political—just us meeting together is a political action." But because she doesn't look disabled
or have any very obvious signs of cognitive difficulties, she meets with
"some suspicion." Because she is more ambulatory than others present
she is conscripted into the role of the aide or facilitator, which leads
her to wonder whether she is disabled enough really to be entitled to
the services, even to the classification of disabled. She might be trying to pass as disabled. Those problems among other disabled women
intersect with and exacerbate the problems of disability credibility she
encounters in the able-bodied world, with her difficulty in asking for,
specifying, and justifying forms of assistance, at school for example.
Instead of having to prove what she *can* do, she is in the unenviable
position of having to demonstrate what she *can't* do, or at least that she
has to work her ass off to do it on a good day.

If Elise is concerned with never feeling disabled enough, others are
fine with not being identified as disabled at all and/or feel no sense of
identification with other disabled people. The stigma associated with
being so identified is one, but only one, reason for this. Brain injuries
are often invisible, and that leads to a set of pragmatic questions about
passing in certain contexts. By way of transitioning to accounts of other
contexts and grounds for authoring of meaning and identity, some
words about an "age-old question":

CINDY: We've got a woman that we're working with now who's an architect, and *really* derives great benefit from the peer support group, the women's support group, and from being affiliated with the Women's Center. But she's in a constant dilemma about the need for getting the benefits and yet, the lack of willingness to identify herself as head-injured in the architectural community. And, head injury, you're going to run into that, you know. It's, yeah, an age-old question. That's a benefit that spinal cord injured and wheelchair users—you know, I means it's just up-front. And, really, head injury's got all these connotations to it. Plus, she's not superconfident about her architectural abilities. So I think that that kind of, if she got more comfortable with herself she'd find ways to—and this is what I tell the women that come to me—in time you will either learn how to compensate for, either by doing something else, *or* hiding whatever it is that you feel is not in your social interest. Um, and that time, you might or might not be comfortable with identifying yourself as hav- ing, you know, cognitive, or, uh, you know head-injured effects.

If you don't have to, why should you identify as brain injured, given that it may not be in your "social interest"? "Head injury" does have a lot of connotations. As Abby and Elise have pointed out, it also lacks the benefit of being up-front. But this woman, at least in Cindy's account of her, experiences a "constant dilemma" in that she derives benefit from being affiliated with the Women's Center and support groups while not identifying herself as head-injured in her professional community. Cindy avoids being prescriptive here, suggesting that "hiding whatever it is you feel is not in your social interest" is a legitimate strategy. But at the same time, she also indicates that there is a problem of not being comfortable with oneself, and that can make it difficult to make deci- sions about whether to do something different or even to find ways to compensate for impairments. Cindy's point is not so much that it is imperative to identify publicly as head-injured—that is a strategic deci- sion—but more that unless or until this woman gets *comfortable with herself* it will be difficult to finds ways to make decisions about compen- sation strategies, changing jobs, passing, or identifying as head-injured.

For Tom Shakespeare (1996) there is not just a political but also a qualitative relational and psychological difference between those who claim disability identity and those who do not. Attempts to pass, he argues, create "compromised identities" that are costly to personal happiness and safety, while "positive disability identities" reject oppression and develop new narratives of self and political relationships (100). Cindy makes a similar point about a compromised identity. But Cindy is not issuing an indictment because, as she says in chapter 4, "you don't see it right away. There's no way, there's *no way* you can embrace the totality of that at one time or in one encounter. It just doesn't work like that."

Transactions

"Disability is an inconstant experience, its significance to the story of self requiring multiple retellings, repeated narrative shaping" (Mintz, 2007, 4). These retellings and shapings involve a variety of contexts, relationships, and contests for meaning and identity. There is a process, actually process*es*, involved in coming to terms with disability and in developing a disability identity (if that is what one does come to develop). Negotiating a relationship to a newly acquired and stigmatized identity is unlikely to happen immediately or all at once, and that's aside from the many preoccupations presented by simply getting a handle on one's impairments. Beyond that, however, we all want to fit when and where we can. There must be a psychological and political difference between trying to become the round peg one is not, or denying a misfit exists, and making strategic decisions about when there is meaningful misfit or if it really matters in certain contexts.

Getting comfortable with one's self and asserting a positive disability identity is a process that takes time. But it also complicated by the intentions of others and by contexts and relationships that may be central to one's identity but are far from comfortable. Abby is fairly active in the disabled women's community through the Women's Center, and she is working toward an advanced degree in rehabilitation services. Both of those steps took Abby some time to take, but she has become fairly comfortable and found some camaraderie in this community. However, there are places and ways of knowing herself in which she is not so comfortable in her own body. As this became clearer in the course of the interviews, I asked why she wasn't self-conscious walking across her college campus but felt acutely uncomfortable attending her hometown church almost ten years after her stroke:

> ABBY: I think it's, um, it would be, I think I would, I would be more likely to do, what God wants of me, than, than, um, than I am now. I have a problem with, um, the fact that my body isn't, my body isn't, whole? I mean, well, my body isn't, isn't, um, I've had a stroke. And it changes things? For me. Um, and I find that I get very embarrassed, you know. And I find that I can't even, I think that you have to be like, just like this normal person. That doesn't sound right, but you have to be like dedicated, I think. And I'm not dedicated to anything right now. I went to church for the first time, since just after my stroke, this year. And, um, I was very nervous. Um, and I remember we went into the church, and, um, there were still people there that knew me, and they were, you know, very happy to see me. Um, but my arm was like, my arm was closed really tight, and I was like really nervous, tense. Um, I was just very nervous. And, we got out of there pretty soon. Um, and, um, people were very nice. But, it wasn't, I didn't feel much, you know. I felt like, nothing really. I mean, I was so worried about myself, you know about myself being there and other people seeing me, you know? [ES: Mm] That I really didn't get the chance to get really into religion.

Abby's difficulties feeling comfortable in her church come up again, with fuller context, in the next chapter. Trying to reconcile her disability with her religious beliefs and desire to be a part of the church community continues to be a struggle for her, even ten years after her stroke and despite her disability consciousness. The problem here seems to be what her body signifies in church and to the congregation: what she thinks it signifies of course, but also what this specific religious narrative says it signifies, namely some fault or sin on her part. Abby sees her body as the problem and the sign of problems. And, apparently, she needs to be "whole" and "normal," as well as "dedicated," to do what God wants of her. Based on other things Abby has said, "dedicated" also seems to mean that she shouldn't be tired and want to stay home on Sunday mornings, that she should somehow be happier, more active and accomplished, and shouldn't be angry that she's disabled. Abby's body betrays her, but in a sense so does this community.

If community provides a site and set of relationships for authoring identity and meaning after brain injury, it may be exactly by means of experiencing difference and distance within that community that such an authoring is enabled. For Diana Fuss (1995), "identification with" is a "detour that defines self"; it is, then, "a process that keeps *identity at a distance*, that prevents identity from ever approximating the status of an ontological given, even as it makes possible the formation of an illusion of identity as immediate, secure, and totalizable" (2, emphasis added). Disability identity and identification with other disabled people are, then, a kind of "inside/outside movement" that enables a distance from a bestowed and totalizing identity and an "inherited vocabulary" in place for people with disabilities (such as of the medical model or the abjection narrative). That critical distance offers the possibility of effecting change both in that vocabulary and in one's relationship to self as disabled; of "turning them inside out, giving them a new face" (Fuss, 1991, 7). Even as one is looking for a place among others who are "just like me," it is the ways in which that is not found, the various failures of "identification with" that create opportunities for creating new meanings and new opportunities for identity. That is, such an inside/outside movement prevents individuals from being tied to an identity in a constraining way. It enables them to refuse the scientific and administrative inquisitions that determine who one is (Foucault, 1983, 212).

If disability community as political construct and as personal relationships don't equate, there are, of course, critical overlaps. As many of the accounts testify, there are real, tangible benefits to women with disabilities being, working, and identifying with other people with disabilities in a broad sense. There are also the referrals to enlightened care and service providers, social and professional networking, validation, and all of the things that come from being with people who "have been there." A disability identity and community also provide unique grounds for experiences of mattering, of reciprocity, and fitting. In these relationships and roles, though, there was always an element of misfitting, of difference and, frankly, of how one was not impaired. But even if one is not *in* it, or self-consciously identified with disability community, the fact and idea of it does help with resisting or countering the discourses and practices that define the disabled as less than human, a burden, and/or somehow to blame for their circumstances. Even at a distance, it provides a "strategic place" that can serve as a base from which relations with and a perspective on an "exteriority" can be managed or resisted, a resistance that is difficult until a space and position has been defined *by* rather than *for* the subject. In other words, disability identity offers a strategic kind of "otherness" that is not individual but collective and is also collectively theorized (de Certeau, 1984). In different ways, each of the women described the kind of inside/outside movement that Fuss points to as central to possibilities for political change and for evading the totalizing kind of classification that ableist ideology ascribes to people with disabilities.

And

Not every woman I interviewed had embraced a disability identity or a disability community. Sarah and Tracy are both fairly early on in their processes of recovery, still getting a handle on their impairments and whether they are permanent. Neither of them is at the point of crafting a long-haul narrative. They are also at some *physical* distance, by virtue of their rural locations and extremely short inpatient rehabilitation experiences, from other disabled people. Neither was passing in any sense, and both were working to integrate their disabilities with their community identifications. At the time of the interviews, Tracy was about six months post-injury and her doctors were suggesting the likelihood of a more or less complete recovery. Her community of reference is her high school friends:

> TRACY: I went with my parents to talk to a lawyer, to see about getting some of the medical bills paid for, because the accident wasn't my fault. So, he said what about taking off this year—because I wasn't back in school yet—just not going back to school this year and going back next year. And mom looked at me, and my dad looked at me, and we all looked back at him: "It's not an option. This is all the friends I've grown up with and we've gone through a lot together." Like, I just don't hardly talk to the other class. So, but, I, um, the past two years I've gone out for track and I was planning on going out

again this year, then I found out I couldn't. So, you know, everybody's asking me why not. And, I'm like well, the doctors said I can't do track because the high jump is my event, they don't want me landing on my head. And they're like, "Aren't you over that yet?" [*Laughs*] I'm like, "Nooo, not yet." So they don't understand that I'm still limited on some stuff I can do.

Skipping a year of school isn't an option because these are her people, her history, and her identity. These are also the people with whom Tracy wants to go through recovering from her injuries. If she hardly talks to the "other class" a year behind her, it's not surprising that she's not looking to connect with a group of strangers based on brain injury. For Tracy and her friends, she is simply recovering from a car accident. Aside from sorting out some problems related to social perception and changes in how some of her classmates related to her, the main concern for Tracy and her friends is how soon she'll be able to go out for track. Rather than feeling marked by her impairments, she has to remind her friends that she's still limited. It is all largely a matter of "not yet," so there is no apparent need to reauthor identity or identifications. No need, clearly, to develop any kind of disability identity. For a high school student such a thing would be, in fact, anathema; the pressures of normalization at work in a rehab setting pale in comparison to those operative in high school. Technically speaking, because of the severity of her injuries and the age at which they occurred Tracy does have a *legal* disability. That may or may not become relevant to her as time goes by, but for now she and some of her doctors are thinking in terms of a more or less complete return to pre-injury functioning. She also maintains fairly engaged and reciprocal relationships with her family, friends, and community.

Sarah's story is different. Her injuries were quite severe and pervasive, both physically and cognitively, and her doctors are not predicting anything like a complete recovery. She was also, and this not insignificant to matters of identification, still largely housebound most of the time because of her tracheotomy and motor difficulties. For Sarah, however, medical opinion is low in the real hierarchy: her spiritual faith is what determines her relationship to and expectations about her injuries and recovery. That faith has a tremendous influence on how she relates to the people in her small town and how they relate to her:

> SARAH: Well, regarding the collision and repair phase, I have *not one* regret about any of it. I perceive the way Spirit's using all of it to glorify God. And the joy, just in the immediate community is *so amazing* to me. It feels like I, I'm more connected with each of the parts. Before the collision occurred, people in town or, you know at Unity church, it's like they held me up on a platter, like I [*laughs*] do I mean platter?
>
> ES: Maybe. You *are* delicious. Maybe you mean pedestal though?
>
> SARAH: Pedestal! [*Laughs*] But it was like I wasn't one of them, like I was an outsider that was doing good. And they liked that, it warmed their hearts. There were some that helped me out, but, it's as if now, because they see this person that they used to hold up on a platter as person that also *suffers*—they say suffer—that I'm more one with them, that I'm not *above* them. I'm more, well, more touchable, more approachable. And, although I don't really have a large community *contact*, it's as if I receive their thoughts. It's like I know they hold me warmly in their hearts. It *feels* good. So in one sense, it's like I'm less part of the community, because I'm not active like I was before. Before the collision I was *so* active in the community, that's pretty much what I did. But, you know, this is a small town, five hundred people, and there were five of us, five women from town on the way to a wedding, so almost everybody in town was involved in the collision. And the effects just rippled through, and I was the most seriously injured. And that all seemed to bring people together, as they watched us recover, watched me recover—I was in a coma so long, after everyone else was home. And they watched my family. So, the community shifted its view, and I think they got to understand that I really *live* the spiritual. So it's been fascinating. Because I think they used to look at me, like, you know she's *nice*, and she says these things, but I was an outsider in a lot of ways, and they kind of observed me. Now, I'm kind of observing them, watching them experience Spirit. And, here's an example. A woman who took me to lunch last week, on the way home, she actually spoke the words

that she felt like I was here to teach truth to people. It's like she knew
that. That really amazed me. She was my piano teacher, before the
collision.

Sarah is quite articulate, and the passage provides its own interpretive frame. Sarah is also very charismatic; when I was with her I was
as caught up in her faith and her story as I imagine the people she
describes here are. Her optimism and warmth are *formidable*, as is her
effectiveness at negotiating a meaning to her injuries and a relationship
to her community. In other words, there is credibleness to her assertion
that her experience—and her experience of that experience—are bringing joy to her immediate community. In case it isn't completely obvious,
her narrative is resonant with Christianity, particularly in the redemp-
tive (and transient) quality of suffering: because she also "*suffers*—they
say suffer—that I'm more one of them, that I'm not *above* them." From
her injury-imposed distance Sarah is observing and "watching them
experience Spirit."

I am obligated, I believe, to say something here about the "indifference reaction" associated with severe right brain injuries, the lack of
awareness of deficits (anosagnosia) and denial of their impact that is
sometimes displayed in the early stages of RBI (see, for example, Lezak,
Howeisen, and Loring, 2004). That is, from a neuropsychological perspective, Sarah's faith in a complete recovery and her perceptions of
others as sharing that perspective are best understood as symptoms of
organic deficits. No doubt, Sarah is still at a fairly acute stage of recovery, as she herself will tell you. She can also enumerate her various cognitive and physical difficulties—she is not unaware and she is not completely indifferent (see chapter 3). But, or also, her beliefs about what
happened to her and *why* it happened are also completely in line with
her pre-injury worldview and relationships, including her relationship
to herself. I—of little faith—am not convinced about Sarah's metaphysical belief in a complete or transubstantiationalist recovery; when I'm
away from her, that is.

But, then, that isn't really the point here. Sarah's account illustrates
how her community is taking up her injuries and her interpretations of
them—and vice versa, how Sarah is taking up her community in relation to her experience. This not Dickens's Miss Havisham alone and

isolated and fixed in the past. She is connected to community. Medicine and critical theory are not the alpha and omega of brain injury narration. (And neither is without its own metaphysics or anticipated miracles.) If disability community can provide a kind of transcendence—transcendence of isolation and of a pathology-saturated medical and cultural narrative—other kinds of transcendence remain significant, if not necessary. There remains a "higher authority" to whom some of the women feel accountable and, importantly, whom they hold to account.

Before turning fully to the metaphysical, though, I want to make or reiterate some points about meaning-making and relational strategies and trajectories to conclude this consideration of community. First, I want to be clear that although I and many of the women I talked to do think that in one way or another "embracing" a disability identity and community is valuable, I don't want to imply that there is an imperative or inexorable teleology to that valuation. Other strategies are possible, perhaps even preferable; so nothing here should be taken to mean that people who don't become part of a disability community aren't experiencing a real sense of community. Nor are they suffering under the influence of an "indifference reaction" or internalized oppression. That is simply not a judgment that can be rendered independent of particular contextual and interpretive circumstances. Second, and related to that point, is that there is no all at once—or any once and for all—to recovery from brain injury or living with disability. So it would be as problematic for people who are dealing with brain injury to be subjected to a political or ideological test of where they are in comparison to where "they ought to be" as it is when that test is cast in medical terms and ideals. Time and process (and ethics and autopoetic aesthetics) have to be honored, as does the fact that there is no single or ideal trajectory for people with brain injuries (Sherry, 2006). I have followed the accounts of many of the women here in placing a fair amount of emphasis on the role and importance (and challenges) of disability community; that also reflects my own inclinations as a community psychologist and a fairly politically minded person.

Sarah has her own ways of countering disqualification and a medicalization of her experience and identity, and it is based in spiritual beliefs and spiritually informed relationships that are robust and probably flexible. Neither medicine/rehabilitation nor disability community were *sufficient* contexts, explanations, or relationships for any of the women in this study. Even for those women like Cindy who are deeply, even emotionally, involved and active in disability issues and community, that relationship is not defining of identity but a strand—sometimes a thick one, sometimes somewhat thin—of identity and identification. Other communities and commitments are critical to the women's identity: family, work, cultural communities, romantic involvements, or psychotherapy were often equally important, even if they didn't generate as much discussion in the interviews. However, discussions of religious and spiritual beliefs and affiliations (and difficulties) did generate considerable discussion, and in some cases those communities figured as or more prominently as did disability community, and the two were sometimes entwined.

6

Wrestling with an Angel

Most of the women discussed spiritual or religious commitments, beliefs, and/or communities as important to their identity and their recovery. Tracy was regular churchgoer and believer but didn't see a connection between that and her injuries; the car accident was "just one of those things." Beth is the only participant who *dis*avowed any spiritual or religious beliefs. She describes herself as a Hobbesian materialist, sometimes as a pantheist. To remind the reader, Beth was injured when she was caught in gun crossfire while driving to a conference, about six years prior to this interview. Here, I was asking for her thoughts about post-injury meaning or sensibility:

> ES: I'm wondering, and you might have already answered this in
> telling me about being a "stoic midwesterner," but I was wondering
> about the experience of it, you know, the day-to-day of it, what got
> you through it? The way you make sense of it?
> BETH: Oh, well there's no meaning.
> ES: Yeah? There's no meaning?
> BETH: No. no meaning.
> ES: Yeah?
> BETH: You know, life is random.

ES: Okay. [*Both laugh*]

BETH: Random events. Umm [*twenty-second pause*] Yeah, it was, um—no, I don't ascribe meaning.

ES: To the *event*. No, no. I guess I meant—

BETH: Or to?

ES: I suppose to the fact that your life is altered, and in a fairly profound way. [Beth: Yes] So a lot of the things that were meaningful, or important, do those things apply, or has—

BETH: Some things are better, like I said, but it's an unconscious process. [ES: Huh] Umm [*twelve-second pause*] uh, a few of my professional friends have become, we've become closer, or more intimate, or whatever. You know. I think it's partly that I've been given some of the tools to work with, [ES: Uh huh] um, and some insight, through various professionals. They make a few statements, and you have time to reflect on it and, uh, think about it. Then if necessary I call them back three months later and ask [*both laugh*] is this really what you meant? [ES: Uh huh] [*thirteen-second pause*] And with regard to—people frequently ask me if I have, uh, anger, and, uh, oh say want revenge toward the guy who shot me. [ES: Yeah] And, it doesn't even, that doesn't even occur to me. [ES: Huh] He's in jail and probably going through something worse than I'm going through. I'm a little obsessive-compulsive but not in that, um, global, or, uh, it's beyond the galaxy, so . . . ?

ES: Cosmic?

BETH [*LAUGHS*]: Yeah. No. Just so people will clean up after themselves around here, that's enough order for me. [*Both laugh*]

Beth initially took my inquiry as about a meaning to the injury and the way it was incurred, perhaps because people do frequently ask about it and if she has anger or wants revenge. Beth was quick and clear in saying that there is no meaning to the incident and her injury, life is "random events." The quickness of her initial response indicates that there is no equivocation in her position, she doesn't "ascribe meaning" and doesn't give thought to a "why" of the injury—except when others ask her to.

If Beth doesn't see it as a matter of ascribing meaning or crediting the injury, she does go on to say that some things are better. Her friendships and her relationship with her family have become more intimate ("or whatever"). She attributes those changes to the tools she's been given to work with and the insight she's gotten from working with professionals. Echoing other statements of Beth's presented in previous chapters, she also sees the *time* she now has, to reflect and think about things people have said, as having been a major contributor to those positive changes in her personal relationships. So while she declines to ascribe meaning to the injuries or the event, she can identify the ways that relationships are better and ascribe value to those changes. That Beth describes this as "an unconscious process," not a project of intentional meaning construction or extraction, is interesting because some of the women draw an intentional distinction between the meanings they have purposefully constructed post-injury versus those that were in some sense inherent or ordained in them. Beth may be a "little obsessive-compulsive" but not in any cosmic way: "Just so people will clean up after themselves around here, that's enough order for me."

In a relatively short passage she introduces concerns or motifs recurrent in many of the other women's accounts. One is the question of a purpose or meaning to the injury, including how it happened and, to an extent, the placing of blame. A second and related question is about the question of justice or order—worldly or cosmic—that is raised by having been injured, and what appears to be the accessory problem of what to do with the anger about being injured or impaired—the loss, if that is how it comes to be construed. Third, Beth asserts here (and elsewhere) the importance of interpersonal relationships and how they and her perspectives on them have been changed following the injury. Fourth, she points to the work of reconstructing life and meaning post-injury, and finding the "tools" necessary to that endeavor. And, fifth, she mentions the time needed for that reconstruction work.

Beth is unique in her dispensation of questions of meaning and in her resistance to metaphysical framings, as well as in the way she discusses an "unconscious process." But the centrality of relationships is a common and generally central aspect of all of the women's accounts, of the ascription of a meaning to their injuries, and of the process of reauthoring identity. Some of the women ascribe a crucial or even primary spiritual relevance to their interpersonal or community relationships;

in other cases, these relationships pose a significant dilemma to religious or spiritual reconciliation and meaning.

The ways those relationships are taken up in accounts to follow are often intertwined with a certain metaphysics of "my old personality" or pre-injury self, as well as of a "future self" that might have been (or may still be), which haunt or inspire the women's experience. That is, these accounts bring up something about handling a "non-coincidence of facts and meaning," as well as about a relationship of subjectivity with truth, and with relationships of facts and subjectivity to ethics (de Certeau, 1984; Foucault, 2001). Of course, dilemmas of the noncoincidence of facts and meaning, questions about the relationship of subjective experience to the "truth" of medical and cultural "facts," and the basis and place of an ethical protest against those facts, have been themes in all of the previous chapters. But where those chapters presented those dilemmas in terms of the limits (or metaphors) of academic theory and methodology, of medical knowledge and practice, or of the politics of disability rights and disability community, in varying ways the accounts here involve "a different discourse, a discourse one can only *believe*— just as an ethical reaction must believe that life cannot be reduced to what one sees of it" (de Certeau, 1984, 17, emphasis in original).

Most of the women needed a place from which to protest the unacceptability of an established order. Rose, for example, mentioned God twice in the course of recounting her experiences with the mental health professions. Both times it was to invoke God as a witness or judge, a standard by which right actions and right relationships can be determined: "I kept thinking that if I could just talk to God, if I could just make my case, then I could work this out." Rose's head injury went misdiagnosed as various psychiatric disorders for over twenty years; her sanity and personhood were often put in question by doctors and teachers—and by Rose—during that time. God, though, was not the cause of her troubles, or those of the people with whom she now works. In discussing her own research on trauma and community, she cited a proverb she had come across in her reading: "God provides but He doesn't distribute." Rose is not anticipating miracles or divine interventions, but she does find in God a position from which to fight the factual contingencies of injustice, as well as a position from which to validate the truth of her experience.

The rest of the women, in one way or another, wrestled with the question of a purpose to their injuries—why they happened and what the ultimate meaning of them might be—and of responsibility, God's, their own, or people's. Susan was injured when she was drove her car into a tree, thirteen years prior to this interview. She was twenty at the time and "smoked grass all the time, popped pills" and did all "sorts of stupid things." Susan never clearly stated to what degree she was impaired behind the wheel, but she has done public speaking in schools ("pouring my heart out to little kids") on drinking and driving since she left rehab. She recounts the night in this way:

> SUSAN: I was driving. And my friend that was in the car. I woke him up out of his, he was stone drunk, and I forced him out of bed at twelve o'clock and said get your butt moving, we're getting out of this house because we need some fresh air. "Yeah, okay, I'm coming." And that was the last thing I remember, is picking him up. I don't remember the drive, I don't remember the accident. I just—I went through a yellow light, someone hit my back end, I hit the brakes, spun around, hit a tree. That's what stopped me from spinning. I hit my rearview mirror and got this huge dent [*touches her forehead*], where they put a probe in my brain. So that's my story. I was in a coma for nine weeks then in a half coma for another nine weeks.
>
> ES: Was your friend hurt?
>
> SUSAN: He broke some bones, and then he went to college, all because of—the government paid for him to go to college. So he should be thankful to me, that I got him to go to college. He found his wife, became an engineer. Last I heard. So, the guy should be thankful to me, he shouldn't hold it against me. But he won't talk to me, so I don't know.

Early in the interview, when I had asked her about how she had incurred her injuries, Susan opened the discussion by telling me about a *reason* for the accident:

> SUSAN: I was twenty years old at the time of the accident. I think there was a reason for the accident.
>
> ES: You do?

SUSAN: See, I was confused, about where I was going, what I was
doing with my life. So, but I was, I *know*, I remember going to the
university and applying for a job in radiology, because I was looking, I didn't know what I wanted to do. And I was lost. And I was—I
think going back to college after the injury helped me, find where
I was going, where I should have gone. But, I took the long way
around finding it.

ES: So you think the accident was pivotal in leading you to make the
decisions you made?

SUSAN: Mhm. I think so. I *want* to think so. I'm trying to look at it
optimistically, and positively. It's where I should have gone.

It is unclear whether this is a matter of making the best of a bad situation or something like the lost prodigal being put on the right path.
It is where she "should have gone," implying a correct path, but it's not
clear if that "should" is a matter of pragmatism or of preordination.
Susan framed the "reason" for her injuries by first telling me about her
wild ways, the drugs and all the "stupid things" she did before the accident. She only very briefly touched on how that may have precipitated
the injuries to herself and her friend. In fact, she says that he should be
thankful—to her. She got him into college, a career, and a marriage. That
is, she puts his experience in the same terms she frames her own, finding a way as a reason for the accident. But, as I began to understand her
as saying that there had been a *plan* at work in the accident—she had
mentioned God in her heart very early in the interview—the account
became more complicated as she talked about God's actual role:

ES: So, um, how would you say that your, um, faith in God has
affected your recovery process?

SUSAN: I [*seven-second pause*] I don't think God makes a preference
in that? [ES: Uh huh. Huh] I think, I know how I feel, and I know
that I, I hope and pray that He's there. But even if He isn't, it's up to
me. And, as long as I have the strength I can make it. I mean God can
be there for you, or He doesn't have to be there. I, I just know how I
feel and it's up to *me*. Not to anything else or anyone else. You know,
so. God come and help those—He can't even help those that are
depending on Him. It's up to *you*.

ES: So God's not directly intervening [Susan: No] on your behalf. But, um, has just having faith that God exists been strengthening for you? I mean has it been a source of [*Susan shakes her head*] strength for you? No.
SUSAN: No, because I don't believe that way. Because I know that it's up to me. And that's all I can depend on. And if He's inside, within me, then we'll work together. But it's me first, and He'll help. If He can. That's all. So, God doesn't have anything to do with it.

While there was a reason for the accident, it's not clear whose reason it was. It helped her find where she should have gone—and apparently also put her friend on course. Yet God doesn't make a "preference." Susan hopes and prays He's there, but either way it's up to *her*: "He can't even help those that are depending on Him." He'll help if He can, but, finally, "God doesn't have anything to do with it." My efforts to clarify what I saw as contradictions, between her ascription of purpose to the accident and an apparently uninvolved and powerless God, and the equivocation on whether He can or can't help, only met with impatience on Susan's part; I'm pretty sure that she thought I was just dense.

Not to draw too much psychological inference here, but it is worth noting that the accident, by Susan's own account, was the result of her being under the influence (though she only indicates that indirectly). It was, in that regard, caused by *her*. That *may* be why there is some ambiguity in relation to why the accident happened and what its purpose was; she is, though, clear that accident did lead her out of her confusion about where she was going with her life. The accident put her on the right path and it is up to her to stay there. That she ends up by saying "it's up to me" is similar to the point many of the other women arrive at. But that Susan was driving recklessly is at least a dimension of comparison with the other women's accounts of their injuries, some of which were caused by a crime or criminal act (Beth and Cindy, or Elise who was hit by a hit-and-run drunk driver), some by biological vascular problems or defects (Abby and Nancy's arteriovenous malformations), and some by more purely random accidents (Tracy, Rose, Lydia, and Sarah).

Lydia also believes her car accident happened for a reason, but she is less equivocal in how she talks about it: "The Lord had other plans for me." Lydia attends church regularly and she discusses her church community and activities as central to her life. They are by her own account her primary community of reference (though she had to changes churches several times before she found one that treated her as full member rather than a "charity case"). At the start of our first meeting she gave me a written "personal statement of faith," something she does with most people she meets:

ES: You say here in your statement of faith that in 1969 you drifted away from God. And, when did you, I mean at what point did you feel like you, um, came back, to God? Was it immediately after the accident, or was it..?

LYDIA: Oh, *well.* You know, um, a lot of these scriptures—when I was, um, back then I was very, very religious and I led the city's Presbyteria, I was moderator of that. And, so, I um, I figure that that's why, maybe, I don't know, that—I guess I think a little differently now. You know I don't believe that the Lord actually *caused* my car accident to happen. You know, He sets laws for nature in, into effect but He's not going to *change* anything. And what He did was He made, um, made my rehabilitation easier. Put therapists in my path, you know I'd meet physical therapists, occupational therapists, I mean they had a lot that was amazing. I'd meet people, and the friends I made, it was amazing. People helped me.

ES: And were you aware, I mean were you attributing that to God at the time or was that something that you thought about after?

LYDIA: Well, no. See I wrote that in '75, after, it was only like three years after, I realized, at that point that the Lord was blessing me. And I shared it with all my therapists, I gave copies of that to all of them. I passed it out to everyone. Because I was so overjoyed, because I realized what a miracle my whole recovery was. I *knew.* I wasn't supposed to walk, and I am walking. And, *then*, at that time, I attributed all of that to the Lord. You know, like *"I'm allowed,"* to tell everyone about miracles, because all good things come through the Lord. On the other hand, all bad things don't come through the Lord either. What is put in motion, certain laws of nature and He doesn't change the plan. Shit happens.

ES [*LAUGHS*]: Yeah. Yeah?

LYDIA: That was the neatest thing. I was, um, thirty-five, I met this girl who was a graphic artist and, uh, she developed MS. She couldn't walk anymore. She had this sign, she made tee shirts and signs for people? [ES: Uh huh] She made this sign, "Shit Happens." I'll never forget that. So, you know, but I do get angry, really angry. Under everything, there's a level of anger. [ES: Is it anger about—] Anger at life. I have to work on my anger all the time. Or like I'm having a pity party, "I'm really dumb, and half my brain has been wiped out by a car accident and there's nothing left." A whole scenario, a whole tirade. And I'm pretty sure that's why I'm really being angry at God-dess. [*Laughs*] You know, like that's my anger some days, at Goddess is the only, because, like, where else, who else? [*Four-second pause*] But, that's just another day on the street. I'd like things to be different, you know, we'd all like things to be different. Shit happens. [*Fourteen-second pause*]

ES: Will that be your concluding statement? [*Both laugh*] I remember you have to get out of here by four, and that might be—

LYDIA: Yes! Shit happens. *The end* [*laughs*].

For Lydia, God (or Goddess) is actively involved. He (or She) made her rehabilitation "easier," though it took twelve years and Lydia described it as far from easy. God put amazing people in her path. Yet she also describes a kind of Deist God who put the laws for nature into effect but who wasn't going to *change* anything. This is a much more helpful deity than Susan's, and Lydia does identify the ways the Lord blesses her. S/he apparently *does* have a preference in Lydia's rehabilitation, and all good things come through the Lord. *Why* the accident happened, though, is that "shit happens" and that realization was "the neatest thing." Again, it was help that she got from one of the people she met, this one a graphic artist with multiple sclerosis, who made "shit happens" signs and tee shirts.

But if God has helped by making rehab easier and putting amazing people in her life, and if the rest is just the fact that shit happens, Lydia immediately brings up that she does get really angry: "Under every-thing, there's a level of anger." I didn't need to finish my question, it is "anger at life." And she has to work on that all the time or it becomes a pity party, "a whole scenario, a whole tirade." This problem is not unique to Lydia, though the way she sets it in this particular context and her eloquence about it is distinctive. Because of what her anger is *about*, Lydia is pretty sure she's "really being angry at Goddess . . . because like where else, who else?" I'm not sure what to make of the gender switch there, why *He* made rehabilitation easier, blessed her, and put people in her path, but it is *She, Goddess*, that is the focus of Lydia's anger. "We'd all like things to be different." Shit happens. "*The end.*"

Lydia is negotiating questions about *why* her injuries happened and, within a metaphysics that does include God, how she understands causality, order and, by extension, blame. In the attribution of cause and meaning, she is also wrestling with anger. Lydia seems to be okay with allowing herself to be angry at Goddess ("who else?"), but also with it all being "just another day on the street." I find that final *we* significant as it makes it a shared problem: shit happens to *us*, not just to her. Another important element of Lydia's discussion is how she can reconcile her belief in a benevolent God(dess) with terrible events and loss, and that she can let some ambiguity (or mystery) be.

Cindy was raised Catholic and converted to Judaism when she became engaged to the man who is now her husband. She frequently refers to her "rich dream life" as an integral part of her authoring process; in fact, she discusses having had a sense that a traumatic challenge "in the horrible category" was in store for her prior to the injury because she was having "death-related dreams" at the time. But the question of why the assault and her injuries happened, along with the implications of the crime for a sensible world, became pressing for Cindy when she got pregnant, about six years post-injury: "You know, I thought if there was evil, it [the assault] probably was evil. I kept wondering, you know, how this could happen. And I struggled to make *sense* of this philosophically, you know? Because I was about to bring a life into the world." Cindy spent a fair amount of time on these dilemmas, using her training in analytic philosophy, her psychotherapy, and in explicitly spiritual explorations. But she found particular help in a book:

CINDY: But, I found this one book really helpful, not something I would have picked up on my own probably, Rabbi Kushner, do you know him?

ES: Oh yeah, um, *When Bad Things Happen to Good People*?

CINDY: That's it. It's a book somebody just gave me. People give you all sorts of books when, you know, you get disabled, uh, traumatically anyhow, or these things happen. But, you know, *he* takes the point of view that his God, you know, is all-loving. He kind of uses loving as the defining attribute, this kind of omni-loving *but* not all-*powerful* God. Okay? [ES: Yeah] So, he makes this trade-off between, um, it's one that you have to make if you want to keep free will in human beings. You have to keep the control, the will, the personal will, in the individual, as overriding. So, when something really, really *bad* happens, particularly if it's generated by another human being, um, like what happened to me, *or* if it's just even a random event like what happened to the Rabbi's son, which was a disease occurring by chance, God is not the one to blame, you know or responsible in any way. There are things beyond God's control. Human actions are beyond God's control. I don't know what his concept of God was, but I kind of bought into this thing about God not having any—I mean I didn't look at why God did this to me, or why did God allow this. You know, that's a real common thing, something a lot of us struggle with. I always looked at it more like there was a larger part of myself, that, uh, was probably attuned to things that were going on, or going to happen, that were important for my growth. And that these tools would always be there for me, I just had to find out what they were, and, you know, *believe* that I could use that somehow. So, his framework helped me at least think about responsibility and blame, for really bad things, I mean *bad* things like people killing one another or trying to kill somebody. Um, and that was very freeing for me, just because I'm a very logical and analytical person? [ES: Right] And I had to somehow come to terms with that piece of it. In the larger scheme of things, it might have always been something that somehow, at some level my larger self knew I would take on the challenge of, but I didn't, you know, I don't [*six-second pause*] I've always thought that if you're going to argue that things happen for a reason you have to argue that things could happen for *multiple* reasons, and how would you ever know? [*Laughs*] How would you *ever* know? I mean there's an infinitesimal multiplicity of reasons that anything could ever happen. So it always boiled down to *no* reason for me. So, that, I really think, that helped take the responsibility from *me* and from *God*, and it just, that's a big struggle for a lot of people.

Cindy links several themes together in her telling. First, it is worth reiterating that questions about evil, about God's power and responsibility for events, and about a sensible world took on a focused salience for Cindy when she was about have a baby: "because I was about to bring a life into this world." She had to make "*sense* of this philosophically." The press for meaning and sensibility is also related to her opening point about the fact that other people impose their own press for meaning, and for you to make particular meaning of being disabled, when "these things happen." The point is worth marking. Beth alluded to it in discussing her friends' questions to her about anger and revenge and, as will be clear below, other people's explanations, or need for them, were significant in the accounts and dilemmas of some of the other women.

For Cindy, the "trade-off" Rabbi Kushner (1984) makes, preserves a sense of agency, control, and personal will in human beings. When "something really, really *bad* happens," God is "not the one to blame." The idea that human actions are beyond God's control was resonant and very freeing for Cindy: she didn't have look at why God did this or allowed it to happen to her. And that question is "a real common thing, something a lot of us struggle with," "us" being people with disabilities. As an analytical person she had to come to terms with the fact that really, really bad things do happen to people and are done by people. Things do happen for a reason, but if "there's an infinitesimal multiplicity of reasons that anything could happen . . . how would you ever know? [*Laughs*] How would you *ever* know?" For Cindy, the laughable unknowableness of why came down to *no* reason. That realization took the responsibility from *her and* from God—the big struggle for a lot of people.

There is, of course, a mystery left here in that there is no knowing why. But why doesn't or, in the context of her account, *can't* matter. This resolution is not very different from Beth's "random events" or Lydia's "shit happens." It is also not very different from Susan's conclusion that it's up to her because God doesn't have a preference. These events and, indeed, human actions are beyond God's control, though for Cindy and Lydia they are not beyond God's love. This is, as Cindy says, a "trade-off" in that it preserves free will in human beings but also troubles questions of order or justice and gives considerable play to randomness. Yet (paradoxically) it is the abandonment of reasons in the world that lets Cindy make sense of events.

But then how does a God who exercises no power over events or human actions in the world operate in the world? That is, what is the role of God—whom Rose, Susan, Lydia and Cindy all invoke—in a world governed by randomness and human caprice (or freedom)? Perhaps this is my own preoccupation, but it does seem to hang as a loose thread in these metaphysics. Cindy weaves Rabbi Kushner's trade-off with her own perspectives. There is a larger, attuned part of Cindy's self that is important for her growth. The tools would always be there; it is a matter of finding out what they were and believing. In fact, she believes the assault and its sequelae were events that at some level her larger self knew were going to happen and that they would be a means for growth. Here is God, then, knowable and available through tools, attunement, belief, and a larger self, and for the purpose of growth.

"Up to me" is actually a key point in all of the accounts so far, as are tools and growth. But that "up to me" and the emphasis on—if not the need to assert—agency is often juxtaposed with relationships to and dependence on other people. In the last passage Cindy emphasized agency, personal will, and growth. She went on to discuss growth and her spiritual sense in relation to responsibility and interconnectedness with others:

CINDY: I don't think of my spiritual life as being Catholic or Jewish, I never really have. I feel like I'm still learning about that. But I feel that, um, [seven-second pause] I, I feel like that my spiritual sense has to do with, um, things that are very *compatible* with my values, that are Jewish. That reverence for life in general, and its interconnectedness, and, and for human life in particular, that, that life is, in the here and now. That, that's the other thing! About Judaism, which does, I, I think coincide with my sense of what we do here and now, the differences we can make now. [ES: Uh huh] It's not that I'm, I don't know about the after life, you know, I never really focused on it that much to begin with, you know. Uh, so, I try to do as much as I can to make the differences now. Plus, I was almost not here now.

[*Laughs*] *And there are a lot of differences to make!* I still see spirituality as being deeply connected with interconnectedness, among
people, and keeping that reverence, um, the reverence for life a, a
focal point. And, so, that's, um, the last major thing I wanted to say
about my sense of spirituality is, I mean I still go back to the sense
that we're all community, which I still center really with the disabled
community—and we're lucky here because it's pretty tight and it's
pretty flexible and pretty open.

Cindy considers Judaism to be her "public faith," but she draws a
distinction between that and her "spiritual sense," even though the
two are compatible in a reverence for the interconnectedness of life
and the here and now. "I was almost not here now. [*Laughs*] *And
there are a lot of differences to make!*" There is, then, an ethical and
social imperative that rests on interconnectedness among people and
a reverence for life. But Cindy goes on to give what might otherwise
seem like an abstraction a location and specificity: "I mean I still go
back to the sense that we're all community, which I still center really
with the disabled community." Throughout her account, even when
discussing very personal experiences, Cindy brought most things
back to her work with other disabled people. Every resolved problem—spiritual, logistical, social, physical—was something useful and
available to other women and women with disabilities. Her participation in the disability community is a spiritual experience and a spiritual practice.

This particular aspect of Cindy's spiritual narrative is one that has
developed along with the process of coming into identification as a
disabled woman. As much "coming out" as disabled, then, there is a
conversion experience involved. It is hard not to think of the road to
Damascus in relation to her account of "coming into" disability community (though Cindy becomes Jewish in the end). Cindy's sense of community, her identity, and her spiritual sense have developed together.
"Pretty tight," "pretty flexible and pretty open" is how she describes the
community "we're" lucky to have; it also fairly describes the spiritual
narrative that doesn't just operate alongside the facts of the world, but
introduces a political analysis into her reconciliation of a noncoincidence of facts and meaning.

Elise had no difficulties identifying with disabled people or with being a troublemaker, but she did contend with a crisis of faith in relation to her injuries and the accident that caused them. Elise went through a period of several years when she was depressed, wished to be dead, felt completely "stuck" and "globally angry." Particularly galling was the paralysis of one her vocal cords, derailing her scholarship and career in vocal performance, as well as her faith:

> ELISE: After the crash, I had been practicing, well, I had been kind
> of a practicing Catholic. I'm baptized Lutheran, didn't have much of
> a denominational upbringing, just generic Christian. Um, went to
> Catholic school and when I was there decided I was an atheist. [*Both
> laugh*] I started dating a woman who was Catholic and found ways
> to deal with being a lesbian and being Catholic, and all of this. [*ES
> laughs*] Yeah! [*Laughing*] I know, go figure. Um, through that, um,
> and I was also singing at the church—the one good thing I got out
> of Catholic school was the choir. [ES: Ahh] I sang there throughout
> even my most down and out times in school, when I was just miser-
> able and when I hated everybody and everything, you know, and
> hated school. Um, it had been, music had been my survival through
> the darkest of days. And, um, so to have that taken away, at the *very*
> darkest of days, was extremely detrimental. But, um, so through
> singing every week in choir, and through dating her, and, um, I had
> sort of professed myself a Catholic. But, after the crash, you know
> I was seeking an answer as to *why* this would happen to me. Um, I
> had decided that my voice would be given to the service of the Lord,
> since the Lord had "given it unto me." [ES: Uh huh] Um, and then
> here He took it away, and, um, I wanted to know why [*laughs*] you
> know? [*ES laughs*] It just didn't make a whole lot of sense. I give you
> a gift and you blow it off!?

Elise's sense of having been betrayed by God is fairly singular here, and it was quite targeted. The story she tells, which it should be acknowledged is also a story of her adolescence (and first love), is complicated, involving a number of identity formations and relationships. But it is hard to overlook the (almost biblical) irony of her vocal cord being singled out for damage in an accident caused by a hit-and-run drunk driver. God took away the gift she was going to use in His service; Elise wanted an explanation.

Catholicism may initially have been a matter of circumstances, but, given the passion of her anger and her year or so of struggling with her sense of betrayal, her belief in God was very real. Most of her fellow Catholics told her to wait to see what "spiritual opportunities" the accident would offer her. But, waiting did not help her recovery, and she ended up wanting nothing to do with the spiritual promise:

ELISE: So, um, well my girlfriend gave me the Book of Job, [ES: Really?] suggested I read the Book of Job, are you familiar at all with that?

ES: Oh, yeah.

ELISE: Um, [*laughing*] Job's story is a pretty sad one. [*ES laughs*] That, actually, reading the Book of Job is what just killed my faith in God, Christianity, Catholic Church, organized religion, all of it. Because I was nobody's pawn piece, and that was not—what was I supposed to do? Just, "Thank you sir, may I have another?" [ES: Uh huh] Which is what Job did. And Job is lauded for that? What did he get out of it? So, um, that's, that was happening to me at the same time that I met a woman who practiced Buddhism. I was still considering myself Catholic and trying to fight with that, and I got so hopeless, as a Catholic [*ES laughs*] that, um, you know, like the Book of Job, God could just do this to me, that this could just happen to me. Even *though*, I'm doing everything right, even *though* I'm doing everything I can do, you know, this can still be happening *to me*. [ES: Right] Then I, I just gave up in therapy, stopped working at anything, didn't care because why bother? Why improve? You know? I felt *trapped*, and stuck in what I was doing. I felt, um, that, you know, I was so angry that this had happened to me, and I was so confused and frustrated, and wasn't, um—my girlfriend at the time was, um, was the primary person who was afraid of me. She had gotten advice from people that she ought to treat me with kid gloves for a while, and so she wasn't really my girlfriend. [ES: Uh huh] So, and I didn't really understand why, why she was treating me this way. So I felt bad about myself, I consequently took that on myself, I must be a bad person, or I must be, you know, there must be something wrong with me that she's doing this.

Job's story catalyzed rather than resolved Elise's sense of God's injustice (or ingratitude, or capriciousness). The faithful might argue that she missed the point, but the fact remains that Elise took God and the Bible seriously enough to be outraged. Actually, I don't think she did miss the point, she just found the point of Job unacceptable: "God could just do this to me." Job may not have been a well-considered prescription for a nineteen-year-old in any case, but it was all the less apt for Elise, who already was clearly averse to being anyone's pawn and who was already trying hard to figure out what to do next. Elise was very angry and had no place to direct it within this Catholic framework. She felt "stuck," and she gave up on therapy and working at anything: "why bother?" In fact, she went through a long period of blaming the neurosurgeon for having saved her life. Her anger was pathologized and her confusion was disqualified; people were obviously "handling" her—with kid gloves.

It is true that people recovering from brain injury can be difficult to live with, and at least part of Elise's anger, depression, and social perception were organic effects of the injury. But there seems to be plenty of blame attributable to the scant information she was given about what to expect, as well as to the clumsy responses of others to her frustration and anger. At any rate, the effect was that she thought she was "a bad person." By chance, she encountered Buddhism, which seemed to have allowed her to both accept and stop accepting:

ELISE: Buddhism found *me*. I had hired a woman to do a portrait of me for my girlfriend. By the time the portrait was finished I no longer had that girlfriend. [*Both laugh*] Um, but she was a practicing Buddhist, and I would arrive sometimes for photo sessions, or just to discuss something, and she would be chanting and I would hear it. At first it was just the sound that attracted me. I was feeling very scattered at the time, very confused. My thoughts were, it was just all *jumbled*, it was all confused and angst-ridden, and the chanting helped just soothe that and calm it. So, it took me a while before I sort of committed myself to it. But Buddhism has a couple of, um, philosophies, a couple of tenets, that really spoke to me at that time and that made me start trying again, gave me a reason to try again. One of them was the Ten Worlds; that idea helped me "unstick" myself, that you can always let go of whatever hell you're in. Another thing was that what really matters is *from this moment forward*. What are you going to do *now*? Yes, this happened to you, don't worry about why. *Why* is karma, cause and effect. But don't worry about that, worry about what you do with it now. How you create value from this moment forward. And, um, not having to worry about *why*, not having a person to blame for why, changed my life dramatically, totally changed my life. You know, it was only up to me to do that, and that wasn't something that I was hearing from anybody in my environment. [ES: Huh] You know, they were, I can't say whether or not another neuropsychologist would have, um, done anything in that area, but I can tell you that the neuropsychologist that I saw for five years never really offered that kind of information to me, or that kind of perspective. It was more about, you know, trying not, not to make me feel so bad, instead of really giving me tools to get out, um, listening to how bad I felt instead of helping me to not feel bad anymore, telling me that I didn't have to feel bad. [ES: Huh] Anyway, he was very helpful in a lot of ways, but that was something that I got out of Buddhism, and from my practice thereof, and from other members of the organization.

It was the chanting of this particular school of Buddhism that first caught Elise's attention. It helped soothe and calm her "jumbled" thoughts, the confusion and angst she was experiencing. It was something she could *do*, and it's also a fair inference that it appealed to her as a singer. Beyond the practice, to which she gives a lot of credit, it was the tenets that really spoke to her and gave her reasons to try again: what really matters is *from this moment forward*; and, this happened to you, don't worry about why. As it was, in slightly different ways, for all of the women so far, letting go of why was an important turning point for Elise, it "totally changed" her life. Things became a matter of creating value from this moment forward. These were not the kinds of things Elise was hearing from anybody else in her life at the time; it was up to her to do that. Others had tried not to make her feel bad, rather than giving her tools or telling her that she didn't have to feel bad. It was liberating to hear that she could always "let go of whatever hell" she was in. Those were tools she got from Buddhism and the other members of the organization.

A Religious Scene

The next three accounts involve a more explicit or traditional religious faith. God is an active agent rather than the absent, powerless, or non-interventionist deity of the accounts so far. These three accounts are about *religion*.

In the technical use of the term, Nancy's injuries were not due to a trauma to her brain. Like Abby's, Nancy's brain injury was due to an arteriovenous malformation (though actually her injuries were more proximally due to complications during the second surgery to correct the malformation). In that sense, Nancy's and Abby's injuries were more or less the result of "natural" causes rather than violence, recklessness, or a random accident. Nancy reiterates dilemmas already identified in the preceding accounts, but introduces a different framing:

> NANCY: Everything was really clicking and then, boom, it was gone. And *that* pissed me off! In a big cosmic way, I was really angry about that. Um, *bizarrely*, I had been baptized, let's see, four weeks before my surgery, my second surgery. Um, and that was, it made such a difference. Um, I really can't, *constantly*, even when I was desperately depressed and wanted to die I still, I could fall back on faith. And um, I remember several times when I was in the hospital lying in my bed and being upset and crying and um, one of these nurses being there and me looking up at the ceiling and saying, "I *love* Jesus, I love Jesus." And she would say, "He loves you too, just keep it up." It was really that nurse. Um, and when I got to the Rehab Center I was much more mobile because I got to be in a wheelchair and um, that's always a plus, and I could go to the, uh, services in the chapel, and I did that every Sunday because it was such a source of comfort. And my priest came to see me and, um, various chaplains from the hospital. Um, they just, it gives me the chills that I can't, can't believe that there was mere coincidence—that literally a month before all of this happened, spontaneously, it was a very spontaneous decision to be baptized. Um, it's just the timing of it. I just can't believe that it was just a coincidence. I haven't quite figured out what I'm supposed to do with it, what, what the project is. Or maybe it's extremely obvious. But still, I just can't feel that it was a coincidence [*fifteen-second*

pause]. Um, and I, almost immediately I realized that this is a test. You know, this is a test of faith, quite simply. You know, I could be angry at God and, and say "why me!" You know, *or* I can say, "Okay, this has happened, it's awful, I'm upset that this happened to my life, *but* there's a reason and I don't have to go through this alone" and put my faith in my doctors and my nurses and with God.

Nancy woke up and realized the extent of her physical injuries—it took a little while to realize her cognitive difficulties; everything that had been clicking was "boom," gone. She was pissed off in a cosmic way, and also desperately depressed and wanting to die. Yet she could fall back on faith "*constantly.*" From her descriptions of this early period, how miserable she was and must have seemed to others, one might not have known that she held the belief that what was happening was part of a divine plan, that she had no doubts about Jesus. Her faith didn't dictate how she had to behave or feel, she could feel okay and not at all okay together. Her faith also never stopped her from fighting with her doctors for attention to her distress, asking questions about her care and her surgeon. (Nancy, by the way, is the only woman who mentioned the hospital chaplains or services—many mentioned their nurses.)

Nancy doesn't, in fact can't, believe that her spontaneous decision to be baptized, *bizarrely* one month before all of this happened, was a coincidence. She was noticeably moved in telling this story, as the fifteen-second pause might indicate. If Nancy hadn't quite figured out what the project is, she did immediately see it is a test of faith, "quite simply." That there *is* a reason, that God *did* cause this to occur, as a *test* no less, stands in contrast to the conclusions drawn by all of the women in the previous accounts. (It is, in fact, exactly the interpretation that Elise found so infuriating.) I found this very intriguing (maybe because I don't have the same faith): that Nancy could be angry, depressed, even suicidal, and fully confident in Jesus at the same time; she could decide to take it that God had done this as test and could still have faith, *and* be angry. Nancy did receive quite a bit of social support, including from the priest and congregants of her new church, and from her fiancé's Catholic church. People were supportive of both her anger and her faith. But, still:

ES: It sounds like you didn't have a real problem being angry and upset *and*, and at the same time still really believing that this was happening for some sort of purpose, like—

NANCY: Yeah, um, well, I'm still, part of me is pretty peeved, you know. Um, but yeah, somehow I was able to reconcile the fact that it's okay to be upset about this. Um, but it's a very traumatic thing, and your life as you imagined it would be isn't going to happen. Um, and I think, you know, that's, um, that's difficult to deal with, because everything, you know, should have happened the way I wanted it to happen. Um, but yeah, I could be angry in a general sense if this was happening to me and still feel like okay, *but*, there's a reason why this is happening. I've *got* to have faith. You know, this is a test and I don't know what it's for, um, it's going to teach me a lesson on multiple levels. Um, but [*laughing*] I can still be upset that it's happening.

ES: Uh huh. And, uh, at whom, or at what, do you get to direct the anger?

NANCY: Initially it was directed at my surgeons. [ES: Uh huh] Um, not so much because I actually believed they had done something wrong. Because I checked on that actually, [*both laugh*] I asked around. Um, but because I guess there was really no one else to blame it on. Um, and I don't know if I necessarily need someone to be angry *at*. Um, I can, I can be angry in general that this is happening and know that, okay, this is God's design for my life. There's a reason. This is, you know, He knows what He's doing. Um, and I can be angry and upset that this is happening, um, but not necessarily angry at Him. Because that, that's never occurred to me to be angry at God. So, yeah, it's—I don't know, I just, I really don't think I have to blame anyone. I can just be angry in general. [*Both laugh*] I don't know. It's an interesting question, wonder what my priest would say about that? I wonder if he told me, you know, there has to be some object that you're directing at, like, if it's no one in particular, then it must be God because He's designed your life. Um, I don't necessarily, I wouldn't see it that way, but who knows, he probably wouldn't say that.

That doesn't seem to require additional explication. I had really just wanted her to speak to how she managed what I saw as a paradox, maybe just the ambiguity that all of the women here had confronted in different ways. The question of why or for what purpose appears to be inevitable in the process, and because the effects are enduring—"your life as you imagined it isn't going to happen"—it is an inevitably recurrent question. But, especially within religious and spiritual frameworks, assigning meaning or purpose to the injury and disability only seems to raise further questions about one's self, one's ascription of meaning, God, or all three. Nancy's answer is exemplary faith: "He knows what He's doing." To reach back to previous chapters again, that faith, the "project," has also informed her volunteer work at the Rehab Center, her participation in disability community, and her battle with and her new perspective on the corporate culture she returned to post-injury.

Nancy's discussion of how she reconciled being upset about her injury with her faith in God and belief that her injuries happened for a reason, indeed as a "test" of that faith, provides a relevant comparison to Abby's account. They share a strong faith in Jesus and the belief that God had caused their injuries; they also both had arteriovenous malformations, though Abby's wasn't diagnosed until after a major stroke. Both women are young, ambitious, and their careers were just starting to click when they had the injuries. They also share a certain pride in their education and cognitive abilities. But there is sharp divergence in how they came to author the relationship between their faith and their injuries, and in how their church communities responded to those injuries.

Abby's story foregrounds relationships between meaning and practice, and between disability, religion, and identity. As a teenager she chose to join the Southern Baptist church in her hometown (her mother attends a different, less fundamentalist church). Abby also identifies that church as her main connection to the African American community, a connection she considers very important. Reconciling these commitments with the stroke and subsequent impairments has been difficult for Abby; it occupies much of her account, and it was the sole topic of the three-hour interview from which the following dialogue is excerpted.

> ABBY: I really tried hard to be a good Christian. I had always had
> problems with, and I also always struggled with that, you know. And

so it was like, um, it was always a struggle going on with me, like living up to the Ten Commandments? I mean I literally took it, I took religion as everything that it said that you should do in the Ten Commandments. And of course I had problems with them. [*Both laugh*] Um, but anyway, so I think, um, then I, um, then I had my stroke, and, um, I was very upset. I was very upset because I thought God had let me down. That God, um, that God wasn't there when I needed Him, you know? [ES: Uh huh] And that God, had, um, had um, had had turned His back on me, you know. [ES: Right] And I felt like that was true about *Him*, but I also felt that that was true about *me*, you know. I thought it was true about me *and* Him, you know? [ES: Huh] So I started going back, going, and I even met a lot of the people I went to church with, um, a lot of the mothers—that's what we would call them, the, uh, older women that go to your church, [ES: Ahh] um, *mothers*. And, so, um, a lot of the mothers would like say to me, say, yeah, you know, would say that I'd done something wrong. [ES: Mmm] That, that I had been doing who knows what, what's wrong, what I did was wrong. But, um, something like that for me, for my having a physical disability, you know what I mean? God was punishing me, you know. [ES: Wow] And, um, I never really got to that point, I never got to—I'm not so sure! I don't know! I mean, like I don't know. Maybe that's true. I mean, maybe. You know what I mean? Um, maybe. [*Seven-second pause*] Maybe, I don't know. Maybe, maybe, not that it's true because now I don't believe that. I mean *now*, I don't know what I believe. But, now, I'm, I'm, I don't know what I believe, you know? [ES: Mhm] And, um, but I want to, um, I still want to become close to God. And, um, there are times when I need someone, you know? [ES: Uh huh] That foundation to fall back on? [ES: Right] Um, but I really can't fall back on that, I really can't fall back on it. I can't really do that anymore because then, because I have a problem with praying now. When I start to pray, I, um, I always bump into, I bump into, "where have I been all these years?" since I've been getting better for ten years. [ES: Uh huh] I mean, like how come now? How come I only need God when I think I need Him, you know what I mean? [ES: Mmm] When I'm, when it's right for *me*, you know. And, um, we, yeah, that's a big problem for me.

Before the stroke, Abby had struggled with being a good Christian and living up to the Ten Commandments. Abby also lived in a small town with a smaller African American community; like all of the young members of her church her behavior was surveilled by the older members, and she got frequent reminders of the ways she wasn't living up to expectations. That back story is further complicated by the fact she went to a predominantly white high school, dated white boys, and chose to attend a predominantly white university rather than attending the historically Black college that her church and family had expected her to attend. She also had a reputation in her church for being "smart" (not in a good way) and "fast." It's worth reiterating that this is a church Abby had selected for herself, in part to be connected to "the community." In other words, a lot was bound up in her relationships to this church, matters of identity, community, and expectations that extend beyond scripture. All of that provides some background for the response of Abby's church mothers: "That, that I had been doing who knows what, what's wrong, what I did was wrong. But, um, something like that for me, for my having a physical disability, you know what I mean? God was punishing me."

Abby is obviously ambivalent about this interpretation of events; she says "I don't know" five times, and "maybe" six times in five lines of that passage. She doesn't want to believe that it's true, but *now*, she doesn't know what to believe. *Now* that she's away from the church and her hometown and the mothers, and now that her recovery has progressed, she's not so sure about this interpretation or the reasons behind it. There are, however, at least two relationships being discussed in this passage (there is a third, perhaps a fourth, but this will become more apparent in the passage that follows). There is Abby's relationship to the church, or the church mothers and their ascriptions of fault, about which she is not so sure. There is also, not entirely separate, the relationship with God that seems to be a more fundamental dilemma: "I was very upset because I thought God had let me down. That God wasn't there when I needed him, you know? And that God, had, um, had um, had had turned his back on me, you know." So God had failed *her*, and when she needed him most. But, for Abby the failure was mutual: "that was true about *Him*, but I also felt that was true about *me*, you know. I thought it was true about me *and* Him."

This relationship is remarkably palpable, as may be apparent from the terms Abby uses to discuss it. Abby was also noticeably emotional about the topic; some of the false starts and the many "um"s in this passage and the next should be taken as reflective of the emotional valence of this discussion. Working out the estrangement in this relationship is also bound up with Abby's recovery. She wants to become close to God. She needs to fall back on that foundation but can't: she has problems with praying because where was she these ten years when she was getting better? Abby is acutely aware of her responsibility for holding up her side of this relationship and not just when it's right for her. But it is a problem of *relationship*, of her *and* Him. Abby is coping with estrangement in a relationship that is fundamental to her sensibility.

There is for Abby, I believe, a genuine question of *authenticity* (not a word I use often); she needs to do things like praying, or being there, in good faith or not at all. There is something terribly genuine—and terribly exacting—about her commitment to her faith, and the centrality of working it out to her life, identity, and in many ways to her sense of being recovered:

ES: So how do you think disability and your recovery has been affected by, uh, or is involved with your faith, by your relationship with Jesus, as estranged as it is?

ABBY: Yeah, um, actually, um [*five-second pause*] I think that, um, my recovery hasn't been *helped* by my, you know, my, all these ifs and whats and, you know, that go along with religion for me. Because, um, because, um, instead of letting myself *be*, and letting myself, you know, be handicapped or be whatever—*this is me*, instead of doing that, I've put up walls. You know, walls where, walls where I think they have to be. [ES: Huh] And, so, it's hard for me to become more religious because I've got all these walls up, all these little *codes*, you know, that I'm not fulfilling. And, um, and it's hard for me to be religious and, and, um, and have a disability. [*Four-second pause*] That's not—maybe that is true, I mean maybe, I don't know. I kind of don't like that, what I just said, about having a disability and being religious. [ES: Uh huh] I think, um, I think that you can have a disability and you can be religious, *if* you're not me. [*Both laugh*] If, um, if I could get through all these codes, you know little—then I think

I'd be doing a lot better, in my recovery. I don't think, now that I look back on it, so far, I've been struggling, you know, trying to make my recovery work for me, and it's been really hard, um, without, without giving into, you know, my religious nature. [ES: Huh] And so it's kind of, it's kind of like I'm, I'm just fighting against this little, just fighting against something. But it's, it maybe would be better if I would just, you know, *at ease*. And, um, if I allowed, um, religion, to come in, you know.

That was the end of the long interview; Abby was ready for a break but also, as may be apparent from how she was reflecting on her own responses in that passage, wanted to think for a while, alone. Abby's recovery has not been helped, but as she explains, the problem is not her religion per se but all the walls up where she thinks they have to be, and all the little "codes" she's not fulfilling. Those go along with religion for Abby and make it hard for her to be religious. And disability is a big part of this difficulty, but (again) in a complicated way: disability seems to interfere with being able to fulfill the codes, yet religion also seems to interfere with accepting being disabled: "I think I'd be doing a lot better in my recovery." Abby is in the middle of this breach: "I think that you can have a disability and you can be religious, *if* you're not me."

But before this is left as simply a matter of being Abby, it is important to consider how "being Abby" is crowded with the intentions of others. It is the case that Abby is exacting of herself, and she also compares herself often to her pre-injury self and the person she would have become if not for the stroke. It is also the case that left-brain injuries are associated with a perhaps fixated attention to deficits and anxiety about them; they also seem to leave people who have them at the mercy of what might be called the right brain's endless generation of contingencies (a contrast to right-brain injury will be apparent in Sarah's account, which follows). I don't think it is accurate to interpret these problems as all in Abby's brain, however. There are plenty of discourses and metaphors in the culture at large, and at work in the responses of Abby's fellow congregants, that support the experience of disability as failure—of will, of faith, of discipline or character. At least part of Abby's difficulty with reconciling disability and religion is emblematic of these cultural formations and the anxieties of others. All of the women in this study faced the problem of accepting being disabled, of "letting myself, you know, be handicapped or be whatever—*this is me.*"

If Abby's struggle is with religion or her religious nature, it is an important site because religion is so important to her; again, everybody here had some difficulty reconciling being disabled to being something or other that was central to their identity. In that passage, as she hears, reflects on, and responds to her own statements, Abby is articulating the process of recognizing, trying out, and trying to resolve competing discourses or narratives about being disabled and about being religious: "you know trying to make recovery work for me, and it's been really hard, um, without, without giving into, you know, my religious nature." She has been fighting against *something* (consider the accounts of most of the other women on this point), but it is not clear if she ought to resist (not give "in to her religious nature") or let go (allow "religion to come in"). Both her disability and her religious nature are sites of struggle, and those struggles complicate one another. The absolute factuality of both for her, along with Abby's exacting attitude toward herself, her unwillingness to elide or gloss over contradiction, not to mention the ministrations of others, present real authorial dilemmas.

It is difficult to tease apart Abby's problems with the interpretations of her church mothers, which also echo many implicit cultural messages about illness and disability, Abby's relationship to herself, including her prior self and her current high expectations of herself, and Abby's relationship to Jesus and religion. The last relationship had been an important and—if one takes Abby's faith seriously—valid site of struggle before her stroke. Abby is herself working to tease those knotted problems apart. But because the terrain is so overpopulated with intentions of others, it is difficult to let herself "be handicapped or whatever—*this is me,*" or to open the space to clearly attend to her relationship with God and let "religion come in."

Furthermore, it may be important to recognize the ways that a relationship with God and a spiritual life would entail a legitimate struggle rather than a clinical or rhetorical problem to be resolved. That is, it is not clear that religion or spirituality is meant to make things *easier.* The point is important because it allows for distinctions among Abby's struggles in her relationship to God—including the kinds of work she feels she must do in the service of that relationship, and that God may also need to do—from the other problems she contends with in relation to her own and culture's discourses about disability, and those difficulties related to impairments due to her brain injury.

That is, it seems pertinent to make the case that not every form of suffering or experience of confusion requires diagnosis or fixing. From many perspectives, spiritual as well as political, there is a price to be paid for the truth. Given that metaphysics are at play in the other discourses applied to the treatment and experience of people with disabilities, it is only fair to attend to a venerable spiritual tradition of labor and renunciation, of a necessary transformation of oneself, as the "cost" for gaining access to the God. A spiritual life, at least in some traditions, involves the "researches, practices, and experiences, which may be purifications, ascetic exercises, renunciations, conversions of looking, modifications of existence" that are, for "the subject's very being, the price to be paid for access to the truth" (Foucault, 2001, 15). There can be no truth without a conversion or transformation of the subject. Access to God, then, involves the work of the "self on the self, and elaboration of the self by the self, a progressive transformation of the self by the self" by which one takes responsibility in a long labor (16). A concern for that kind of work of the self on the self, a transformation, and a responsibility for the labor, seem obvious in Abby's account.

Love is also a part of this conversion, "an ascending movement" of the subject herself toward truth, or else a movement by which the truth comes to her and enlightens her (Foucault, 2001, 16). Abby is facing some dilemmas in this movement of love, in the ways that she and God are and are not "there" for one another. That movement of love is obviously complicated by the stroke, but the relationship is clearly eminent in her life even if the immanence of this movement is uncertain. Love and labor, then, are the two major means by which the subject must be transformed in order to become capable of knowing truth, or God. An act of knowledge—or simple obeisance to law or rules—in and of itself could not provide access to the truth, unless it was "prepared, accompanied, doubled, and completed by a certain transformation of the subject." Not of the individual but the subject herself, in her being, as subject (Foucault, 2001, 16).

The point of that diversion through Michel Foucault's genealogical analysis of spirituality is not simply to validate Abby's struggle—though that was part of the intention. It was also to redeem, so to speak, spirituality and spiritual struggle (even suffering) from being construed as essentially problematic, as a personal or cultural pathology. It is also to salvage spirituality from the fairly bland, neutered, or mechanistic (even pharmacological) terms in which it is frequently framed in the social science literature on illness, disability, and recovery (and, increasingly, on psychotherapy). In those literatures spirituality and religion are often reduced to measurable variables: hope, positive expectations, prayer or other "acts" such as attending services, and/or sometimes membership in a congregation or community. Or, spirituality may be philosophized into a sense of connection, of being part of something larger than oneself—the transcendent as the "transpersonal." Not that there's anything wrong with framing or experiencing spirituality in terms of community and relationship to others (several women here did), of faith and positive expectations, of some sense of transpersonal meaning, or of considering particular behaviors or practices like prayer or attending services. Rather, it is that such operationalizations and ascriptions do leave a lot behind—admittedly much that is difficult to make work as prescription or as methodology. They leave behind the ways in which suffering and struggle might be seriously meaningful, even fundamental, to someone's spiritual experience and relationship to truth, not something to be alleviated or treated. In another way, making spirituality solely a function of community neglects the ways that community may actually create problems for reconciling disability with spirituality (as it did for many of the women here, Abby being the proximal example), or perhaps create problems for a spiritual process (in demands, for example, for other kinds of transformations, or access to different kinds of truth).

Some consideration of those points also seems required in anticipation of Sarah's account, to which I turn now. Sarah's experience exemplifies de Certeau's case for the role of the "supernatural" in response to the facts of the world: "Without diminishing in any way what one sees everyday, the stories of miracles respond to it 'from aside' with irrelevance and impertinence in a different discourse, a discourse one can only *believe*—just as an ethical reaction must believe that life cannot be reduced to what one sees of it" (de Certeau, 1984, 17).

Sarah believes her injuries are part of a grander design for her life. Far from challenging her long-established and fully intertwined spiritual and identity narratives, her injuries and the subsequent coma are (maybe must be) taken as confirmation of them. The severity of her injuries indicates that the fact that she is alive and so engaged *is* something of a miracle. Sarah framed and prefaced her discussion of the injury and her current life with an autobiography structured by three prior epiphanic moments or turning points; these were episodes in which she—and others—were *inspired* to decision or action. The first of these moments was when Sarah decided to adopt her son, even as she was in the process of divorcing her first husband. This transpired in the 1970s in rural Idaho, so it was no small act of faith or love, or of bravery. The second event, more literally epiphanic, was when she decided to sell everything she owned and move to Arizona. She was working as an interior decorator and driving with a client on a day trip from Scottsdale to Sedona:

> SARAH: So, as we got up to the area where we start entering the rocks I heard a voice in my head—first time—it was so loud and gigantic I assumed everyone could hear it. [*Laughs*] And it said, "Welcome home, dear one." And it was like all-consuming love, and I felt it, it was just wonderful. It was the first time anything like that happened. Of course it got my attention. We finished the day and did our thing and went back down to Scottsdale, and I went back to Cincinnati, which is where I was living. *Sold everything*. Packed everything else, got to Sedona. I was living there three weeks later. It was like I just knew I was going to live there. I knew all the details would be taken care of, that I wouldn't have to worry about it, which is *the right thing to do*.

Here the voice of Spirit let her know that Sedona was her home, and that she was dear: "an all-consuming love." She knew the details would be taken care of; it was obviously "the right thing to do." Sedona is where Sarah became the center, or teacher, of a fairly large group of similarly spiritually-minded people, and those relationships—and Sarah's importance to them—were still very vibrant at the time of our interviews. The third epiphanic moment for Sarah came when she decided to marry her third and current husband, Gary, and move to a small farming town in the Midwest (Hamlet). Sarah's coma, more than the actual collision, represents the fourth major spiritual event in Sarah's life:

SARAH: The coma was literally to die for. It was awesome. It's like all understanding that I had, I got to experience the *truth* of it in the coma. It's like all that I knew, that I understand, I got to experience. It's like I experienced oneness with all that is, which is what I *intellectually* knew before, that we aren't separate. Any thought I had was just, you know, it was just going to do what it did. Now I know my thoughts are quite powerful. Before I didn't know that. So it really just assisted me with knowing what I already knew. I got to become what I knew. So, I'm closer to being my spiritual self. I feel as if I'll be used in ever increasingly spectacular ways. And I don't know all those ways yet. I've seen visions of me speaking in front of large groups, of *travel*, of traveling to groups. And, what I'd say about my background is that I've been well-prepared to be in front of a group. I have no fear of standing in front of a group, to opening my mouth and letting the words fall out of it. It's like that would be the greatest joy for me. [ES: Mhm] I'll say it this way: it *will* be the greatest joy for me. I, from my coma experience, I know that my body, physically, will function well beyond what it was functioning at. It's as if I will have more strength and energy, and dexterity and all the—you know, restored. I'll be *well* restored. So that my body's not a limitation. I could actually see that in the coma. I'm undergoing physical changes, genetically. It's as if genetically I'm achieving the whole potential, the blend of genetics. So it's not like my physical body's *changing*, it's like it's becoming what it *could* be.

Sitting across from Sarah I could believe that God has spoken to her and that she probably will be (or ought to be) restored. However, reading this excerpt with her injuries in mind is somewhat difficult, certainly poignant, especially in light of the limitations on her speaking and her mobility. This interview, our second, took place about eighteen months after the injury, Sarah had developed some strategies for handling her cognitive problems, was more mobile and active, and more fully participatory in the interviews than she had been at our first meeting six months earlier. But she was resisting surgery that would allow her to dispense with the tracheotomy tube or to have a glass eye fitted to replace the one that had been bisected in the collision. She believed that these would interfere with the transformational process she was undergoing.

This is not a private, idiosyncratic perspective; it is supported and perhaps demanded by people in Sarah's life, her family but also by those who are part of her spiritual circle or following. One of these friends, Rob, was visiting Sarah and participated in part of that interview. Rob followed up on Sarah's account of her experience of the coma by elaborating on its effects on those around her:

> ROB: Not just here in Hamlet, in many places too. What happened caused a lot of us in Sedona to be forced through some severe and intense spiritual growth. Uh, there are several of us who, our meditation slash teaching group in Sedona that Sarah was a part of, we always considered Sarah so close to God that we got immediately confused to how God could let this happen to her. [ES: Uh huh] And we had to work through that, and she wasn't there to counsel us because she was in a coma. [*Sarah and Rob laugh*] So, uh, and she's convinced that this is all part of the plan, therefore I've watched all of the repercussions of this, that have happened and enhanced, have enriched other people's lives. I *see* that part of it, and I know that she still sees more of it than I do, because she sees further into the resolution of the whole thing. I'm just reporting what I've seen so far. And the healings within her family and all that started to happen as we, severally or separately, were standing around her bed when she was unconscious. It seemed to break all the barriers between people and people started getting real. That, uh, repercussed through her friends and her family. In terms of opportunities to, uh, seize additional levels of understanding about our relationship not only to God, but our relationship to each other, as human and as sons and daughters of God. So, Sarah teaches even when she's unconscious. [*All laugh*]

Sarah's experience is not just Sarah's experience, and the "resolution of the whole thing" will have repercussions for friends and family; repercussions for *their* meaning making, for their relationships to God and to each other. With due deference to the ways in which these people and their love for Sarah have been supportive of her through the injury and recovery, it is also very apparent how they are invested in—perhaps even dependent on—Sarah's accounting of the injuries and on a particular resolution. It is fair to say that it places a particular burden on Sarah. It certainly puts significant weight on her own authoring process, given that her identity and role as spiritual teacher, counselor, and one "so close to God" are so bound up. People were confused about how God could let this happen to her, but because Sarah is convinced of a plan, their lives have been "enriched" and "enhanced"—except for her son, whose response is presented in chapter 3; he is missing the beauty and goodness of his pre-injury mother. Sarah's recovery is heavily populated with the needs and intentions of others.

Sarah's neuropsychologist Dr. Austerlitz provided another perspective on the relationships between Sarah's organic injuries, the concerns of others, her spiritual narrative, and identity. From a neuropsychological perspective, Sarah's relationship to her injuries and impairments could be considered symptomatic *of* her RBI. But here Dr. Austerlitz frames the lack of awareness of and indifference toward impairments that are classically characteristic of brain injury as more or other than symptomatic; they are a transcendent function:

DR. AUSTERLITZ: Almost in all brain injuries, okay, right hemisphere, left hemisphere, there are awareness deficits. So, in a sense, you don't have to transcend anything, because [*laughing*] the brain has already done it, it has transcended reality, and creates its own delusions, as a healing strategy.

ES: Okay, that's an interesting way—

DR. AUSTERLITZ: No, it's a biological fact. And I will say to people, you know God has a way [*laughs*] of protecting people. Because families are intensely anxious about the emotional pain the person will experience, that the *family* is already experiencing in anticipating this life change. So, uh, they will frequently ask you many questions about what should we say, what should we do when they argue, you know, should we argue with them? And so on. And I say, "Well, you know this is God's way of protecting people from this," and as time goes on their awareness will get different. And, uh, they will get depressed, or you know, then you reframe it as, "Well that's good. I hate to see you in pain in addition to everything else, but then we know the brain is working normally." But, for now, in the meantime, "God has this way of protecting people." And if the patient thinks it's okay, if they have come to some transcendence of the loss, saying, "Well, I'm going to get my drivers license," or something, and they feel like it's together now, then who's to argue? Um, with an understanding that in a year they might come back with a very different perspective. And, I guess one might consider that another metaphysical, uh, perspective that does get communicated, and that's the impermanence of it all. The good, the bad, the ugly. Some way, it comes, goes, it comes back again. But, specifically about Sarah, um, the last time she was here, the thought process hasn't quite found its anchor. She's up, she's down, just in a short time frame. And I, you know, to reflect back to her humanness, her ability to recover from those moments when her narrative is self-defeating, and come up with another way. Sarah is not devoid of therapeutic insights. You know, time, and the nature of them and, uh, the fleetingness of them, uh, may be an issue. But, to reframe the pain of it, the pain of the negative narrative, in a human way—and Sarah *can* do that very well. Because she's aware when the narrative's not working. She wants to know why! [*Both laugh*] Right? So, uh, I just try to help with that notion of impermanence, the impermanence of effectiveness, impermanence of the state, of that moment of misery or fear. That's transcendence. I don't try to change the dialogue or the syntax, the meaning of what they're saying, or try to get them to think of Kierkegaard or whatever. [*Both laugh*] I just try to shift from that moment of misery, get them into the impermanence of it all. They don't know, I don't know, where it will lead. And, with Sarah, you know, she can say "Spirit's work," so, uh, then, I can say to her, "just let spirit work."

Dr. Austerlitz weaves together neuroscience, Buddhism, existentialism, and the pragmatics of psychotherapeutic strategy. Materialism becomes metaphysics and vice versa: "the brain has transcended reality." It is a biological fact and it is God's way of protecting people. It is "delusion" and it is "healing strategy." If there is subtle didacticism to the way Dr. Austerlitz discusses this, it is noteworthy how there is no trace of pathologizing the process and experiences. Without changing their syntax or their meaning he tries to get them into the impermanence of it all: of the effectiveness of particular narratives or strategies, of the state, of the misery and of the fear. It could be said that while Sarah relies on a suspension of *dis*belief, he is invoking here a kind of suspension of belief. Yet they converge in as much as both his and Sarah's reconciliations are assertions of faith: "They don't know, I don't know, where it will lead. And, with Sarah, you know, she can say 'Spirit's work,' so, uh, then, I can say to her, 'just let spirit work.'"

But Dr. Austerlitz begins his accounting by discussing the problems experienced by the family, about their intense anxiety and emotional pain in anticipatory response to what the patient will experience as awareness begins to return: what should we say, should we argue with them? His response is that this is God's way of protecting people from anxiety and pain. If the patient has come to some transcendence of the loss, if they feel as if it's together, "then who's to argue?"

But this particular way of framing the relationship between the family and the patient, the relationship between the family's and the patient's distress, and the direction of dependence between them, misses a dynamic that seems central in Sarah's case. That is, Sarah's family and friends are apparently dependent on Sarah to reduce their distress and their sense of loss; their "awareness" is also problematic for Sarah as she tries to find the "anchor" for her own "thought process." It is no more a private process than Sarah's spiritual narrative is a private one. In part that's because being the mouthpiece of Spirit and helping other people find their way had been so major to Sarah's role in other people's lives; those others are invested in—dependent on—the restoration of *that* Sarah.

Dr. Austerlitz, for his part, tries to direct Sarah back to her humanness, to her ability to recover when her narratives fail and come up with another way. Sarah is "not devoid of therapeutic insights." They may be transitory or at odds with reasonable expectations, but when it comes to reframing the pain of it in a human way, Sarah *can* do that very well. She knows when the narrative is not working. "She wants to know why! Right?"

When I first met Sarah, not long after the collision and only a few months after she had been released from the hospital, I took her expectations of a miraculous transubstantiation as symptomatic of her injuries. Even during the second interview I was still concerned with what would happen to Sarah's spiritual and identity narratives—they seemed to be one—if (actually, in my mind, *when*) there were no miraculous cure, no remission of her physical and cognitive problems. I had already talked to a number of people who had pointed out how holding on or holding out for a "cure" often kept people from "moving on" with their lives. Sarah's faith and the narrative of complete restoration seemed to be too completely at odds with reality, too contingent on a particular outcome and too at odds with the course of events.

Rather than responding with "irrelevance and impertinence in a different discourse" to what one sees everyday and believing "that life cannot be reduced to what one sees of it," Sarah did not seem to have a place "aside" (de Certeau, 1984, 17). Life would need to go a certain way in order for her narrative to remain viable, ethical. But while any or all of those assumptions might still bear some relevance, over time and in the course of more interactions and observations, it became apparent that the many intentions of others, as well as the heterogeneity of perspectives by which Sarah was variously imaged and valued made it very difficult for Sarah—and in variant but similar ways, Abby—to respond in a different discourse. The needs and anxieties of others, the judgments of others, the myths and imperatives of perfectibility that often adhere to medicine, religion, and critical theory, those cultural beliefs about a reason if not a warrant for bad things happening to people, and the ways all of those impinge upon and constitute identity—all would challenge faith, acceptance, and "being human." And, these are intentions and perspectives that would have to be managed while struggling with the organic effects of the injuries.

Metaphysical meaning making, certainly religion, is entangled in social relationships, impositions, and demands, so there remains the task of social negotiations, including with one's self. Developing and maintaining a place for ethical protest is, then, also a matter of the intentions of others. Cindy addresses this problem succinctly and links a particular form of metaphysical narrative back to community building and to medical discourse:

CINDY: Another thing that I found it very difficult to deal with, um, is this concept of, I mean I deal with these people that want to *cure* you. [ES: Uh huh] I mean, you just get, I mean it's just a really difficult thing. I mean I've really dealt with two different kinds of people, major reactions. There are people that actually do, like have, um, their own skewed sense of, because this happened to me that I

was a bad person, or something, like this makes *me* bad. [ES: Right]
You know, *very* strange. And, um, and there's people that somehow
kind of dump this whole thing on me that if I only had more faith, I
only, if I only believed *more*, that I would, you know, not have to live
like this. [ES: Uh huh] And, it's very difficult, you know. And I think,
sometimes I feel like we as disabled people, particularly women, I
mean I think we're kind of magnets for that kind of thing. You know?
[ES: Yeah] And that gets very frustrating, and I think again that's
where it helps to have a sense of community that's built around a
non-medical model. Because that, um, way of thinking, you know, of
relating to *yourself*, even, actually just pathologizes everything more,
and reinforces the *negative* aspects.

Cindy makes identification with a community of disabled people,
particularly women, central here. Being a magnet for the various forms
of victim blaming and disqualification because of disability—and gender—is not unique to religious and spiritual narratives and communities. The idea that "if I only believed *more*" or differently can also be
a feature of political and critical theoretical characterizations of people with disabilities (Siebers, 2008). Medicine and rehabilitation may
also convey the message that failures of recovery are failures of will or
morality (see, for example, Ingstad & Whyte, 1995; Sontag, 2001). Negotiating this, resisting, rejecting, or challenging these discourses requires
a certain amount of support and critical reflection, which Cindy finds
or finds best in a community of other disabled women—a set of relationships and a place in the world that is not structured around diagnoses, shared pathology, or common failure.

Many disability theorists and researchers have pointed out how disability and chronic illness inspire anxiety, fear, or even dread in the
nondisabled. The fact that disability is really ultimately a universal
experience—a question not of *if* one is disabled but if one is disabled
yet—rather than a minority experience is no doubt part of that anxiety.
It also contributes to the press to configure disability as a minority and
minoritizing experience, as distant and individual: as other. The apparent need to adhere to a belief in a just world makes it almost irresistible
to locate the cause and effect of disability in the disabled person. Randomness—let alone a capricious God—is difficult to fully accept, as are

the vagaries of human experience and the frailty and idiosyncrasies of the human body.

Metaphysicians

Cindy's friend Dr. Larsen sees disability community—in a local, relational sense—as very important to the renegotiation of meaning. She considers such relationships and contexts as offering a place in the world based on shared experience, caring, and cooperation, and as a site for voicing an ethical protest. But she has reservations about how pat answers can create problems for the kind of reflection she thinks is necessary to negotiating disability:

> DR. LARSEN: Well, sometimes, I think, with some people, the answers may be too pat. Or, you may feel you *have* to accept the answers because you're part of that faith, rather than doing the kind of stepping back and questioning that I think is really important and beneficial for people. Um, I guess also as we're talking, I'm also very aware of how my own sense of spirituality is not necessarily tied to an individual religion. And I think that's true for other patients I've worked with, where the idea of some sort of self-actualization or, being more introspective and, um, learning from one's life circumstances and growing, is something that I would say almost every patient does. And I, I almost consider that spirituality, in the broader sense. And, um, I think that value readjustment that people go through when they've been disabled is a very important part of that. And the pace of life, the change in the pace of life that occurs, is a very important step. We move at such a fast pace in this society, I think when you *can't*, you've got to attend much more to what's going on around you, and interpersonal dynamics, that you've got to be much clearer about your priorities for a day. And the other thing that I think happens is the investment in relationships. I am so impressed when I look at what I call the disability community, at the strength of the bonds, the caring, the compassion, the support. I mean it's really tremendous, I think, in terms of looking at what a community can be. And, I see something, in a broad sense, spiritual about that. But, that, we view ourselves still largely as a religious society. And yet

we're a very selfish society. And the churches have been fairly silent on a lot of these issues. Individual churches have been *awful* because they are protected or *exempt* from the ADA, as religious organizations. And so it's still not at all uncommon that somebody may have been a member of a church for twenty years and they can't get into the church without being carried up the stairs, and it's such an inconvenience and embarrassment that they quit going to church. And the church says they can't afford to put the ramp or elevator in. So, I think in the sense of the role that organized religion can be *playing*, is a tremendous role that's sort of untapped.

Here and elsewhere Dr. Larsen emphasizes how our culture's emphasis on individualism is one of the major things people with disabilities have to free themselves from. She does emphasize the need for self-actualization, introspection, learning, and growing; that kind of stepping back and questioning, the value adjustment that a person goes through when they're disabled is "spirituality, in the broader sense." Dr. Larsen, though, is offering an individual "change of mind" perspective, a change that she sees as both facilitated and necessitated by disability. But as she continues, she shifts to an emphasis on the selfish nature of our society, something to which the disability community offers an alternative or antidote: "the strength of the bonds, the caring, the compassion, the support. I mean it's really tremendous, I think, in terms of looking at what community can be." There is also something, "in a broad sense, spiritual about that." So the change that has to take place is both personal and social. No need to amplify her well-articulated perspectives on organized religion.

Both doctors see questions of meaning and purpose (or "love and work"; they both cited Freud) as critical to recovering from brain injury and living with disability. But while they are both interested in quality of life and optimal outcomes, Dr. Austerlitz also explicitly disavows any interest in the "ghosts and goblins" and the "magical" aspects of religion, potentially problematic because of its "structure and dogma." He does, however, see a critical role for the "meta-physical":

DR. AUSTERLITZ: In essence brain injury and the physical disabilities, uh, have to be transcended, *meta*-physically. Right. Which is not, uh, and spirituality, uh, you could say, really, what spirituality is, is this metaphysical perspective. [ES: Okay] Uh, it may in fact be something else, or just a small part of the metaphysical perspective. You said trans*personal*, may be another, I don't know another term for meta-physical, uh, but they may have different meanings and different, uh, heuristic value, uh, pregnant meanings as one were to think it over, over time. So I think about it as whether people are, uh, metaphysi-cal. Uh, because in fact, uh, because most religions are, uh, adherents to structure and dogma, uh, you might even find an inverse relation-ship between that concept of spirituality, and, uh, this ability to be meta-physical, and, uh, transcend the physical, uh, impact on your life. [ES: Uh huh, huh] So, it comes up, it does come up both in this spiritual sense, and it comes up in this metaphysical sense, and if it doesn't come up, you try to infuse it. The term, um, the term, the phrase that has rung in my ears over the years was from, uh, I think it was the movie *Little Big Man*, and he says "a human being," that was the highest thing you could be. So, I cannot tell you how effec-tive, these people tell terrible, terrible tales—"*You're human.*" And, uh, that connects them with a broader sense of experience than just the experience of themselves and this other, this everyday life. Now, for some people that's very threatening, because they're very rooted in the uniqueness of the self at that moment. And that, you have to work on that, because that is part of the thing that keeps you, if I might say this metaphysically, in the wheel of dependent origination.

Dr. Austerlitz finds his metaphysical perspective summed up by Charging Bear: "'a human being,' that was the highest thing you could be." It is an effective response to terrible, terrible tales, "*You're human.*" It connects people with a broader sense of experience than just the experience of themselves and "this other, everyday life." By this "other, everyday life" I took Dr. Austerlitz to mean the preoccupation with their *physical*, unique, and impermanent state, that which keeps them separate, isolated, and trapped in the (Buddhist) "wheel of dependent origination." This is not so different, though put in different terms, from Dr. Larsen's emphasis on stepping back and relationships.

There is in both accounts an interesting and important allusion to the problem of separateness, and the problems involved in the ways that disability and separation are so entwined, if not synonymous. The experience of separateness and the need to overcome it run through all of the women's accounts in one form or another. For some of the women it was the way they feel or felt separated from humanity or particular communities and relationships, for others it was feeling separated from themselves, and for others it was separation from God or, in a metaphysical sense, from humanity.

Overcoming the problem or illusion of separateness is a central theme of many religious and spiritual systems and narratives. But it is also central to the arguments, analyses, and strategies of disability rights and disability studies, for instance in the ways that medical and rehabilitation practices objectify people; invite patients to become special cases, isolated by the uniqueness of their physical or cognitive conditions; to view their problems as "personal"; and to become independent. It is also central to disability rights struggles to challenge the exclusion and pathologization of people with disabilities and to reframe disability as a cultural rather than a personal deficit. It is also central to disability studies' arguments about the universality of human fragility and vulnerability, and the uses to which the marginal framing of the disabled is put in various discourses of economics, citizenship, and power.

These are metaphysical struggles insofar as they must be responded to "from aside," in "a different discourse, a discourse one can only *believe*—just as an ethical reaction must believe that life cannot be reduced to what one sees of it." "Constantly repeated facts, the relationship of forces do not become anymore acceptable by virtue of being reinscribed." It is that which is not yet and is not to be known by the established state of affairs and the repeated facts that creates a place for protest (de Certeau, 1984, 17). Stories of miracles are indispensable as a site for the possible: "In spite of everything, they provide the possible with a site that is impregnable, because it is nowhere, a utopia. They create another space, which coexists with that experience deprived of illusions. They tell a truth (the miraculous) which is not reducible to the particular beliefs that serve it as metaphors or symbols. They exist *alongside* the analysis of facts, as the equivalent of what political ideology introduces *into* that analysis" (de Certeau, 1984, 17, emphasis in original). Such counternarratives, even by virtue of their fantasticness, can then provide the possibility and material for an authoring process that transcends repetition, replication, and reinscription.

Coda

Just because it was a constantly repeated fact, this relationship of forces did not become anymore acceptable. The *fact*
was not accepted as a *law*, even if it remained inescapably a
fact. Trapped in dependency, forced to submit to the facts,
this conviction is nevertheless opposed to the *statutory* fact
of an order presenting itself as natural, a goal of non-accep-
tance, and to its fatality, an *ethical* protest.
de Certeau, 1984, 16, emphasis in original

People with brain injury are most often spoken *about* by others, in the
terms of others and in relation to the concerns and interests of others.
Whether as intention or effect, the perspectives and vocabularies—
just the third person-ness—of these representations problematize and
exclude those of whom they speak. This book has been, then, a project of "narrative retrieval" to re-present the identities, strategies, and
relationships that ten women with brain injury were creating (Garland-
Thomson, 2005). If it has been successful, these women were present as
agents engaged in social action on a variety of fronts. Rather than things
to be managed or problems to solved, these women are creative—if
encumbered and shifting—authors of self, meaning, and relationships.
It is, after all, the women, not their "service providers," who must create
and live their lives and who must negotiate disability.

The second aim of this book has been to contribute to a "resymbolization" (Eiesland, 1994) of brain injury and disability more broadly,
to foreground the need for a "different discourse" (or discourses) for
living with brain injury. In the long run the marginalization, disqualification, and embarrassment—in fact the processes of subjectification—imposed by culture were more disabling for these women than
were their impairments. The struggles were personal, in the sense that

the women confronted them in their everyday, situated lives; they drew on different biographical experiences and priorities in their responses. In one way or another, most of them said that it was up to them. The struggles were personal, too, because they were so often made personal and individual by others. They involved the facts of being alive: work, school, church membership, health care, transportation, intimacy, and status and value as a person and citizen. But those struggles were framed as personal, private, and idiosyncratic problems by narratives of individualism, economic pragmatism, and normalization. That is, practices and discourses of individualization and separation continually worked to construct their struggles as private, physiological, or intra-psychic, even as moral failures, and thereby often deny them grounds for legitimate resistance or refusal, to position them as isolated strangers, and to recruit them into disdain for their post-injury self.

The women's narratives, identities, and communities contribute to critical frameworks for identifying and challenging complicated and intersecting ideologies—the dominant narratives of ability, gender, race, age, and the economy, along with those about vulnerability and dependence—from which social injustice, segregation and oppression derive their energy and legitimacy. That is, the women's accounts illuminate the ideologies that construct reality, for the disabled and nondisabled alike, and that entangled and destabilized—but did not negate—their agency. The women required, and often deployed, different kinds of critical consciousness about their social position in the reauthoring of identity, relationships, and meaning post-injury. Clearly, critical consciousness (political and metaphysical) and the forms of oppositional counternarratives they enabled weren't acquired evenly or at once, nor were they evenly deployed over time and contexts; it was an ongoing, social process that involved contradictions and iterations. Critical consciousness, which I am concluding is necessary to reauthoring a habitable and affirmative identity post-injury, depended largely on connections and engagement with other people with disabilities, and time.

The reauthoring of identity post-injury entailed an ongoing and complex set of negotiations that married adaptation to opposition (Gramsci, 1971). The women did have to adapt to new functional limitations and the realization that their lives would now be different, and differently difficult, both materially and socially. The authoring process involved negotiations of how much and how long to fight against their own bodies and brains versus accepting and adapting to limitations. Realizing the nature, extent, permanence, and consequences of new impairments took time. It didn't happen all at once and it isn't once and for all; because the women, their injuries, and their circumstances varied, there was no single resolution or "outcome." The women also had to identify the source and workings of the cultural barriers and configurations already in place for them as women with disabilities. Authoring a meaningful, positive, and habitable identity post-injury meant opposing disabling roles and narratives. Confronting the nature, extent, durability, and effects of these significations took time and assistance and involved ongoing negotiations that weren't resolved at a pass or in a singular way.

Conceptually, this is fairly straightforward: it is the impairment/disability distinction articulated and refined for over twenty years by disability rights and disability studies. The many battles faced by people with brain injury cannot be reduced to or ascribed to their impairments. Culture disables all of us, disabled and those who consider themselves nondisabled alike, and in complex, insidious, and seemingly natural ways. What is less straightforward is how particular people with particular impairments can come to identify those disabling narratives and practices, let alone negotiate them and the ways they work on everyday life and relationships, while also negotiating the embodied consequences of their impairments.

Also fairly straightforward in a conceptual sense is a right to be recognized as an individual, in all the ways one is truly individual—that is, as a person—without having the problems associated with brain injury *individualized*. That is, people with disabilities do not benefit from being defined and related to in terms of deficits or biological anomaly, from personalizing as organic or psychoemotional symptoms what are better understood as the effects and ascriptions of culture, from being relegated to and devalued by social comparison and categorization, or from being disappeared altogether. This is not a new critique: it has been lodged by different groups and disciplines for decades and is the thrust of the social and cultural models of disability (Michalko, 2002; Oliver, 1990, 1996). In fact, both the impairment/disability distinction and the critique of individualization should be familiar to anyone with even a nodding acquaintance with feminist psychology or the sex/gender distinction (see, for example, Fausto-Sterling, 2012; Rubin, 1993; Samuels, 2011). What is not so straightforward is how particular people work out both resisting being relegated to the pathological heap of the disabled assembled through individualization *and* constructing an affirmative identity that incorporates disability and other disabled people. How does a person come to correctly locate the source of "disdain" for a disability identity and overcome it?

For all the reasons that Freud could never figure out "what women want," the shift to a protest stance must involve terms and positions different from those that created the problem. Many of the accounts referenced how sources and resources of help were also laced with the unhelpful traces of ableism, of disqualification, objectification, or disempowerment (as in rehab, at church, work, or school, even among other disabled people). Merely consulting with disabled people about what they want does not remedy a history of diminished autonomy (Barnes, 2003). Holistic or social neuropsychology, client-centered care, sensitive psychotherapy, community reintegration projects, or even emancipatory research, do not evade the social problematic at the heart of disability: if disabled people are subject to the internalization of dominant definitions and values of disability just like those who are nondisabled, then "asking clients about their personal goals is not a pat solution" (Snyder & Mitchell, 2006, 8). This is particularly true to the extent that these practices and questions are anchored in the acute medical context.

Confronting the ways the women have been objectified, divided against themselves and from others, and recruited into particular subjectivities is a struggle of identity and of identification. In one way and location or another, they had to assert their uniqueness and affirm their difference, to be seen and responded to as individuals. They had to find ways and grounds to refuse everything that isolated them through a reduction to a singular and individual pathology and classification, everything that worked to embarrass them, to objectify them, to make them abject, and to constrain their identities. That is, struggles for a positive disability identity involve both an affirmative recognition and valuation of difference *and* a resistance to diminished, flattened and isolating forms of subjectification: the right to be different *and* the right to be the same, without submitting to distortions or rejections of/by self and of/by others (Rappaport, 1981).

Learning to live with brain injury—constructing meaning, relationships, and an affirmative sense of self—is then identity politics (Alcoff, 2006; Siebers, 2008). Many of the women experienced being divided: from their bodies and their "former selves"; from family, society, community, and from disabled and nondisabled others; from God, truth, or meaning; divided within themselves in terms of identity, aspirations, and acceptance versus refusal. Because living with brain injury is so bound up with working out identity and relationships in the context of a objectifying, pathologizing, and disqualifying narratives and practices, connection to a disability community seems to be a safe prescription. It mattered a lot to the eight women who had found or created that connection. These women discussed the resources, information, tools, and affirmation they obtained in these relationships, a site where they could get right down to work on the issues that mattered to them. Most of them mentioned or alluded to being able to provide help and experience to others; that is, they got to be knowers and givers, and to experience a sense of rapport, intimacy, even of wholeness that they didn't experience in the same way elsewhere. In short, they were members of the community, not objects of ministration or sympathy, not projects or mascots, but full, mattering, contributing, and emotionally engaged members. That is, they experienced a sense of community. All of the women valued other sites and forms of community (such as church, school, work, neighborhood), but disability community provided a strategic position and a critical consciousness about disability that helped sort out the difference between impairments and the disabling effects of cultural discourses and practices and, in that, the difference between authoring an identity that affirmatively incorporates disability and being reduced to it; it was empowering (Collins, 2000; Cornell Empowerment Group, 1989; Gamson, 2002 Rappaport, 1981, 1993, 2000).

That brings up something else that is conceptually straightforward but challenging in its phenomenology: heterogeneity. Even among the women who were connected to disability community, there were negotiations of similarity and difference within it: resonances, distinctions, hierarchies, and distances. Impairments and their consequences vary greatly, along with the significations that attach to them. Obviously, too, the women had multiple identifications and commitments based on a heterogeneity of factors that include but extend beyond age, sexuality, cultural identity, class and means, religious and political commitments, and plain old individual differences. Also, people enter (and exit) the classification of disabled at different times and places. That, though, is actually the point of a disability community—that it can enable one to *step into* and so *step back* from disability identity, to reflect on it from a strategic position and see the difference between the cultural configurations of it and one's lived experience. It is a site of its own reconfiguration, even its undoing. Furthermore, that disability community and identity are crosscut and partly structured by ideologies and experiences of economics, "race" and cultural identity, sexuality, gender, age, and regional provenance (and so on), means the possibilities for common cause and cross-fertilization of critical perspectives are enabled, rather than foreclosed on. Disability is a "category in flux," but it is no less significant for that fact (Siebers, 2008).

But heterogeneity matters in a different way. Two of the women, because of lack of access or lack of interest, weren't in any way identified with other disabled people. This may be "elective," and it may just be a function of being so early in the recovery process and (for better or worse) expecting to exit the category before it even matters for identity and identification—that is, a matter of time and timing. But it is the case that disability community, at least in a physical and face-to-face sense, is not an evenly distributed resource. Rural locations, for example, or the kinds of impairments that limit mobility, participation, and other kinds of freedom in major ways pose considerable barriers to participation in a disability community (or any community). But disability community does exist, virtually and textually, as a resource and set of counternarratives potentially available regardless of geography. It is also available to those who act as advocates and carers for those people with particularly profound impairments.

That leads to another point about heterogeneity, which is how it ought to militate against single standards of normality and deviancy, and so against uniform solutions and conceptualizations for care, treatment, and settings—or even of definitions. If the problems are complex, even paradoxical, then the solutions ought to diverge rather than converge (Rappaport, 1981; Seidman & Rappaport, 1986). Both identity and disability are temporal, relative, and relational, functions of context and person-environment mis/fit, of resources and roles (Campbell, 2009; Garland-Thomson, 2011; Kelly, 2006). Identity and disability meant something different in rehab than they did "out in the world" and in new relationships to self and others. And, all of us may find that we "fit here today and misfit there tomorrow" (Garland-Thomson, 2011, 597). *Disability* is not just for those currently designated as disabled.

The Metaphysical and Resymbolization

Beyond the necessary legislative, economic, and social changes, meaningful inclusion for people with disabilities will require a resymbolization that acknowledges disability as the human condition, and the reality of human interdependence and mutuality of care (Eiesland, 1994; Garland-Thomson, 2005). It is a different discourse, one that asserts the facts of human vulnerability and dependence to challenge the often repeated meanings imposed by ableism and individualism (and economics). Feminist analyses and practices—they're not just for women— might also provide an accessible counternarrative useful for disability: in the articulation of body/culture relationships, in forms of praxis, and the foregrounding of care, embodiment, reciprocity, and intersubjectivity, along with developed considerations of heterogeneity, multiplicity and intersectionality. Feminist insights and values follow naturally from an emphasis on community (or is it the other way around?) (see, for example, Kristiansen & Trausdottir, 2004; Thomas, 2007). So, too, might Buddhism, with its emphasis on impermanence, interdependence, compassion, and the illusion of self; or Marxism—disability and health care are so bound up with critical materialism, class-consciousness and community, the political economy and production. And so on; postcolonial studies and queer theory also offer powerful analytics of rationality and subjectivity and ability and normalization. Without diminishing the value of technical, medical expertise for recovery from brain injury (Rose's account makes that value clear), disability and, in fact identity, is perhaps ultimately an ethical matter.

A cultural model of disability studies, community psychology, and narrative were obviously emphasized in this volume; the aim has been to foreground the ethical, the intersubjective, and the aesthetic, along with the contextual and open-ended nature of identity, meaning, and relationship construction. But the range, complexity, and situatedness of the experiences recounted here, along with the ways the phenomena spanned levels of analysis, ought to underscore the need for inter- and extra-disciplinarity in a resymbolization of living with brain injury (and the human condition).

Listening to Stories (Conclusion)

An array of counterpractices and counternarratives, the deployment of different authoring strategies, and the identification of different audiences and constituencies were apparent in the women's accounts. Every woman said it was hard, that it took time and iterations, involved finding or creating tools, and in one way or another they all said it was up to them, even as they ensembled themselves with, and assembled themselves in relation to, others. They all engaged in agentive struggles and worked strategically, relationally, and resourcefully to reauthor identity, meaning, and places in the world. They identified, excavated, or drew upon forms of knowledge—subjugated, authoritative, autobiographical, political, spiritual, moral, relational—to counter the disqualifying or disenfranchising narratives and classifications they encountered. In and as the end, then, I want to return attention to those accounts and the rich implications and arguments they offer, richness and complexity that I do not claim to have exhausted in my framing and analyses. The last word ought properly to belong to the women known here as Abby, Beth, Cindy, Elise, Lydia, Nancy, Rose, Sarah, Susan, and Tracy.

Brief Summary of Participants' Demographics and Injuries

(Note: Age and years post-injury are at the time of the first interview.)

Abby: Single; African American; thirty years old; ten years post-injury. Stroke (arteriovenous malformation) affecting left occipito-parietal and temporal areas; moderate cognitive difficulties and right hemiplegia.

Beth: Married; white; forty-eight years old; six years post-injury. Random gunshot and penetrating wound affecting right temporal and parietal and left temporal areas; widespread moderate to severe sensory and motor deficits, temporal lobe epilepsy, moderate to severe memory and cognitive difficulties.

Cindy: Married; white; forty-six years old; eighteen years post-injury. Assault causing open-head injuries affecting right parietal area; left hemiplegia, left visual and hearing deficits; moderate cognitive and affective difficulties and trauma-related anxiety; chronic pain.

Elise: Single, self-identified lesbian; white; twenty-six years old; seven years post-injury. Car accident causing trauma to brain stem and diffuse vascular injuries affecting mainly right temporal and parietal areas; mild to moderate motor and sensory deficits, right vocal cord paralysis, mild cognitive difficulties.

Lydia: Single; white; forty-eight years old; tewnty-five years post-injury. Car accident causing fracture and hematoma affecting right occipital and left occipital, temporal and parietal areas; partial right hemiplegia, motor and sensory deficits; moderate to severe cognitive and affective difficulties, chronic pain.

Nancy: Engaged; white; twenty-seven years old; one year post-injury. Arteriovenous malformation and surgical complications affecting right occipito-parietal and temporal areas; partial left hemiplegia and motor deficits, mild cognitive difficulties.

Rose: Single; African American; forty-one years old; twenty-eight years post-injury (four years since correct diagnosis). Blunt force trauma (from a baseball) affecting right parietal area; moderate cognitive and affective difficulties.

Sarah: Married; white; fifty-four years old; fourteen months post-injury. Car accident causing right temporal, parietal and frontal injuries, crushed pelvis, and loss of left eye; right hemiplegia and vocal cord paralysis; moderate to severe motor and sensory deficits, moderate to severe cognitive and affective difficulties.

Susan: Engaged; white; thirty-three years old; thirteen years post-injury. Car accident and open head injuries affecting right parietal and frontal areas; partial left hemiplegia, moderate motor deficits, moderate executive and moderate to severe cognitive difficulties.

Tracy: Single; white; seventeen years old; six months post-injury. Car accident causing right parietal fracture, left and right occipito-parietal hematoma, and left frontal concussion; moderate cognitive and affective difficulties (possible personality changes).

REFERENCES

Aber, M. S.; Maton, K. I. & Seidman, E. (Eds.). (2011). *Empowering settings and voices for social change.* New York: Oxford University Press.

Alcoff, L. M. (2006). *Visible identities: Race, gender and the self.* New York: Oxford University Press.

Atkinson, P. & Delamont, S. (2006). Rescuing narrative from qualitative research. *Narrative Inquiry, 16,* 164–172.

Balcazar, F. E.; Suarez-Balcazar, Y.; Taylor-Ritzler, T. & Keys, C. B. (Eds.). (2010). *Race, culture, and disability: Rehabilitation science and practice.* Sudbury, MA: Jones and Bartlett.

Barnes, C. (2003). What a difference a decade makes: Reflections on doing "emancipatory" disability research. *Disability and Society, 18,* 3–17.

Brody, H. (1987). *Stories of sickness.* New Haven: Yale University Press.

Brown, W. (1995). *States of inquiry: Power and freedom in late modernity.* Princeton, NJ: Princeton University Press

Brownworth, V. A. & Raffo, S. (1999). *Restricted access: Lesbians on disability.* Seattle: Seal Press.

Bury, M. B. (1991). The sociology of chronic illness: A review of research and prospects. *Sociology of Health and Illness, 18,* 451–468.

Butler, J. (1997). *The psychic life of power: Theories in subjection.* Stanford, CA: Stanford University Press.

Campbell, F. K. (2009). *Contours of ableism: Territories, objects, disability, and desire.* London: Palgrave Macmillan.

Chan, F.; McMahon, B. T.; Cheing, G.; Rosenthal, D. A. & Beyzak, J. (2005). Drivers of workplace discrimination against people with disabilities: The utility of attribution theory. *WORK: Journal of Prevention, Disability and Rehabilitation, 25,* 77–88.

Chase, S. E. (1995). Taking narrative seriously: Consequences for method and theory in interview studies. In R. Josselson & A. Lieblich (Eds.), *Interpreting experience: The narrative study of lives* (1–26). Thousand Oaks, CA: Sage.

Chase, S. E. (2005). Narrative inquiry: Multiple lenses, approaches, voices. In N. K. Denzin & Y. S. Lincoln (Eds.), *The Sage handbook of qualitative research,* 3rd edition (651–679). Thousand Oaks, CA: Sage.

Chronister, J. A.; Johnson, E. K. & Berven, N. L. (2006). Measuring social support in rehabilitation. *Disability and Rehabilitation, 28,* 75–84.

Clare, E. (1999). *Exile and pride: Disabilities, queerness, and liberation.* Cambridge, MA: South End Press.

Clucas, C. & St. Claire, L. (2010). The effect of patient role and feeling respected on patient health-related outcomes. *Applied Psychology: Health and Well-Being, 2,* 298–322.

Coffey, A. & Atkinson, P. (1996). *Making sense of qualitative data.* London: Sage.

Collins, P. H. (2000). *Black feminist thought: Knowledge, consciousness, and the politics of empowerment.* New York: Routledge.

Cole, J.; Nolan J.; Seko, Y.; Mancuso, K. & Ospina, A. (2011). GimpGirl grows up: Women with disabilities rethinking, redefining, and reclaiming community. *New Media & Society, 13* (7), 1161–1179.

Connor, D. J. (2008). Not so strange bedfellows: The promise of disability studies and critical race theory. In S. Gabriel & S. Danforth (Eds.), *Disability and the international politics of education* (201–224). New York: Peter Lang.

Corker, M. (1998). Disability discourse in a postmodern world. In T. Shakespeare (Ed.), *The disability reader: Social science perspectives* (221–233). London: Cassell.

Corker, M. (1999). Differences, conflations, and foundations: The limits to "accurate" theoretical representations of disabled people's experience? *Disability and Society, 14* (5), 71–76.

Corker, M. & French, S. (1999). Reclaiming discourse in disability studies. In M. Corker & S. French (Eds.), *Disability and discourse* (1–11). Philadelphia: Open University Press.

Cornell Empowerment Group (1989). Empowerment and family support. *Networking Bulletin, 1,* 1–23.

Crossley, M. (2003). Formulating narrative psychology: The limitations of contemporary social constructionism. *Narrative Inquiry, 13,* 287–300.

Davis, L. J. (1997). *Enforcing normalcy: Disability, deafness, and the body.* London: Verso.

Davis, L. J. (2001). Identity politics, disability, and culture. In G. Albrecht, K. D. Seelman & M. Bury (Eds.), *Handbook of disability studies* (535–545). Thousand Oaks, CA: Sage.

de Certeau, M. (1984). *The practice of everyday life.* S. Rendall (Trans.). Berkeley: University of California Press.

Ditchman, N. M. (2011). Factors contributing to sense of community for individuals with brain injury. Doctoral dissertation (UMI # 3437410). Ann Arbor, MI: Pro-Quest/UMI Dissertation Publishing.

Doidge, N. (2007). *The brain that changes itself: Stories of personal triumph from the frontiers of brain science.* New York: Penguin.

Douglas, J. M. (2012). Social linkage, self-concept, and well-being after severe traumatic brain injury. In J. Jetten, C. Haslam & S. A. Haslam (Eds.), *The social cure: Identity, health and well-being* (237–254). New York: Psychology Press.

Duggan, L. (2003). *The twilight of equality: Neoliberalism, cultural politics, and the attack on democracy.* Boston: Beacon Press.

Dunn, D. S. & Elliott, T. R. (2008). The place and promise of theory in rehabilitation psychology research. *Rehabilitation Psychology, 53,* 254–267.

Eiesland, N. (1994). *The disabled god: Toward a liberation theology of disability.* Nashville, TN: Abbingdon.

Ellis, C. (2004). *The ethnographic I.* Oxford, UK: AltaMira Press.

Esterberg, K. (2002). *Qualitative methods in social research.* London: McGraw-Hill.

Ezzy, D. (2002). *Qualitative analysis.* London: Routledge.

Fausto-Sterling, A. (2012). *Sex/gender: Biology in a social world.* New York: Routledge.

Fine, M. & Asch, A. (1988a). Disability beyond stigma: Social interaction, discrimination, and activism. *Journal of Social Issues, 44,* 3–22.

Fine, M. & Asch, A. (Eds.). (1988b). *Women with disabilities: Essays in psychology, culture and politics.* Philadelphia: Temple University Press.

Fineman, M. A. (2005). *The autonomy myth: A theory of dependency.* New York: The New Press.

Finger, A. (2004). Writing disabled lives: Beyond the singular. *PMLA, 120* (2), 610–615.

Fisher, A. T.; Sonn, C. C. & Bishop, B. J. (2002). *Psychological sense of community: Research, applications, and implications.* New York: Kluwer Academic/Plenum Publishers.

Foucault, M. (1983). The subject and power. In H. Dreyfus & P. Rabinow (Eds.), *Michel Foucault: Beyond structuralism and hermeneutics,* 2nd edition (208–226). Chicago: University of Chicago Press.

Foucault, M. (2001). *The hermeneutics of the subject: Lectures at the College de France 1981–1982.* F. Gros (Ed.) & G. Burchell (Trans.). New York: Picador.

Frank, A. (2004). *The renewal of generosity.* Chicago: University of Chicago Press.

Fraser, N. (2000). Rethinking recognition. *New Left Review, 3,* 107-120.

Freund, P. (2001). Bodies, disability, and spaces: The social model and disabling spatial organization. *Disability & Society, 16,* 689–706.

Fries, K. (Ed.). (1997). *Staring back: The disability experience from the inside out.* New York: Plume.

Fuss, D. (Ed.). (1991). *Inside/Out: Lesbian theories, gay theories.* New York: Routledge.

Fuss, D. (1995). *Identification papers.* New York: Routledge.

Gamson, W. A. (2002). How storytelling can be empowering. In K. A. Cerulo (Ed.), *Culture and mind: Toward a sociology of culture and cognition* (187–198). New York: Routledge.

Garland-Thomson, R. (1997). *Extraordinary bodies: Figuring disability in American culture and literature.* New York: Columbia University Press.

Garland-Thomson, R. (2002). Integrating disability, transforming feminist theory. *NWSA Journal, 14,* 1–32.

Garland-Thomson, R. (2005). Feminist disability studies. *Signs, 30,* 1557–1587.

Garland-Thomson, R. (2011). Misfits: A feminist materialist disability concept. *Hypatia, 26,* 591–609.

Ghai, A. (2006). *(Dis)embodied forms: Issues of disabled women.* Delhi: Shakti Books.

Goffman, E. (1963). *Stigma: Notes on the management of spoiled identity.* Englewood Cliffs, NJ: Prentice Hall.

Gonzalez, M. L. (2008). Getting to know reality and breaking stereotypes: The experience of two generations of working disabled women. *Disability & Society, 24* (4), 447–459.

Goodley, D. (2001). "Learning difficulties," the social model of disability and impairment: Challenging epistemologies. *Disability & Society, 16,* 207–231.

Goodley, D. (2011). *Disability studies: An interdisciplinary introduction.* Los Angeles: Sage.

Goodley, D. & Lawthom, R. (2005). Epistemological journeys in participatory action research: Alliances between community psychology and disability studies. *Disability & Society, 20* (2), 135–151.

Goodley, D. & Lawthom, R. (2006). *Disability & psychology: Critical introductions and reflections.* New York: Palgrave Macmillan.

Goodley, D.; Lawthom, R.; Clough, P. & Moore, M. (2004). *Researching life stories: Method, theory, and analyses in a biographical age.* New York: Routledge.

Goodley, D. & Tragsakis, C. (2006). Storying disability and impairment: Retrospective accounts of disabled family life. *Qualitative Health Research, 16,* 630–646.

Gracey, F. & Ownsworth, T. (2012). The experience of self in the world: The personal and social contexts of identity change after brain injury. In J. Jetten, C. Haslam & S. A. Haslam (Eds.), *The social cure: Identity, health and well-being* (273–295). New York: Psychology Press.

Gramsci, A. (1971). *Selections from the prison notebooks.* Q. Hoare (Ed. & Trans.). New York: International Publishers.

Gubrium, J. F. & Holstein, J. A. (Eds.). (2001). *Institutional selves: Troubled identities in a post-modern world.* New York: Oxford University Press.

Gubrium, J. F. & Holstein, J. A. (2002). From the individual interview to the interview society. In J. F. Gubrium & J. A. Holstein (Eds.), *Handbook of interview research: Context and method* (3–32). Thousand Oaks, CA: Sage.

Hall, D. E. (2004). *Subjectivity.* New York: Routledge.

Hall, K. Q. (Ed.). (2011). *Feminist disability studies.* Bloomington: University of Indiana Press.

Haslam, C.; Holme, A.; Haslam, S. A.; Iyer, A.; Jetten, J. & Williams, W. H. (2008). Maintaining group memberships: Social identity continuity predicts well-being after stroke. *Neuropsychological Rehabilitation, 18,* 671–691.

Heinemann, A. W. (2005). Putting outcome measurement in context: A rehabilitation psychology perspective. *Rehabilitation Psychology, 50,* 6–14.

Heller, W.; Levin, R. L.; Mukherjee, D. & Reis, J. P. (2006). Characters in contexts: Identity and personality processes that influence individual and family adjustment to brain injury. *Journal of Rehabilitation, 72* (2), 112–131.

Hochschild, A. R. (1983). *The managed heart: Commercialization of human feeling.* Berkeley: University of California Press.

Hogan, A. (1999). Carving out a space to act: Acquired impairment and contested identity. In M. Corker & S. French (Eds.), *Disability discourse* (79–91). Philadelphia: Open University Press.

Holstein, J. A. & Gubrium, J. F. (2000). *The self we live by: Narrative identity in a post-modern world.* New York: Oxford University Press.

Holstein, J. A. & Gubrium, J. F. (2004). Context: Working it up, down, and across. In C. Seale, G. Gobo, J. F. Gubrium & D. Silverman (Eds.), *Qualitative research practice* (297–311). London: Sage.

Holstein, J. A. & Gubrium, J. F. (2005). Interpretive practice and social action. In N. K. Denzin & Y. S. Lincoln (Eds.), *The Sage handbook of qualitative research*, 3rd edition (483–506). Thousand Oaks, CA: Sage.

Hughes, B. (2009). Disability activisms: Social model stalwarts and biological citizens. *Disability & Society, 24* (6), 677–688.

Hughes, B. & Paterson, K. (1997). The social model of disability and the disappearing body: Towards a sociology of impairment. *Disability and Society, 12* (3), 325–340.

Hughes, R. B.; Lund, E. M.; Gabrielli, J.; Powers, L. E. & Curry, M. A. (2011). Prevalence of interpersonal violence against community-living adults with disabilities: A literature review. *Rehabilitation Psychology, 56,* 302–319.

Hunter, K. M. (1991). *Doctors' stories: The narrative structure of medical knowledge.* Princeton, NJ: Princeton University Press.

Ingstad, B. & Whyte, S. R. (Eds.). (1995). *Disability and culture.* Berkeley: University of California Press.

James, J. C. (2011). Gwendolyn Brooks, World War II, and the politics of rehabilitation. In K. Q. Hall (Ed.), *Feminist disability studies* (136–158). Bloomington: Indiana University Press.

Jetten, J.; Haslam, C. & Haslam, S. A. (Eds.). (2012). *The social cure: Identity, health and well-being.* New York: Psychology Press.

Johnson, E. P. & Henderson, M. G. (Eds.). (2005). *Black queer studies: A critical anthology.* Durham, NC: Duke University Press.

Jones, J. M.; Haslam, S. A.; Jetten, J.; Williams, W. H.; Morris, R. & Saroyan, S. (2011). That which doesn't kill us can make us stronger (and more satisfied with life): The contribution of personal and social changes to well-being after brain injury. *Psychology and Health, 26,* 353–369.

Jones, J. M.; Jetten, J.; Haslam, S. A. & Williams, W. H. (2012). Deciding to disclose: The importance of maintaining social relationships for well-being after acquired brain injury. In J. Jetten, C.; Haslam & S. A. Haslam (Eds.), *The social cure: Identity, health and well-being* (255–271). New York: Psychology Press.

Josselson, R. (2006). Narrative research and the challenge of accumulating knowledge. *Narrative Inquiry, 16,* 3–10.

Kelley, R. D. G. (1997). *Yo mama's dysfunctional! Fighting the culture wars in urban America.* Boston: Beacon Press.

Kelly, J. G. (2006). *Becoming ecological: An expedition into community psychology.* New York: Oxford University Press.

Kent, D. (1988). In search of a heroine: Images of women with disabilities in fiction and drama. In M. Fine & A. Asch (Eds.), *Women with disabilities: Essays in psychology, culture, and politics* (90–110). Philadelphia: Temple University Press.

Kincheloe, J. L. (2001). Describing the bricolage: Conceptualizing a new rigor in qualitative research. *Qualitative Inquiry, 7,* 679–692.

King, M. L., Jr. (1968). The role of the behavioral scientist in the Civil Rights Movement. *Journal of Social Issues, 24,* 1–12.

Klein, B. S. (1992). 'We are who you are': Feminism and disability. *Ms.,* November–
December, 72.

Klonoff, P. S. (2010). *Psychotherapy after brain injury: Principles and techniques.* New
York: Guilford Press.

Kögler, H-H. (1999). *The power of dialogue: Critical hermeneutics after Gadamer and
Foucault.* Paul Hendrickson (Trans.). Cambridge, MA: MIT Press.

Krieger, L. H. (Ed.). (2003). *Backlash against the ADA: Reinterpreting disability rights.*
Ann Arbor: University of Michigan Press.

Kristiansen, K. & Trausdottir, R. (Eds.). (2004). *Gender and disability research in the
Nordic countries.* Lund, Sweden: Studentlitteratur.

Kumar, P. & Clark, M. (2005). *Clinical medicine* (6th ed.). Edinburgh, UK: Saunders.

Kushner, H. S. (1984). *When bad things happen to good people.* New York: Anchor.

Laclau, E. (Ed.). (1990). *New reflections on the revolution of our time.* New York:
Verso.

Lalljee, M.; Laham, S. M. & Tam, T. (2007). Unconditional respect for persons: A social
psychological analysis. *Gruppendynamik und Organisationsberatung, 38,* 451–464.

Leonardo, Z. & Broderick, A. A. (2011). Smartness as property: A critical exploration of
intersections between whiteness and disability studies. *Teachers College Record, 113*
(10), 2206–2232.

Lester, J. C. (2002). The disability studies industry. *Libertarian Alliance,* September 26,
www.la-articles.org.uk/dsi.htm

Levack, W. M. M.; Kayes, N. M. & Fadyl, J. K. (2010). Experience of recovery and
outcome following traumatic brain injury: A metasynthesis of qualitative research.
Disability and Rehabilitation, 32 (12), 986–999.

Lezak, M. D.; Howeisen, D. B. & Loring, D. W. (2004). *Neuropsychological assessment
(4th ed.).* New York: Oxford University Press.

Linton, S. (1998). *Claiming disability: Knowledge and identity.* New York: New York
University Press.

Linton, S. (2007). *My body politic: A memoir.* Ann Arbor: University of Michigan Press.

Lloyd, M. (2001). The politics of disability and feminism: Discord or synthesis? *Sociology, 35,* 715–728.

Lorenz, L. S. (2010). Discovering a new identity after brain injury. *Sociology of Health
& Illness, 32,* 862–879.

Lynch, K.; Baker, J. & Lyons, M. (Eds.). (2009). *Affective equality: Love, care, and injustice.* Basingstoke, UK: Palgrave Macmillan.

Lyotard, J-F. (1989). Time today. *Oxford Literary Review, 11,* 3–20.

Mankowski, E. & Rappaport, J. (1995). Stories, identity and the psychological sense of
community. In R. S. Wyer (Ed.), *Advances in Social Cognition, 8* (211–226). Hillsdale, NJ: Lawrence Erlbaum.

Marks, D. (1999). *Disability: Controversial debates and psychosocial perspectives.* London: Routledge.

Marx, K. (1956). *Selected writings in sociology and social philosophy.* T. Bottomore (Ed.) New York; McGraw-Hill.

McGrath, J. C. & Linley, P. A. (2006). Post-traumatic growth in acquired brain injury: A preliminary small-scale study. *Brain Injury, 22,* 767–773.

McMillan, D. W. & Chavis, D. M. (1986). Sense of community: A definition and theory. *Journal of Community Psychology, 14,* 6–23.

McRuer, R. (2002). Critical investments: AIDS, Christopher Reeve, and queer/disability studies. *Journal of the Medical Humanities, 23,* 221–237.

McRuer, R. (2003). As good as it gets: Queer theory and critical disability. *GLQ: A Journal of Lesbian and Gay Studies, 9,* 1–23.

McRuer, R. (2006). Compulsory able-bodiedness and queer/disabled existence. In L. Davis (Ed.), *The disability studies reader,* 2nd edition (301–308). New York: Routledge.

Meekosha, H. (1998). Body battles: Bodies, gender and disability. In T. Shakespeare (Ed.), *The disability reader: Social science perspectives* (163–180). London: Cassell.

Meekosha, H. (2012). *Body battles: Disability, representation and participation.* London: Sage.

Michalko, R. (2002). *The difference that disability makes.* Philadelphia: Temple University Press.

Miller, G. (1997). *Becoming miracle workers: Language and meaning in brief therapy.* New York: Aldine de Gruyter.

Miller, P. J.; Hoogstra, L.; Mintz, J.,;Fung, H. & Williams, K. (1993). Troubles in the garden and how they get resolved: A young child's transformation of his favorite story. In C. Nelson (Ed.), *Memory and affect in development: Minnesota symposia on child psychology, Vol. 26* (87–114). Hillsdale, NJ: Erlbaum.

Mintz, S. B. (2007). *Unruly bodies: Life writing by women with disabilities.* Chapel Hill: University of North Carolina Press.

Mishler, E. (1986). *Research interviewing: Context and narrative.* Cambridge, MA: Harvard University Press.

Mitchell, D. T. (2002). Body solitaire: The singular subject of disability autobiography. *American Quarterly, 52,* 311–315.

Mitchell, D. T. & Snyder, S. L. (1997). Introduction: Disability studies and the double bind of representation. In D. T. Mitchell & S. L. Snyder (Eds.), *The body and physical difference: Discourses of disability* (1–31). Ann Arbor: University of Michigan Press.

Morris, J. (1996). *Encounters with strangers: Feminism and disability.* London: Women's Press.

Moya, P. M. L. (2002). *Learning from experience: Minority identities, multicultural struggles.* Berkeley: University of California Press.

Moya, P. M. L. & Hames-Garcia, M. R. (Eds.) (2000). *Reclaiming identity: Realist theory and the predicament of postmodernism.* Berkeley: University of California Press.

Murphy, R. F. (1987). *The body silent.* New York: Henry Holt.

Nafstad, H. E.; Blakar, R. M.; Carlquist, E.; Phelps, J. M. & Rand-Hendriksen, K. (2009). Globalization, neo-liberalism and community psychology. *American Journal of Community Psychology, 43*, 162–175.

Nelson, G. & Prilleltensky, I. (2004). *Community psychology: In pursuit of liberation and well-being.* New York: Palgrave Macmillan.

Nochi, M. (1998). "Loss of self" in the narratives of people with traumatic brain injuries: A qualitative analysis. *Social Science and Medicine, 46*, 869–878.

Nochi, M. (2000). Reconstructing self-narratives in coping with traumatic brain injury. *Social Science and Medicine, 51*, 1795–1804.

Oliver, M. (1990). *The politics of disablement.* London: Macmillan.

Oliver, M. (1996). Defining impairment and disability. In C. Barnes & G. Mercer (Eds.), *Exploring the divide: Illness and disability.* Leeds, UK: The Disability Press.

Olkin, R. (2009). *Women with physical disabilities who want to leave their partners: A feminist and disability-affirmative perspective.* Los Angeles: California School of Professional Psychology and Through the Looking Glass.

Paget, M. A. (1983). Experience and knowledge. *Human Studies, 6*, 67–90.

Plummer, K. (1995). *Telling sexual stories.* London: Routledge.

Plummer, K. (2005). Critical humanism and queer theory: Living with the tensions. In N. K. Denzin & Y. S. Lincoln (Eds.), *The Sage handbook of qualitative research*, 3rd edition (357–373). Thousand Oaks, CA: Sage.

Polletta, F.; Chen, P. C. B.; Gardner, B. G. & Motes, A. (2011). The sociology of storytelling. *Annual Review of Sociology, 37*, 109–130.

Rappaport, J. (1981). In praise of paradox: A social policy of empowerment over prevention. *American Journal of Community Psychology, 9*, 1–25.

Rappaport, J. (1993). Narrative studies, personal stories, and identity transformation in the mutual help context. *The Journal of Applied Behavioral Science, 29*, 239–256.

Rappaport, J. (1995). Empowerment meets narrative: Listening to stories and creating settings. *American Journal of Community Psychology, 23*, 795–808.

Rappaport, J. (1998). The art of social change: Community narratives as resources for individual and collective identity. In X. B. Arriaga & S. Oskamp (Eds.), *Addressing community problems: Psychological research and intervention* (225–246). Thousand Oaks, CA: Sage.

Rappaport, J. (2000). Community narratives: Tales of terror and joy. *American Journal of Community Psychology, 28*, 1–24.

Rappaport, J. & Seidman, E. (Eds) (2000). *Handbook of community psychology.* New York: Kluwer/Plenum Publishing.

Richardson, L. & St. Pierre, E. A. (2005). Writing: A method of inquiry. In N. K. Denzin & Y. S. Lincoln (Eds.), *The Sage handbook of qualitative research*, 3rd edition (959–978). Thousand Oaks, CA: Sage.

Ricoeur, P. (1984). The creativity of language. In R. Kearney (Ed.), *Dialogues with contemporary continental thinkers.* Manchester, UK: Manchester University Press.

Ricoeur, P. (1988). *Time and narrative, Volume 3.* K. Blamey & D. Pellauer (Trans.). Chicago: University of Chicago Press.

Ricoeur, P. (1991). Narrative identity. In D. Wood (Ed.), *On Paul Ricoeur.* New York: Routledge.

Ricoeur, P. (1992). *Oneself as another.* Chicago: University of Chicago Press.

Ricouer, P. (1996). Reflections on a new ethos for Europe. In R. Kearney (Ed.), *Paul Ricouer: The hermeneutics of action.* London: Sage.

Riessman, C. K. (1993). *Narrative analysis.* Newbury Park, CA: Sage.

Riessman, C. K. (2002). Analysis of personal narratives. In J. E. Gubrium & J. A. Holstein (Eds.), *Handbook of interview research: Context and method* (695–710). Thousand Oaks, CA: Sage.

Riessman, C. K. (2003). Performing identities in illness narrative: Masculinity and multiple sclerosis. *Qualitative Research, 3,* 5–33.

Rose, G. (1992). *The broken middle.* Oxford, UK: Blackwell.

Rosenthal, D. A.; Chan, F. & Livneh, H. (2006). Rehabilitation students' attitudes toward persons in high- and low-stakes social contexts: A conjoint analysis. *Disability and Rehabilitation, 28,* 1517–1527.

Rosenwald, G. C. & Ochberg, R. (Eds.). (1992). *Storied lives: The cultural politics of self-understanding.* New Haven, CT: Yale University Press.

Rubin, G. (1993). Thinking sex: Notes for a radical theory of the politics of sexuality. In H. Abelove, M. A. Barale & D. M. Halperin (Eds.), *The lesbian and gay studies reader* (3–44). New York: Routledge.

Samuels, E. (2011). Critical divides: Judith Butler's body theory and the question of disability. In K. Q. Hall (Ed.), *Feminist disability studies* (48–66). Bloomington: Indiana University Press.

Sander, A. M.; Pappadis, M. R.; Davis, L. C.; Clark, A. N.; Evans, G.; Struchen, M. A. & Mazzei, D. M. (2009). Relationship of race/ethnicity and income to community integration following traumatic brain injury: Investigation in a non-rehabilitation trauma sample. *NeuroRehabilitation, 24,* 15–27.

Sarason, S. B. (1974). *The psychological sense of community: Prospects for a community psychology.* London: Jossey-Bass.

Schriempf, A. (2001). (Re)fusing the amputated body: An interactionist bridge for feminism and disability. *Hypatia, 16* (4), 53–79.

Scully, J. L. (2008). *Disability bioethics: Moral bodies, moral differences.* New York: Rowman and Littlefield.

Seidman, E. & Rappaport, J. (1986). Framing the issues. In E. Seidman & J. Rappaport (Eds.), *Redefining social problems* (1–8). New York: Plenum.

Shakespeare, T. (1996). Disability, identity and difference. In C. Barnes & G. Mercer (Eds.), *Exploring the divide: Illness and disability* (94–113). Leeds, UK: Disability Press.

Sherry, M. (2004). Overlaps and contradictions between queer theory and disability studies. *Disability & Society, 19,* 769–783.

Sherry, M. (2006). *If I only had a brain: Deconstructing brain injury.* New York: Routledge.

Shildrick, M. (2007). Dangerous discourse: Anxiety, desire and disability. *Studies in Gender & Sexuality, 8,* 221–244.

Siebers, T. (1992). *Morals and stories.* New York: Oxford University Press.

Siebers, T. (2008). *Disability theory.* Ann Arbor: University of Michigan Press.

Singer, E. (2008, May). Brain trauma in Iraq. *Technology Review, 53*–59.

Smart, J. (2001). *Disability, society, and the individual.* Austin, TX: Pro-Ed.

Smith, B. & Sparkes, A. C. (2002). Men, sport, spinal cord injury, and the construction of coherence: Narrative practice in action. *Qualitative Research, 3,* 143–171.

Smith, B. & Sparkes, A. C. (2005). Men, sport, spinal cord injury and narratives of hope. *Social Science & Medicine, 61,* 1095–1105.

Smith, B. & Sparkes, A. C. (2008). Narrative and its potential contribution to disability studies. *Disability & Society, 23,* 17–28.

Sneed, S. L. & Davis, J. (2002). Attitudes of individuals with acquired brain injury toward disability. *Brain Injury, 16,* 947–953.

Snyder, S. L. & Mitchell, D. T. (2006). *Cultural locations of disability.* Chicago: University of Chicago Press.

Somers, M. (1994). The narrative construction of identity: A relational and network approach. *Theory and Society, 23,* 605–49.

Sontag, S. (2001). *Illness as metaphor.* New York: Picador.

Sparkes, A. C. & Smith, B. (2003). Men, sport, spinal cord injury and narrative time. *Qualitative Research, 3,* 295–320.

Sparkes, A. C. & Smith, B. (2005). When narratives matter. *Medical Humanities, 31,* 81–88.

St. Claire, L. & Clucas, C. (2012). In sickness and in health: Influences of social categorizations on health-related outcomes. In J. Jetten, C. Haslam & S. A. Haslam (Eds.), *The social cure: Identity, health and well-being* (75–95). New York: Psychology Press.

Stein, A. (1997). *Sex and sensibility: Stories of a lesbian generation.* Berkeley: University of California Press.

Stewart, J. E. (2011). On voice: difference, power, change. In M. Aber, K. Maton & E. Seidman (Eds.), *Empowering Settings and Voices for Social Change* (193–206). New York: Oxford University Press.

Strandberg, T. (2009). Adults with acquired traumatic brain injury: Experiences of a changeover process and consequences in everyday life. *Social Work in Health Care, 48,* 276–297.

Swain, J. & Cameron, C. (1999). Unless otherwise stated: Discourses of labeling and identity in coming out. In M. Corker & S. French (Eds.), *Disability discourse* (68–78). Philadelphia: Open University Press.

Swain, J. & French, S. (2000). Toward an affirmative model of disability. *Disability & Society, 15,* 369–382.

Thomas, C. (1999). Narrative identity and the disabled self. In M. Corker & S. French (Eds.), *Disability discourse* (47–55). Philadelphia: Open University Press.

Thomas, C. (2007). *Sociologies of disability, "impairment," and chronic illness: Ideas in disability studies and medical sociology.* New York: Palgrave Macmillan.

Todd, L. (2006). Enabling practice for professionals: The need for post-structuralist theory. In D. Goodley & R. Lawthom (Eds.), *Disability and psychology* (141–154). New York: Palgrave Macmillan.

Torrell, M. R. (2011). Plural singularities: The disability community in life-writing texts. *Journal of Literary & Cultural Disability Studies, 5*, 321–338.

Townley, G. & Kloos, B. (2009). Development of a measure of sense of community for individuals with severe mental illness residing in community settings. *Journal of Community Psychology, 37*, 362–380.

Tremain, S. (Ed.). (2005). *Foucault and the government of disability.* Ann Arbor: University of Michigan Press.

Tremain, S. (2006). On the government of disability: Foucault, power and the subject of impairment. In L. J. Davis (Ed.), *The disability studies reader,* 2nd edition (185–196). New York: Routledge.

Venn, C. (2000). *Occidentalism: Modernity and subjectivity.* Thousand Oaks, CA: Sage.

Vernon, A. (1998). Multiple oppression and the disabled people's movement. In T. Shakespeare (Ed.), *The disability reader: Social science perspectives* (201–210). London: Cassell.

Warren, L.; Wrigley, J. M.; Yoels, W. & Fine, P. R. (1996). Factors associated with life satisfaction among a sample of persons with neurotrauma. *Rehabilitation Research and Development, 33,* 404–408.

Weinstein, D. & Weinstein, M. A. (1991). Georg Simmel: Sociological flaneur bricoleur. *Theory, Culture & Society, 8,* 246–260.

Wendell, S. (1996). *The rejected body: Feminist philosophical reflections on disability.* New York: Routledge.

Wendell, S. (1997). Toward a feminist theory of disability. In L. J. Davis (Ed.), *The disability studies reader* (260–278). New York: Routledge.

White, M. & Epston, D. (1990). *Narrative means to therapeutic ends.* New York: W. W. Norton.

Whyte, S. R. (1995). Disability between discourse and experience. In B. Ingstad & S. R. Whyte (Eds.), *Disability and culture* (267–291). Berkeley: University of California Press.

Williams, G. (1991). Disablement and the ideological crisis in health care. *Social Science and Medicine, 32,* 517–524.

Williams, G. (1998). Towards a materialist phenomenology. In T. Shakespeare (Ed.), *The disability reader: Social science perspectives* (234–244). London: Cassell.

World Health Organization. (2001). *International classification of functioning: Disability and health.* Geneva: World Health Organization.

Ylvsaker, M. & Feeney, T. (2000). Reconstruction of identity after brain injury. *Brain Impairment, 1,* 12–28.

Ylvsaker, M.; Feeney, T. & Capo, M. (2007). Long-term community supports for individuals with co-occurring disabilities after traumatic brain injury: Cost effectiveness and project-based intervention. *Brain Impairment, 8,* 276–292.

Ylvsaker, M.; McPherson; K., Kayes, N. & Pellett, E. (2008). Metaphoric identity map-
    ping: Facilitating goal-setting and engagement in rehabilitation after traumatic
    brain injury. *Neuropsychological Rehabilitation, 18,* 713–741.
Ylvisaker; M., Turkstra, L. S. & Coelho, C. (2005). Behavioral and social interventions
    for individuals with traumatic brain injury: A summary of the research with clinical
    implications. *Seminars in Speech and Language, 26,* 256–267.
Yudice, G. (1990). For a practical aesthetics. *Social Text, 25,* 129–145.
Zola, I. K. (1994). Communications barriers between the worlds of "able-bodiedness"
    and "disability." In R. Schmitt & T. E. Moody (Eds.), *Key concepts in critical theory:*
    Alienation and social criticism (159–164). Atlantic Highlands, NJ: Humanities Press
    International.

in a patient's connection to, 104, 108, 168–169, 220. *See also* community

disabled women's community: Cindy's involvement, 137–139; feminist analysis of volunteerism and caretaking, 139–140, 150–151; implied hierarchies in, 148; importance of to Elise, 140–141; work in disability services by women, 156. *See also* community

distinctions between people with disabilities: caste system within the community, 160–161; claiming a disability identity or not, 164–166; cognitive versus physical disabilities, 161–163; developmental versus acquired disabilities, 132–133, 160; Elise's experiences with not appearing disabled, 127–128, 163–164; Lydia's frustration over her speech issues, 69–70

doctors. *See* health care professionals

Doctors Hospital, 40

DORS (Department of Rehabilitation Services), 142

Elise: biographical information, 35; crisis of faith after her injury, 189–191; disabled women's community and, 140–141; embracing of Buddhism, 191; experiences with not appearing disabled, 127–128, 163–164; frustration at not living up to unrealistic expectations, 65–66; interview setting, 42; loss of her connection to Catholicism, 190–191; problem with getting acknowledged by the professionals, 65; realization that she had a TBI, 125–126; shaping of her identification with disability rights, 126–128

fight in recovery and rehabilitation: Cindy's experiences (*see* Cindy's fight for services); climate of competition in, 133; "cognitive differences" versus "mental defect," 132–133; concept of waiting and, 91, 115, 117, 118, 122; disability's shift to a relational concern, 98–99; employment discrimination and, 123–125; forcing

of people to advocate for themselves, 117–118; identity complexities when the disability isn't visible, 127–130, 132–133, 163–164; longevity of the struggle for rights, 118–119; Lydia's frustration over her speech issues, 69–70; Nancy's experience, 119–122, 125; nature of the fight, 98, 134–136; personal fights made into community fights, 110–111, 116; requirement of a labeled diagnosis, 126; resisting the shame imposed by others, 9–10; role of community and identity in, 115–116; role of informal settings and networking in, 115, 122; sense of being a burden and (*see* burden associated with disabilities); tiresome nature of asking for help, 130–131, 134

Foucault, Michel, 202

Frank, A., 26

Fuss, Diana, 168, 169

Goffman, E., 3

Gracey, F., 6

Gubrium, J. F., 48

health care professionals: advocacy work being done by, 56–57, 58–59; different framings and expectations by different specialists, 75–76; frustration over availability of services, 53–54, 55–56, 135; inability to predict the extent of recovery, 67; metaphysics' role in recovery, 207–209, 213–214; mismatch of meaning between patients and, 63–64; nurses, 64, 65, 74, 146, 193, 194; patients' resistance to low expectations, 68–69, 74–75; problems with professional disconnect, 61, 65; tendency to downplay risks to patients, 64

Holstein, J. A., 48

Hunter, K. M., 63

identity: authoring metaphor used in relation to, 11–12; coming to terms with disability and, 166–167; communities and commitments critical to, 17–18, 174;

identity (*continued*)
connection with working, 151, 154; critical consciousness and, 7–9, 11, 217–218; critiques of identity-based movements, 107–108; decision to claim a disability identity, 107, 131, 164–166; disability versus other identity-based movements, 148–149; in the early-recovery stage, 83–84, 85; inappropriate standards of perfection and, 124–125; "inside/outside movement" characterizing, 168, 169; issues important in recovery, 4–5, 8–9, 220; personal nature of struggles, 2–3, 216–217; positive disability identity elements, 9, 219–220; Rehab Center's response's impact on Cindy's, 111–113; role in fighting for change, 115–116; sense of being a burden, 118; social identity theory, 5–7; as a social phenomenon, 2; the women's relationships with their pre-injury self, 82–83
integration, 16

Judaism, 187, 188

Kent, Deborah, 140
Kushner, Rabbi, 184, 185

Larsen, Dr.: about, 39; advocacy work, 56–57; frustration over the fight for services, 53–56, 135; on patients' transition to acceptance, 92, 94; on the role of community and organized religion, 212–213
left-brain injuries, 200
Lester, J. C., 108
Lloyd, Margaret, 139, 150
Lydia: anger issues, 93, 183–184; belief that there was a reason for her accident, 181–184; biographical information, 33–34; disappointment with rehab, 70–71; frustration over her speech issues, 69–70; interview setting, 40; search for meaningful work, 155–156

managed care: advocacy work being done, 54–59; consequences of the shift to outpatient care, 55–56; disability framed as an economic issue, 54, 58; issue of amount of care authorized, 53–54; political economy's structuring of ideologies, 58; public policy-level fight for services, 54; sarcasm derived from experiences with, 53; uniqueness of the Rehab Center, 57, 69–70
methodology: the author's interaction with the women, 26–27; author's positioning in the study, 42–43; author's training and disciplinary perspectives, 44–45; biographical information, 29–37; cautions against using abstractions, 43–44; demographics of the women, 29; distribution of the interview material, 37–38; "heroic overcoming" versus quest narrative, 26; interviews and transcription, 46–47; language and term use, 50–51; medical doctors' participation, 38–40; narratives presentation, 47–50; participant selection, 27–28; procedural approach to the study, 45; settings for the interviews, 40–42; storyteller versus story analyst perspective, 48; turning points and, 25–26; use of narrative, 45; use of pseudonyms, 37; the women as narrators, 46; women's injuries described, 29
Mintz, Susannah, 139, 150
misfitting, 14, 15
Mitchell, D. T., 94–95, 96
Morris, Jenny, 139

Nancy: on being both faithful and angry, 193–196; biographical information, 1, 34; critique of her company, 2, 122, 123–125; failure to pursue knowledge about risks of surgery, 62–63; hospital's lack of attention to her, 1–2, 65; injury's impact on her religious faith, 2; involvement with other disabled people, 145–146; new-found link to a community, 149–150; personal nature of her fight, 125; reaction to her post-surgery status, 63, 64; reemployment experience, 119–122, 125
nurses, 64, 65, 74, 146, 193, 194

Oliver, M., 50
Olkin, R., 104
Ownsworth, T., 6

Plummer, K., 45
political economy: city administration's refusal to help, 103; cultural model of disability and, 95–96; disability framed as an economic issue, 54, 58, 95; feminist analysis of volunteerism and caretaking, 151; lack of political savvy by the Rehab Center, 118–119; society's strategy of shifting the problem, 111, 117–118
pre-injury self: Abby's focus on regaining lost abilities, 86–87; acknowledgment of a loss, 90; argument for a refocus of rehabilitation strategies, 95; challenge of simply functioning, 97; Cindy's reflections on her pre-injury self, 84–85; cultural models and narratives of disability, 93–96; difficulty of the shift to accepting the disability, 90–93; early-recovery stage realities, 83–86; economics of rehabilitation, 95; impact of the intentions and needs of others, 89–90; medico-rehabilitation and religious perspectives, 90; rehabilitation process's role in post-injury lives, 96–97; rehabilitation regimen's pushing aside of long-term goals, 86; religious affiliations and beliefs' roles recovery, 87–89, 94, 205–207; the women's relationships with, 81–83

queer theory, 18, 45, 222

RBI. See right-brain injuries
Reeve, Christopher, 94
Rehab Center, 32, 41; advocacy work, 56, 95; inconsistency of its transport position, 109–110, 112–113, 114, 117; lack of political savvy, 118–119; role in the disability community, 57, 69–70, 145, 146, 151, 152, 156, 196; shifting of the problem onto Cindy, 111, 117–118; support of Nancy's employment issue, 120, 122, 123

rehabilitation experiences: anosagnosia and, 66–67; different framings and expectations by different specialists, 75–76; discourse of productivity in, 71, 79–80; doctors' inability to predict the extent of recovery, 67; doctors' tendency to downplay risks to patients, 64; drawing on pre-injury self as a resource, 78–79; feelings of not being heard, 61; impact of expectations on, 62, 65–66, 68–69, 74–75; mismatch of meaning between doctors and patients, 63–64; professional disconnect and, 65, 77–78; resistance to low expectations, 68–69, 74–75; results of not having access to expert services, 61; Rose's injury and late diagnosis, 59–60; Sarah's experience due to her belief system, 75; self-perceptions versus perceptions of others, 70–72, 73–74; socio-economic status related to quality of help received, 60, 62; specter of the premorbid self and, 67–68
religious faith: Abby's relationship with her church post-injury, 134, 167–168, 196–201; Beth on assigning meaning to her injury, 175–177; centrality of relationships to the women, 177–178; challenge of spirituality, 202; Cindy's struggle to make sense of the assault, 184–186; concerns recurrent in the women's accounts, 177; cultural framing of disability as a failure, 200–201; Elise's crisis of faith after her injury, 189–192; framing of spirituality when reconciling it with disability, 203; Lydia on cause and effect, 181–184; medico-rehabilitation perspectives regarding recovery and, 90; metaphysical framing of recovery, 177, 207–209, 213–214; Nancy's faithfulness and anger, 2, 193–196; non-disabled peoples' need to locate the cause and effect of disability, 211–212; other peoples' need

J. Eric Stewart is a Clinical-Community Psychologist and Associate Professor of Interdisciplinary Arts and Sciences at the University of Washington Bothell.